DATE RAPE AND CONSENT

Dedicated to my father, John Cowling, and the memory of my mother, Rosemary Cowling

Date Rape and Consent

MARK COWLING
School of Social Sciences
University of Teesside

Ashgate

Aldershot • Brookfield USA • Singapore • Sydney

Published by
Ashgate Publishing Company
Gower House
Croft Road
Aldershot, Hants
GU11 3HR
England

Ashgate Publishing Company
Old Post Road
Brookfield
Vermont 05036
USA

Ashgate website:http://www.ashgate.com

Reprinted 1999

British Library Cataloguing in Publication Data
Cowling, Mark
    Date rape and consent
    1. Acquaintance rape
    I. Title
    362.8'83

Library of Congress Catalog Card Number:98-72629

ISBN 1 85972 509 0

Printed and bound by Athenaeum Press, Ltd.,
Gateshead, Tyne & Wear.

Contents

Preface

This book represents my attempt to answer a puzzle: according to official conviction rates, rape is a problem directly affecting some four to five hundred very unfortunate women in England and Wales each year. According to some of the surveys I discuss, about one woman in four could be expected to be a victim of rape or attempted rape. It seemed clear to me from the start that the question of how rape is defined and identified must be an important part of the answer to the question of how this massive discrepancy comes into being. Thus philosophical issues concerning the definition of concepts could play an important part in making sense of an important social problem. I cannot pretend to have 'solved' the problem of the extent of rape, or of how it should be defined, but I have presented many of the issues and arguments needed for anyone who wishes to make sense of it.

Along the way I have incurred debts to many people. The School of Social Sciences at the University of Teesside has provided a congenial working atmosphere and some relief from teaching and administration. A whole series of people have offered useful advice, including Professor Roy Boyne, Sue Lees, who was kind enough to comment on an article in which I explored some of the themes of the book,[1] Jill Radford, Paul Reynolds and Roz Waddington who read most of the book and provided detailed comments, Walter DeKeseredy, John Fekete and Katharine Kelly, who took the time to answer letters from me, and the Women, Gender and Sexuality research group of the Centre for Social and Political Research at the University of Teesside, who made many useful comments on a presentation of my work. My daughter Camillia Cowling proof-read the book and found many more mistakes than I had bargained for.

---

[1] Mark Cowling, 'Date Rape and Consent', *Contemporary Politics,* Vol. 1, No. 2, 1995, pp. 57-72.

The staff at Ashgate have been most tolerant of missed deadlines caused by various unavoidable events, and Christine Davis has been a meticulous and helpful proof-reader.

My family have been most helpful in humouring my obsessions and occasional neglect of other tasks.

I should stress particularly strongly that the opinions expressed below are my own, as I know that some of the people who have helped disagree strongly with some of them.

The book is dedicated to my parents, who brought me up with an interest in the rational discussion of difficult and emotive issues.

Mark Cowling
March 1998

1 Introduction

Date rape has been defined by one of the leading US academics studying the area as: 'a specific type of acquaintance rape that involves a victim and a perpetrator who have some level of romantic relationship between them'.[1] I shall discuss this definition further in Chapter 4, but it is a sensible one in that it corresponds quite well with public perceptions. Date rape is an issue which leads a curious life in Britain. Every so often there is a cause célèbre in the courts, most notably in recent years those of Austen Donnellan, the student from Kings College, London, who ended up on trial for rape (he was acquitted) as the end result of his unwillingness to move class times to separate himself from the student with whom the incident occurred, and Angus Diggle, a solicitor who was convicted of the attempted rape of a fellow solicitor after taking her to a lavish ball. Such incidents lead to much press publicity and banner headlines, together with responses from women's organisations to the effect that there is much more date rape than most people realise, and from some commentators suggesting that women have taken to describing bad or drunken sex as rape. Following this, very little more is said, and there is relatively little interest, popular or academic, until the next incident. In contrast, in the United States there is a substantial academic industry devoted to date rape, involving particularly psychologists[2] and, to a lesser extent, lawyers. There is, as can be seen from the bibliography of this book, a very large literature on the issue. In Canada there was a major outcry about various forms of sexual

---

[1] This definition is given by Mary P. Koss and Sarah L. Cook in 'Facing the Facts: Date and Acquaintance Rape are Significant Problems for Women', in Richard J. Gelles and Donileen R. Loseke eds, *Current Controversies on Family Violence*, Sage, Newbury Park, California, 1993, pp. 104-119, quotation on p. 105.

[2] The contrast between the massive US psychological literature and the very limited British psychological literature is very striking. The one British article which is frequently cited is J. Pollard, 'Judgements about Victims and Attackers in Depicted Rapes: A Review', *British Journal of Social Psychology*, Vol. 31, 1992, pp. 307-26. The few other British articles are also largely about attributions rather than surveys of incidents.

violence, including date rape, in 1993, followed by sceptical academic and press commentary, followed by relative silence.

In this book I have two main, interlocking, aims. The first is simply to describe and attempt to make sense of the - largely American - literature on date rape. What can a British audience learn from it? Given that there has been a much more intensive discussion of date rape in the USA for the last fifteen years or so, are there academic pitfalls which we can avoid? The second is to ask philosophical questions about where the boundaries between rape and non-rape should be drawn: what conduct deserves to be called rape, and what should be done about conduct which perhaps has some similarity to rape but should simply be seen as unethical or bad mannered? This second question is very important, and has a considerable overlap with the first. Everyone has to have some kind of an attitude to the second question, from the male chauvinist traditionalist who thinks that British courts convict too many innocent men of rape, to the radical feminist who comes close to identifying all heterosexual sex as rape. The importance of the boundary question for our understanding of the American literature on date rape is that much of the literature offers findings that rape is much more extensive than court or police records show. Plainly, the more all-embracing our conception of rape, the more of it there is to be found. In turn this issue leads on to more practical questions: what can or should be done about the very large number of unreported and unconvicted rapes? How much do the more extensive definitions of rape lead us towards the notion that women commit rape on men, and if we accept that they do, what, if anything, needs to be done about it?

There is a strong case that we in Britain should be taking more of an interest in date rape and in the US discussion of it. Feminist activists and academics have a convincing case that rape is not taken sufficiently seriously by British courts,[3] and there is also a widespread view that for every incident of rape reported to the police many more go unreported. Although there is every reason to think that this view is true, there is less agreement on the exact extent of unreported rape. This lack of agreement has been exacerbated by the partial success of feminists in shifting public assumptions about rape. From a rare crime committed only by maniacs it has come to be seen as a more widespread phenomenon, notably in the recognition that wives should be legally protected from rape by their husbands. There has also been a limited shift towards the feminist view that women deserve the protection of the law from rape irrespective of their previous history, their clothing or where they choose to go and when. In a situation where customs and assumptions are changing it is only to be expected that the boundaries of what counts as acceptable behaviour will also be debated.

We also need to take more of an interest in date rape because there is likely to be more of it in modern Britain. From a situation where sex before marriage was

---

[3] As seen, for example in the Campaign to End Rape, launched in the summer of 1997 - contact at 28, Eaton Road, Sale, Cheshire, M33 9TZ.

frowned upon, we have moved to a society where the average new bride or groom has had five previous partners;[4] fewer people are actually bothering to get married; and our rate of divorce is at a record high. All of this indicates that people are encountering new sexual partners at a much higher rate than hitherto, and are almost certainly bringing a range of different expectations to these encounters.[5] Rather than having a Canadian-style panic about date rape it is better for us to discuss carefully what is involved in sexual consent, hoping to achieve a consensus, or failing that, an understanding of our differences. It would probably be desirable to have a large-scale British survey of sexual assault on the lines of those carried out in the US and Canada. However, given the extent of debate which followed the US and Canadian surveys, particularly concerning the way in which the questions were posed, it would be sensible to clarify our concepts first. This book aims to make some contribution to that process.

This book is a philosophical investigation of date rape, written by a man. Before going into any more detailed account of its contents, some explanation of both of these points is called for. By a philosophical explanation I have in mind one which has as its central focus the investigation, analysis and explanation of concepts. One of the most fruitful and interesting developments in philosophy over the last thirty years or so is the use of precise philosophical investigation to study real problems which cause anguish to ordinary people: abortion, euthanasia, war, civil disobedience, suicide,[6] etc. Things have come a considerable distance since my undergraduate days when ethical discussions used such issues as walking across the grass on the college's quad and taking the last slice of ice-cream as it circulated around the high table. So far, although there has been as we shall see, some philosophical attention to rape it has generally been conceived as stranger rape rather than date rape.

Why does date rape require *philosophical* investigation? Surely rape is a matter for criminologists or lawyers or sociologists? To begin to see the reason for taking a philosophical interest in date rape, consider the issue raised previously about the extent of rape. If rape is conceived only as a crime evidenced by convictions in court, then rape in England and Wales is currently running at around 450 cases a year. Consider, in contrast, the estimates of the extent of rape which I produce by a rather crude method at the end of Chapter 3 on the basis of some of the claims

---

[4] See Wellings, Kaye et. al., *Sexual Behaviour in Britain: the National Survey of Attitudes and Life,* Penguin, Harmondsworth, 1994.

[5] For an American comment on similar lines see Kate Fillion, *Lip Service,* Pandora/Harper Collins, London, 1997, pp. 165-6.

[6] There are now a large number of books and articles in this area. Examples which I have found particularly interesting, without, of course, endorsing all their conclusions, are Peter Singer, *Practical Ethics,* Cambridge University Press, Cambridge, 1979; Janet R. Richards, *The Sceptical Feminist,* Second Edition, Penguin, Harmondsworth, 1995; Jonathan Glover, *Causing Death and Saving Lives,* Penguin, Harmondsworth, 1977; Thomas Nagel, *Mortal Questions,* Cambridge University Press, Cambridge, 1979.

made by psychologists and activists. If their claims about sexual assault are right then there are some 70,000 plus incidents of rape each year in England and Wales. Assuming very modest sentences for rape and attempted rape, I produce estimates of between 110,000 and 270,000 extra prison places being required if all the incidents resulted in court convictions. If current conviction levels are accepted as an account of the rate of rape in England and Wales then the phenomenon is a traumatic tragedy which affects very few women, and the idea that rapists are psychologically abnormal looks plausible. On the other hand, if the higher estimates are even roughly accurate we are living in a society where rape is a very frequent, almost normal experience.

There are, of course, several explanations for the massive discrepancy. To start with, there is a very substantial attrition rate between women complaining to the police of having been raped and court convictions. The major problem here seems to be the way in which rape trials are conducted in England and Wales. In Chapter 2, I give a brief summary of Sue Lees's excellent account of this process. However, assuming that all complaints of rape made to the police are valid, we still have a little under 5,000 incidents of rape a year. The much higher estimates come from surveys conducted by psychologists and activists. Their major conclusion is that very many rape victims,[7] particularly those raped by dates or acquaintances, tell no-one at all. Some victims tell only friends or possibly rape crisis centres, but most either do not define their experience as rape, or acknowledge that they have been raped but feel too embarrassed to tell the police. They think that because they knew the man, or had been drinking, or had agreed to go somewhere suggested by him, or had been wearing 'provocative' clothing, or had slept with him before, that the police would not do anything about the incident. Undoubtedly there is some basis to these claims of a silent epidemic. That said, however, there are a number of other issues. Some of these concern the sampling procedure, or the use of questionnaire items which are cast so widely that they are unable to distinguish between rape and consenting sex after drinking, for example. I discuss this to some extent in Chapter 3 but these are not the *philosophical* issues I have in mind.

The major philosophical issue is the definition of rape. To start with a straightforward point, if rape is defined to include oral and anal penetration,[8] or

---

[7] There is an important distinction in the feminist and therapeutic literature on rape between victims and survivors. A victim is a woman who is suffering the immediate trauma of a sexual assault, and a survivor is a woman who has managed to integrate the experience and can now face the world again. However, the focus of this book is on the process of becoming a victim, and I have therefore consistently referred to 'rape victims', even in some contexts where the term 'survivor' might be appropriate.

[8] Since 1994 rape has been defined in England and Wales to include anal penetration of a woman or a man (Criminal Justice and Public Order Act, s. 142). Thus, assuming the same rate of assault of various kinds, the number of incidents of rape will go up because of an altered definition.

penetration by fingers or objects as well as by a penis, then there will be more of it than if these acts are seen as separate offences. But the major definitional question concerns the concept of consent. If, as is widely (but not universally) accepted, rape is sex without consent, then the way consent is defined becomes very important. Clearly, if non-consent is restricted to 'resistance to the utmost', as in some older US legislation,[9] then there will be much less rape than if, at the other extreme, one accepts a version of the Dworkin and MacKinnon view that all heterosexual sex under patriarchy is suspect. The core of the book is my attempt to get to grips with the concept of consent. In Chapter 4 I break it down into several component parts. All of these turn out to contain ambiguities. As real-life rape incidents are likely to include aspects of all these parts it is little wonder that there is a great deal of debate about the extent of rape. A simple way of putting the question I am asking is: 'Where does rape end and consenting sex begin?'

In discussing this book with feminist psychologists and sociologists I have been made very aware of the difference between a philosophical approach to questions and a psychological or sociological one. Philosophers tend to like discussing simple, extreme cases which prove a point. Two examples should be mentioned. In Chapter 2, I discuss a character called the Mineral Water Fanatic who forces mineral water on his victims. He tends to be seen as a frivolous invention, but my point is simply to find a clear example of someone who commits most of the offence of rape but without its specifically sexual component, and thus to show the importance of this component. Again, in Chapter 4 I offer an example of a woman who never explicitly consents to sex in so many words but who plainly does consent by her actions. My intention is to show that an insistence on explicit verbal consent is not necessary. I am not, however, trying to claim that if explicit verbal consent is written into the law of rape the courts will be flooded with women claiming to have been raped because, despite extensive consenting conduct, they never actually consented in words. Psychologists reading the passage tend to assume I am making such a claim, because they generally deal with what typically happens rather than what could conceivably happen.

There are also differences of language. Philosophers tend to try to liven up their abstract discussions with colourful language about 'doing violence' to concepts, or 'applying Occam's Razor', etc. They also tend to assume that everything they are discussing is suspect in the sense that it may contain ambiguous concepts or flawed arguments. Two of the founders of the discipline are Descartes, who started by doubting everything, but felt he could rely on the fact that he was thinking, and Hume, who showed we are on rather shaky ground in believing that the sun will rise tomorrow. In contrast, the emphasis in the psychological literature I am discussing is on social science, on 'findings' rather than 'claims'. The previous literature is usually reviewed early in an article as a foundation for the current experiment rather than as something inherently fallible. 'Instruments'

---

[9] On this - very unreasonable - requirement see Susan Estrich, *Real Rape*, Harvard University Press, Cambridge, MA, 1987, pp. 29-37.

(meaning questionnaires) are seen as 'reliable' if respondents give the same answers a week later. The possibility that the questionnaires are actually conceptually confused is, of course, acknowledged, but that does not make them 'unreliable' in the technical sense used here. Readers thus need to be aware that putting philosophy and psychology together in the way attempted here involves something of a culture clash, and the language involved may need to be interpreted in a way different from that to which they have become accustomed. In particular, I have tended to use the philosopher's language of 'claims' rather than the psychologist's 'findings', not because I think that work by psychologists in the area of sexual assault is substandard compared to other psychology but because I want to regard *all* knowledge as potentially flawed. If a 'claim' in my terminology is well-supported it is just as good as a 'finding', maybe better given that many 'findings' in fact contradict each other.

Most of the contemporary literature written on rape is written by women. Isn't there something suspect about a man writing about rape? There are several reasons for my interest, but my first motivation, and my bottom line justification is that if there are to be effective reforms of rape laws and real changes in male conduct then the new laws and newly-prescribed conduct must at least be understood by men. It is basically men who commit rape; if there is to be any redress it must come through some combination of the police, the medical and legal professions, all of which remain male-dominated - even though they ideally should not be. Thus although interviews with victims, for example, are doubtless better conducted by women, male understanding does become important where changes in policy are proposed. The route to changes in male conduct surely lies in part through understanding and thought.

A further two motivations are more personal. One is a general and long-standing interest in feminism, stemming originally from a commitment to socialism: if socialism involves a commitment to substantive equality for all, then half of that all are women. Second wave feminism dates from the end of the 1960s. Since that time socialism has generally suffered numerous defeats, whether we consider Britain, with the rise of Thatcherism, or Western Europe, where democratic socialist initiatives in several countries in the 1970s and 1980s foundered under pressure from the international economic system and the multinational companies, or the communist countries, where planned economies have collapsed in the former USSR and Eastern Europe[10] or reverted substantially to capitalism, as in China and Vietnam. In contrast, whilst it could hardly be asserted that patriarchy has crumbled, societies which have remained capitalist have nonetheless introduced a series of reforms in broadly the right direction: equal pay, equal opportunities, employment protection during maternity leave, child care, sexual violence and domestic violence have all been the focus of legislation both in Europe and North America. Along with this, many individual

---

[10] On this see the excellent book by Lawrence Wilde, *Modern European Socialism*, Dartmouth, Aldershot, 1994.

women have moved into senior positions, or into previously largely-male professions, or engaged in a much freer lifestyle than their mothers. My contribution to all this has been the very modest one of teaching courses on feminism at my university at a time when no-one else in my department was teaching anything similar.

My other personal motivation is linked to the previous one: discussions of rape with students have generally been the most fraught area of my teaching. Some years ago I had a discussion about teaching feminist ideas to first year undergraduates with a sociologist colleague. She said that she found male reactions to feminism generally very hostile. In contrast I found that most male reactions were quite favourable, with occasional scepticism or opposition voiced by a few older men. Going into more detail, we found that I had been discussing the number of women in the UK Parliament, which at that stage was well under 5%. Most male students were happy to agree that women should have equal opportunities, that in order to have such opportunities some issues needed legal changes, and that in order to make such changes it would be desirable to have more women in Parliament. My colleague, in contrast, had been basing her discussions on Susan Brownmiller's account of rape as 'a conscious process of intimidation by which *all men* keep *all women* in a state of fear'. Logically this required male students to acknowledge that they were potential rapists, in which case they could not possibly be sympathetic to feminism, or to deny Brownmiller's theory, in which case they were opponents of feminism. On the basis of Brownmiller's theories sympathetic male teaching of feminist ideas about rape is a logical impossibility.

More recent accounts of rape are generally less sweeping than Brownmiller's. However, a promising way of defending something close to Brownmiller's position is to emphasise the research on date and acquaintance rape. In addition to this, it has been repeatedly made clear to me that the possibility of rape frightens very many women in a way which men (myself included) find hard to fully understand: what seems just obvious to women needs to be explained at length to men, or simply has to be accepted as one of those things they do not fully comprehend. This book partly stems, then, from a desire to disentangle an issue which is clearly both important and very divisive. I do not think I have managed to present a clear position on which all decent people could agree, but I do think I have managed to show many of the ambiguities which render the question so fraught.

The structure of the book is straightforward. In Chapter 2, I set the scene for what follows by looking at four important background matters. I start by sketching the current police and court treatment of rape in the UK. I then briefly examine theoretical accounts of rape, emphasising that almost all the discussion of date rape sees it as based on a desire for sex rather than an assertion of power and anger. I summarise the current law of England and Wales on rape, mentioning some ambiguities which have caused problems to judges. Finally, I look at some philosophical accounts of why stranger rape is evil, arguing that the best explanation is that rape is not just any violation of a woman's autonomy but one which has a series of traumatic consequences, typically leaving her with psychological problems to conquer and severely disrupting her relationships, her life at work, her contentment with her living arrangements. My main aim here is to suggest that more marginal offences should be measured against stranger rape by comparing the typical degree of trauma involved.

In Chapter 3, I move on to look at the existing literature on date rape. I start by trying to refine the definition of date rape, arguing that it should include some spousal rape but exclude rape by non-romantic acquaintances. I then discuss the *Ms* survey conducted by Mary Koss, some features of Diana Russell's San Francisco survey and a series of other smaller US surveys. Bearing in mind my fundamental question of the boundaries between rape and non-rape, some issues arise from the surveys. The level of violence used by date rapists in the surveys is generally very slight or non-existent, raising questions about how low a level of violence qualifies for a 'violent' crime; there are strong suggestions that miscommunication plays a major role in many incidents; incapacitation by alcohol is also an issue.

I then discuss some surveys which raise further questions about the Koss and Russell findings. In particular, if one asks male students questions broadly similar to those used in Koss's survey, large numbers of them appear to have experienced various forms of pressure and unwanted sex. As there is no suggestion that these men are deeply traumatised, a question is raised as to whether at least some of the assaults on women are being wrongly-described. A further set of findings concerns communication. There is extensive evidence of women saying 'no' when they are actually willing to have sex, or are at least undecided about the question. At first sight these offer some support to male claims about 'misreading the signals'; they certainly show that the communication of consent and non-consent is an important issue. I then move on to discuss a veritable 'date rape war' which occurred in Canada following the initial publication of findings from Walter DeKeseredy and Katharine Kelly's Woman Abuse in Dating Relationships survey, notably their claim that 81% of women in such relationships suffer 'woman abuse'. Whilst there is doubtless much of value in the Canadian findings, Canada in 1993 offers an excellent model of how not to conduct public debate on date rape.

Next, in Chapter 3 I discuss some British surveys in this area. The British surveys largely avoid the problematic questions which caused so much debate following the US and Canadian surveys. However, the two bigger British surveys used questionnaires distributed to women who showed an interest in 'Women's Safety' rather than random samples, so although they make a lot of valuable points and certainly suggest there is much more domestic and sexual violence than would be thought from police statistics, they are not very useful as measures. A much smaller study by Liz Kelly shows a much greater sensitivity to the problematic boundaries between rape and non-rape than most of the other material considered in Chapter 3, but does not claim to be a representative sample. Finally, in Chapter 3 I briefly look at the implications of the vigorous use of prosecution and prison as a solution to date rape. This suggests that perhaps a quadrupling of the prison population in Britain would be required - which in turn suggests that it would be better if possible to tackle the problem through public education.

In Chapter 4 I move on to consider the concept of consent. One issue is whether a study of consent in non-sexual areas can throw light on sexual consent. I argue that it offers a framework and some sensible questions to ask, but bears only a family relationship to sexual consent. An analysis drawn from the political literature on consent suggests a series of areas to look at. I start by thinking about knowledge of what is consented to, which is obviously a requirement, move on to the question of intention to consent, then look at the communication of consent, and finally examine what it means for consent to occur against a background of free choice. The communication issue includes a lengthy discussion of the concept of communicative sexuality, which is offered as a feminist replacement for current ideas about sexual consent.

When I consider the question of free choice in Chapter 4, I restrict myself to specific, individual or limited-group forms of coercion which render free choice invalid. There remains, however, the argument that sexual consent under patriarchy is not valid because women's choices are too constrained, and this is considered in Chapter 5, Sex on a Sloping Playing Field. This chapter represents my attempt to answer a criticism which could be made of earlier chapters, and, indeed, of much of the literature which they discuss, namely that the pervasive effects of patriarchy are understated. Whether or not patriarchy is a fully valid concept is an enormous issue which I could not hope to tackle. I simply look at some aspects of patriarchy as it is frequently defined and ask first, to what extent any particular aspect applies to all women in relation to all men, and second, to what extent greater male power offers coercive sexual opportunities. What I aim to show is that, while we do not as yet have a level sexual playing field, the general slope which favours men is modified both by some much steeper male-favouring slopes and by some slopes in the opposite direction. This last point leads me to spell out something which has been assumed in this introduction and will be generally assumed through the book: a serious concept of rape is of an act done by men; there is neither any real evidence nor any general sense in society of major male sexual victimisation by women. This in turn suggests that to the extent we are considering forms of coercion which can be (and are) applied by women to men they are probably not best described as rape. However, it also raises the question as to whether analogous forms of coercion applied by men to women should count as rape.

Finally, in the conclusion I suggest some research and policy implications of my analysis, notably the need for better studies of how women give sexual consent and for discussion of how much coercion and of what sorts our society wishes to condemn as immoral or illegal.

2 Stranger rape and date rape

The purpose of this chapter is to set the scene for the rest of the book by looking at the emergence of date rape as an issue against the background of the way public thinking on rape has changed over the last twenty years or so. I start by pointing out that although public attitudes have shifted towards feminist views of rape (for example, that rape is a serious crime, that a woman's general sexual history has no relevance to whether or not rape has been committed, etc.), British court procedures have not kept pace. In particular, there is a vast gulf between the claims made on the basis of various surveys that date and acquaintance rape is very extensive, and the relatively low numbers of convictions in British courts. I then look briefly at some of the theories used to account for rape, noting the changes in the theoretical scene made by feminist interventions since the mid-1970s, but also making some comments on the ability of the theories to explain date rape. I then move on to look at British legal definitions of rape, and ask where date rape might fit. Finally, I justify my approach of considering rape as a moral rather than a legal category. The definition of date rape is a major substantive issue which I wish to leave to the next chapter. For the purposes of this chapter it suffices to recall the definition from the introduction, i.e. date rape is 'a specific type of acquaintance rape that involves a victim and a perpetrator who have some level of romantic relationship between them'.[1] Note that the stress is on some level of pre-existing relationship of a romantic sort, rather than specifically that the event happens on a date, and that date rape will be narrower than acquaintance rape because it excludes non-romantic acquaintances.

Public attitudes to rape in the USA and in countries where American ideas had an influence underwent a major shift with the impact of second wave feminism.

---

[1] This definition is given by Mary P. Koss and Sarah L. Cook in 'Facing the Facts: Date and Acquaintance Rape are Significant Problems for Women', in Richard J. Gelles and Donileen R. Loseke, eds, *Current Controversies on Family Violence,* Sage, Newbury Park, California, 1993, pp. 104-119, quotation on p. 105.

Following the initiatives in the early 1970s, and particularly the publication of Susan Brownmiller's *Against Our Will* in 1975, rape crisis centres were set up by feminist activists and there was a change in police procedures, some legal changes and the general public image became more one of a serious crime of violence and less one of misbehaviour based on uncontrollable male sexual urges.

A good outline account of the shift in the USA is given by Linda Borque. An interesting feature of her presentation of the issue, which is clearly generally sympathetic to feminism, is her comment that the feminist movement started with Betty Friedan's *The Feminine Mystique* in 1963 and the formation of the National Organisation for Women, aimed generally for equal opportunity and equal pay, but 'needed issues to catalyse consciousness-raising and act as rallying points for organisation'. Some attention was initially given to abortion and prostitution, but: 'Only in 1970, when it was clear that prostitution had failed as a mobilising issue, did Susan Griffin and others concentrate their full attention on rape'.[2] The motivations of activists do not, of course, make their claims about the nature and extent of rape untrue, but it is worth bearing in mind that there is a strong political edge to the way rape is defined.[3] This point plainly has a bearing on the issue of date rape: radical feminists will tend to advocate wide definitions of rape, whilst conservatives will prefer narrow ones.

How rape is dealt with in Britain

For Britain, at least, this set of changes has recently been subjected to a searching analysis by Sue Lees.[4] Her book sees the changes in police procedure as real and helpful. Women complaining of rape at British police stations can now generally expect sympathetic treatment and referral on to other services for pregnancy and health checks and counselling rather than the vigorous attempts to break down their story which prevailed twenty years ago.[5] Lees charts a series of significant

---

[2] Linda B. Borque, *Defining Rape*, Duke University Press, Durham, North Carolina, USA and London, 1989, pp. 11-13.

[3] This point is also made in an excellent article on the research implications of the way rape is defined by Charlene L. Muehlenhard et. al., 'Definitions of Rape: Scientific and Political Implications', *Journal of Social Issues*, Vol. 48, No. 1, 1992, pp. 23-44. The women's movement in Britain was seriously divided in the 1970s by the question of how salient should be the issue of violence against women.

[4] Sue Lees, *Carnal Knowledge, Rape on Trial*, Hamish Hamilton, London, 1996. For a critique of earlier US reforms, see Susan Estrich, *Real Rape*, Harvard University Press, Cambridge, MA, 1987, esp. Ch. 5.

[5] It has to be said that police practice is actually more varied and patchy than readers of Lees's book are led to think. (I am indebted on this point to Jill Radford.) More generally, it needs to be recognised that reformed rape laws are only as much practical good as the police officers who enforce them, i.e. old definitions of rape may persist as working

changes to the law in England and Wales: under the Sexual Offences (Amendment) Act of 1976 the victim remains anonymous rather than facing trial by media, and she is not supposed to be asked irrelevant questions about her sexual history. Ludicrously light sentences for rapists are less usual following Lord Chief Justice Lane's guidelines issued in 1986,[6] and marital rape was recognised by the Law Lords in 1991.[7] Many other legislatures have made broadly similar changes. In the United States the legal background prior to 1970 was similar in many states to that in the United Kingdom, thanks to the influence of the background of common law, and particularly its codification in the Model Penal Code, which influenced many state legislatures.[8] Most American states have adopted 'rape shield' legislation, which restricts the use of sexual history evidence, and have made spousal rape illegal. Some US states, together with Canada and New South Wales, have followed the state of Michigan and rewritten the law on rape as a law dealing with degrees of sexual assault.[9]

Unfortunately, in Britain at least, these welcome changes have not been matched by a change of attitudes and procedure in the courts; the bulk of Lees's book is an indictment of a whole series of very serious flaws in the legal process.

Women's confidence in the police appears to have increased, so that while in England and Wales in 1985 1,842 rapes were reported to the police, by 1995 5,039 rapes were reported.[10] Almost certainly, this reflects a change in willingness to report rape and in police recording practice, not a sudden rape epidemic. However, the number of convictions was very similar in each year: 450 in 1985

---

definitions even after a change in the law. See, for example, Rebecca Campbell and Camille R. Johnson, 'Police Officers' Perceptions of Rape: Is There Consistency Between State Law and Individual Beliefs?', *Journal of Interpersonal Violence*, Vol. 12, No. 2, 1997, pp. 255-74.

[6] For details see Jennifer Temkin, *Rape and the Legal Process*, Sweet and Maxwell, London, 1987, pp. 19-21.

[7] On improvements to rape law and practice in Britain, see also Jennifer Temkin, *Guardian*, 15 April 1995. The pattern in recent years seems to be that whilst relatively few rapists are convicted, the sentences given have been rising - see Adam Sampson, *Sex Offenders and the Criminal Justice System*, Routledge, London, 1994, p. 54.

[8] On the Model Penal Code and its influence on US rape laws, see Keith Burgess-Jackson, *Rape: A Philosophical Investigation*, Dartmouth, Brookfield, Vermont, 1996, pp. 72-4.

[9] For a full discussion of legislative changes in Michigan, Canada and New South Wales, all on similar lines, see Temkin, *Rape and the Legal Process*, Ch. 3.

[10] Lees, *Carnal Knowledge*, p. 95, plus HMSO *Criminal Statistics*, 1995. There is a well-supported and widespread view that stranger rape is generally reported at a fairly high rate, and that unreported rapes are largely acquaintance rapes. Even within reported rapes in Britain in the 1980s, however, acquaintance rape features quite substantially. In a Home Office sponsored study of rape in two London boroughs, 39% of offenders were well known to the victim, and over a third of these had had some clear romantic involvement. See Lorna Smith, *Concerns About Rape*, HMSO, London, 1989.

and 425 in 1995, i.e. a rate, compared to reports to the police, of 24% in 1985 and 8% in 1995.[11] It would appear, then, that very many women are going through the traumatic experience of reporting rape to the police to little effect. Lees's impression is that very few of these complaints are without foundation. How does the total get whittled down?

Prior to 1986 rape cases tended to be 'no crimed' by the police, i.e. it was decided to exclude cases from Home Office statistics because the police decided not to proceed. In 1986 a Home Office circular advised that only false complaints should be 'no crimed'; otherwise complaints should enter the statistics even if there was not enough evidence to proceed or the woman withdrew her complaint. Despite this a higher rate of 'no criming' has prevailed in rape cases than in most others. In addition, Lees found that the police tended to re-categorise rape into other sorts of assault and then 'no crime' it; in other words, cases where a variety of charges were possible, including rape or attempted rape, were classified as something else.[12] The next stumbling block is the Crown Prosecution Service, which has to decide whether a case stands a good chance of achieving a conviction. Because rape cases are often thrown out by courts, the CPS tends to be more cautious than it should.

However, Lees's view is that the real problem lies with the courts themselves: the tendency for cases to be downgraded and/or dropped (as already mentioned) happens because of what the police and CPS know about the courts. Lees charts a whole series of problems in court which lead to a low rate of convictions.

One serious point is that the prosecuting counsel is regarded as working on behalf of the public and not as someone seeking justice for the victim. For this reason s/he does not meet the victim to discuss the presentation of her case, whereas the defence counsel meets the defendant. Given the very upsetting nature of the evidence rape victims are needing to give, this failure to offer them any support in court is shameful.[13] Provided the prosecuting counsel takes seriously his or her duty to present the evidence - including relevant matters which do not fully support the case - meeting the victim to prepare the case seems an obvious idea. In addition, the prosecuting counsel needs a better knowledge of the typical circumstances of rape. According to Lees, basic questions which would give an

---

[11] The high rate of acquittals is not reflected in press coverage - see Keith Soothill, 'Another media crime myth', *Guardian*, 13th January 1998. A high attrition rate in rape cases is neither new nor exclusively British, although the current British situation is particularly serious - see Temkin, *Rape and the Legal Process*, pp. 12-16.

[12] Lees, *Carnal Knowledge*, pp. 98-103. The point that fluctuations in official statistics in the rate of rape are currently more likely to be the product of changes in measurement techniques rather than changes in behaviour is made in the US context by Gary F. Jensen and Maryaltani Karpos, 'Managing Rape: Exploratory Research on the Behaviour of Rape Statistics', *Criminology*, Vol. 31, No. 3, 1993, pp. 363-85. See also the discussion in Estrich, *Real Rape*, pp. 10-20. Cf. Sampson, *Acts of Abuse*, pp. 30-31.

[13] Lees, *Carnal Knowledge*, p. 106.

indication of whether the victim consented are often neglected by the prosecution - for example, if sex took place on waste ground, in a car or a lift shaft, was there any discussion of going to either of their homes? Was there any discussion of contraception or of safer sex? What sort of assumptions does the defendant make about consent?[14]

Another unsatisfactory area is the issue of evidence of the victim's sexual history. Despite the 1976 legislation, the tactics of many defence counsel seem to be to introduce any evidence which they can find of the victim's sexual history, relevant or not, in order to persuade the jury that the woman in question has loose morals and would very likely have consented to sex at the time of the alleged rape. This is a complex issue in that some sexual history evidence can be relevant (e.g. of recent consensual sex with the defendant); it is also possible to introduce implied sexual history evidence without mentioning sex (e.g. 'Do you often go alone to city centre pubs near closing time and get drunk?'); and a failure to formally request permission to question the victim on aspects of her sexual history may just be a procedural oversight rather than a substantive breach of the 1976 legislation. However, the overall picture presented by Lees and others is of a calculated defence strategy to denigrate the victim's character, one which all too often works. Put this together with discussion of the victim's menstruation and displays of her underwear handled with rubber gloves in a court where the victim might be more-or-less the only woman present, and one can see why rape trials are often described as a second rape.[15]

Lees proposes that the law on sexual history should be tightened, but any law will work only as well as the judges and counsel who are supposed to uphold it. Judges are overwhelmingly male, elderly, upper-middle class, and public school and Oxbridge educated. They are often appointed on the basis of an excellent record in areas of the law which have nothing to do with rape, and have little training or expertise in dealing with rape cases.[16] Before the 1976 Act on sexual history evidence it was not uncommon to find the judge joining with the defence

---

[14] Lees, *Carnal Knowledge*, pp. 253-4.

[15] Lees, *Carnal Knowledge*, pp. 129-55. Lees is providing further evidence in support of an earlier study by Zsuzanna Adler, *Rape on Trial*, Routledge, London, 1987. A much more detailed study of the use of sexual history evidence, which broadly supports Lees's case, but which looks more carefully at the complexities of court procedure, is to be found in Beverley Brown, Michèle Burman and Lynn Jamieson, *Sex Crimes on Trial: The Use of Sexual Evidence in Scottish Courts*, Edinburgh University Press, Edinburgh, 1993. Scottish law on sexual history evidence in rape and sexual assault trials is different from that in England and Wales, and was designed with perceived flaws in the law south of the Border in mind. The fact that Scottish courts still permit a considerable use of sexual history evidence going well beyond the apparent intentions of the reformed legislation which has applied in Scotland since 1986 strongly supports Sue Lees's next contention, which is that considerable reform and retraining of the judiciary is needed.

[16] Lees, *Carnal Knowledge*, p. 246.

counsel in asking the victim prurient questions of dubious relevance to the case in hand. It is not surprising to find that judges are less vigilant than they should be in excluding irrelevant evidence of sexual history. An additional reason for this is that convictions in cases where sexual history questions are ruled out tend to be overthrown by the Court of Appeal.[17] Lees argues for a series of reforms: judges more representative of the community to be appointed for sexual assault trials, better training for judges, more accountability. Some of her proposals would have effects well beyond rape trials, but would certainly be worth looking at seriously.

Sexual history evidence tends to be introduced in the guise of the defence testing the credibility of the complainant. Normally in non-sexual cases if a defendant attacks the credibility of the complainant he is deemed to have 'thrown away his shield', and the prosecution gains the right to question him as to his previous convictions and character. Rape trials are an exception to this, although sometimes there would clearly be very damaging evidence were the normal procedure followed.[18]

A particularly alarming finding from Lees's work was that the same defendants were sometimes acquitted in several trials where they were accused of assaulting different women on different occasions but in broadly similar circumstances. There is a male nightmare of being accused of rape where the only real evidence is of her word against his, but where this happens on several occasions (seven times in two cases looked at by Lees) in a short interval there is a strong suggestion of serial rape rather than very bad luck. Lees argues that such trials should be held together rather than in series; the law allows for this, but it seems that the similarity criteria are too stringent at present.[19]

Lees's book was published in February 1996 and therefore does not include a further cause for concern which emerged in two trials later that year: excessively lengthy cross-examination of the victim. In one Julia Mason was subjected to a very detailed, six-day cross-examination by her attacker who was defending himself and seemed to relish the chance to re-live the event; she waived her right to anonymity in order to publicise her ordeal and argue that others should be spared a similar experience. In the other trial a Japanese student was cross-examined for twelve days by six separate defence teams, repeatedly going over the same ground. Measures to limit cross-examination to a thorough, rather than excessive, interrogation of the victim are needed.

Lees also argues for a series of measures to make rape trial less traumatic for the victim: avoidance of undue delay during which the victim experiences uncertainty, and, possibly, intimidation from the accused; separation in court waiting areas between victims and defendants and their families; the possibility of

---

[17] Lees, *Carnal Knowledge,* pp. 242-4.

[18] The legislation about attacking the credibility of the complainant is found in Section 1 (f) (11) of the Criminal Evidence Act 1898. The exception in sexual cases dates from Selvey v. DPP - see Lees, *Carnal Knowledge,* p. 156.

[19] Lees, *Carnal Knowledge,* Ch. 6.

hearing evidence in private and of reporting restrictions of victim evidence; the use of screens or of video evidence to prevent victims being intimidated in court by defendants.[20] A further idea, proposed particularly by Jennifer Temkin, is for the rape victim to have her own specific legal representation.[21]

Two points should be stressed in conclusion to this summary of the current British situation. First, I accept Lees's assumption that the vast bulk of the complaints of rape recorded currently at British police stations are genuine and should ideally be prosecuted. Later in this book I shall cast some doubt on some of the claims made about the extent of date and acquaintance rape. However, there is clearly a gulf between accepting claims that there are some 4,600 cases of rape in England and Wales annually and accepting that one woman in four is the victim of rape or attempted rape. Second, the more marginal cases which appear in some of the surveys on rape, together with highly publicised cases such as that of Austen Donnellan, heighten male fears that there is a feminist agenda which would accept all claims of rape and make it easy for virtually any woman to ruin any man by making false claims. This fear in turn plays some role in the high rate of acquittals in rape cases which Lees rightly deplores. There is, however, a considerable distance between the cases Lees considers and the relatively marginal cases which appear in the surveys. A general realisation of this might well raise conviction rates.

Theories of rape

My aim in this section is not to provide a full theoretical account of why rape occurs. It is rather to take existing theories about rape and to make some comments about the way in which date rape is understood.

Before the intervention of second wave feminists, rape tended to be understood as the act of an individual psychopath. This approach has now been abandoned except, perhaps, for the interpretation of a few extremely violent and unusual incidents.[22] The current approaches to rape are summarised in a very

---

[20] Lees, *Carnal Knowledge*, pp. 253-5. Jill Radford points out that the first male victim of rape, under the new definition in the Criminal Justice Act 1994 under which men can be victims of rape, was screened from the defendant, whereas this has never been done for women in the UK.

[21] For her account, see Temkin, *Rape and the Legal Process*, pp. 162-190.

[22] As an exception to this, one recent article does claim a link between student sexual aggression and psychopathy, but this seems more of a technical linking between some tendency to impulsive antisocial behaviour or callous exploitation of others and self-reported sexual aggression than a claim that college date rape is caused by what the public would see as rabid psychopaths. See David S. Kosson, Jennifer C. Kelly and Jacquelyn W. White, 'Psychopathy-Related Traits Predict Self-Reported Sexual Aggression Among College Men', *Journal of Interpersonal Violence*, Vol. 12, No. 2, 1997, pp. 241-54.

comprehensive survey by Ellis.[23] Ellis categorises current theorising on rape into three main perspectives. The first of these is the feminist approach, developed initially by Brownmiller and Griffin. The feminist approach sees rape as aimed not at sexual gratification but at the domination and control of women, i.e. at maintaining patriarchy. This approach tends to be based on a biological distinction, although biology can be accentuated or ameliorated to some extent by socialisation: ...'in terms of human anatomy the possibility of forcible intercourse incontrovertibly exists...When men discovered they could rape they proceeded to do it'.[24] The theory tends to be tied to social inequality between men and women, although, as Ellis points out, it is not clear whether, as men and women become more equal, one would expect rates of rape to rise because men try to reassert their dominance by other means, or fall because they come to respect women as equals.[25]

The second approach Ellis calls the social learning approach. This starts from the idea that repeated exposure to almost any stimulus tends to promote positive feelings towards it. Aggressive behaviour towards women is seen as a learned response. Men learn to rape from direct imitation of life or from the media; they associate sex with violence, having seen the two together repeatedly; they absorb the myths of rape;[26] they get desensitised to pain and humiliation by viewing aggressive pornography.[27] This approach sees rape as a basically sexual act, whilst accepting that anger and domination may play a large part in it. It sees rape as strongly linked to cultural traditions: rape is seen as the extreme end of a spectrum in which men are active and aggressive and women passive; men take the sexual initiative while women set the limits.[28] Almost all the work on date rape discussed in this book fits into this second perspective;[29] its authors would

---

[23] Lee Ellis, *Theories of Rape*, Hemisphere Publishing Corporation, N.Y., 1989.

[24] Susan Brownmiller, *Against our Will: Men, Women and Rape*, Penguin, Harmondsworth, 1976, p. 14.

[25] Ellis, *Theories of Rape*, p. 11. On this cf. Sylvia Walby, *Theorising Patriarchy*, Basil Blackwells, Oxford, 1990, p. 145.

[26] For a classic statement of the myths of rape, see Martha R. Burt, 'Cultural Myths and Supports for Rape', *Journal of Personality and Social Psychology*, Vol. 38, No. 2, 1980, pp. 217-30.

[27] Ellis, *Theories of Rape*, p. 12. The evidence on whether and how pornography of various kinds increases male tendencies to rape is extensive and inconclusive, and not immediately pertinent to the issues discussed here. For further discussion see below, Ch. 4 and Ellis, *Theories of Rape*, pp. 24-7, 35-9.

[28] Lynne Segal's thoughtful chapter in *Slow Motion: Changing Masculinities, Changing Men*, Virago, London, 1990, Ch. 9 basically fits this model, although with more stress on material circumstances.

[29] The one exception to this which I have encountered is Alison West, 'Tougher Prosecution when the Rapist is not a Stranger: Suggested Reform to the California Penal Code', *Golden Gate University Law Review*, Vol. 24, 1994, pp. 169-88, but her claim that

almost all be quite properly described as feminists, so that Ellis could easily have called the social learning approach a second feminist approach.

There are strong attractions in this approach for authors interested in date rape. First, the claim of 'feminist theory' (meaning Ellis's first category) that rape is just about domination is more asserted than demonstrated.[30] Whilst women of any age are raped, the available evidence points strongly to the peak age for rape (however defined) coinciding with the peak age of sexual attractiveness (say, 15-35) as it is usually understood.[31] A crime simply devoted to humiliating women as a sex would presumably be more evenly spread. Groth, in a categorisation of rapes which is widely respected, divides them between rapes based on anger, on power and on sadism. The numerical majority of rapes falls into the power category, i.e. enough force is used to secure sex. In anger rapes, in contrast, rape is used as a form of revenge and the victim is subjected to violence going well beyond what is necessary to secure sex. In sadistic rapes the victim is subjected to a variety of humiliations going well beyond the limits of normal sexual gratification. Finally, and most important from our point of view, the evidence points strongly towards date rape being based on a desire for sex. There is a strong suggestion that date rapists usually try seduction first, turning to rape if it fails, and violence in date rape is usually absent or slight, just enough being used to secure compliance.[32] Of course, Groth does not claim that his categories are watertight, and acts including rapes may be motivated by purposes other than what is being acted out.

Ellis's third approach is evolutionary theory, in which rape is understood as a technique whereby males attempt to maximise their chances of reproducing themselves by mating with as many females as possible, whilst females seek steady and reliable males to help care for their young.[33] It is true, as we have seen in discussing the social learning theory, that the women most often subjected to rape are at the age seen by our society as most sexually attractive, which is also the peak age for having children. However, rape is not usually seen as a direct strategy to maximise offspring. There is no support for the view that women who say they are infertile immediately become unattractive to rapists. Any biological imperative would thus seem to be heavily socially mediated, giving the evolutionary theory at best a background role. Nonetheless, on one point the evolutionary approach achieves good predictions. There is only a very little

---

'rape is a crime of violence and power, not passion or sexual pleasure', p. 186, is more of an assertion than an argued position.

[30] See, for example, Craig D. Palmer, 'Twelve Reasons Why Rape is NOT Sexually Motivated: A Skeptical Examination', *The Journal of Sex Research*, Vol. 25, No. 4, 1988, pp. 512-30; cf. Russell Vannoy, *Sex Without Love: A Philosophical Exploration*, Prometheus Books, Buffalo, 1980, p. 56.

[31] Ellis, *Theories of Rape*, p. 50. I am assuming that peak sexual attractiveness coincides with peak childbearing years.

[32] Ellis, *Theories of Rape*, p. 22.

[33] Ellis, *Theories of Rape*, pp. 14-15.

evidence of violent stranger rape being carried out by women on men.[34] It appears that the commonsense objection that men's erections would fail under threat is in fact false, or partly false. If women were to put their mind to it, then, they would have no great difficulty in carrying out violent stranger rapes on men by operating in groups, using weapons and surprise. If erections failed they could force men to carry out cunnilingus or, if rape is seen as based on sexual humiliation, simply inflict other sexual humiliations on them. Despite these possibilities, violent stranger rape is in fact overwhelmingly a crime carried out by men on women and not vice-versa. Generally, comparisons between men and women point to a much greater degree of overlap than is found here: men may be more violent or better at maths or worse at language skills, but only somewhat and on average. Note that this is a discussion of violent stranger rape. The issue of a female version of date rape is more complex and needs more discussion.

Overall, then, the best approach to date rape is that based on some version of social learning theory.

Legal definitions of rape

The focus of interest in this book is on the boundaries of rape: where does rape stop and bad sex or bad manners begin? What, if anything, should be done about near-rape? How rape is defined thus has a considerable effect on our subject matter. Two examples of how rape is defined in surveys illustrate the point. For the purpose of her survey, Diana Russell defines rape as an act of vaginal, anal or oral sexual contact involving force or the threat of injury, or when the victim is asleep, unconscious, severely drugged or physically helpless. This definition is wider, so far as can be seen, than the general public's definition.[35] It is also, as we shall see below, wider than the English law on rape. The point here is not to minimise the seriousness of acts apart from rape, but to indicate that the statistics generated by surveys will show different rates of victimisation depending on what is counted. Under feminist pressure the law in many places has been amended to recognise the existence of spousal rape, and this will obviously also affect the statistics.

A particularly problematic area is the role of drink. In her survey of women students Mary Koss asked the following question:

---

[34] On this see P.M. Sarrel and W.H. Masters, 'Sexual molestation of men by women', *Archives of Sexual Behaviour,* 11, 1982, pp. 117-31, L. Murray, 'When Men are Raped by Women', *Sexual Medicine Today,* Vol. 20, 1982, pp. 14-16. These articles are based on a very small number of cases, and are interesting because they show the existence of a phenomenon widely thought impossible. Male victims of stranger rape by females seem to suffer traumas similar to female rape victims, together with the problem that they tend not to be believed, or are alleged to have enjoyed the experience.

[35] Ellis/Hamilton p.3

Have you had a man attempt sexual intercourse (get on top of you penis) when you didn't want to by giving you alcohol or drugs, but did not occur? Have you had sexual intercourse when you did because a man gave you alcohol or drugs?

These questions correspond, Koss says, to the section of the Ohio Revised Code which defines rape as occurring (amongst other possibilities) when 'for the purpose of preventing resistance the offender substantially impairs the other person's judgement by administering any drug or intoxicant to the other person'.[36] Under English law a man who comes across a woman rendered unconscious by drink and has sex with her is raping her, but a man who has sex with a thoroughly drunk woman at the end of an evening of encouraging her to drink is probably not. Scottish law refers to the 'will' of the rape victim, so having sex with an unconscious woman, although a serious offence, is not defined as rape (this also has an effect on Diana Russell's definition). Thus the legal definition Koss uses will obviously produce more rape victims than will current English or Scottish law.

English judges have found the boundaries of rape hard to define, and it is debatable whether a contemporary judge might not find ways to modify some of the more arcane findings which follow. The basic English law is that rape is an offence which carries a maximum sentence of life imprisonment (Section I (1), Sexual Offences Act 1956, plus s. 37, Schedule 2). The Sexual Offences (Amendment) Act, 1976, as amended by the Criminal Justice and Public Order Act, 1994, s. 142, states that a man commits rape if:

a. He has sexual intercourse with a person (whether vaginal or anal) who at the time of the intercourse does not consent to it; and

b. at the time he knows the person does not consent to the intercourse or is reckless as to whether that person consents to it.

This formulation codifies the notorious House of Lords judgement in Director of Public Prosecutions v Morgan that an unreasonable belief in consent could be a defence against a charge of rape. The consensus amongst reformers is that this provision should be modified; but the actual operation of the law has not led to a rash of unreasonable belief defences, and this issue tends to be seen as having relatively low priority.[37] Since a Lords decision in 1991 rape can occur within

---

[36] In methodological appendix to: Robin Warshaw, *I Never Called it Rape: The MS report on Recognising, Fighting and Surviving Date and Acquaintance Rape*, Harper and Row, New York, 1988, p. 207.

[37] English legal texts tend to carry extensive discussions of unreasonable belief because lawyers find the concepts involved interesting rather than because this defence acts as a

marriage.[38] '[S]exual intercourse involves the slightest penetration and does not require ejaculation'.[39]

The most important point of interpretation is that of consent. The aim in this section is to try to give an account of the current law in England; this may not entirely match up with what happens in court. For example, more resistance by the victim may normally be required for a conviction than the theoretical minimum, which is none. A tradition stemming from the seventeenth century held that rape was intercourse without consent achieved by 'force, fear or fraud'. The current position, as established by the Court of Appeal, is that the question is simply: 'At the time of sexual intercourse did the woman consent to it?'[40] The prosecution has to prove that she did not, but need not prove 'force, fear or fraud', although 'one or more of these factors will no doubt be present in the majority of cases'.[41]

Let us look at each of these, starting with non-consent without any of the other factors. A woman who is asleep or unconscious from drink can be held not to have consented, although, obviously, she will not have done anything at the time. Intercourse with a girl under the age of thirteen is punishable with life imprisonment, although it may not be defined as rape. The notion here is plainly that girls under thirteen are too young to be able to give informed consent. Intercourse with a girl under sixteen is also illegal, but in practice the courts recognise that there is a grey area here, so that a boy of sixteen having consenting sex with a girl just before her sixteenth birthday would be highly unlikely to face prosecution, whereas a man of fifty who had sex with a fourteen year old girl would be guilty of a serious offence.[42] As with age, there will plainly be a grey area here: perhaps some twelve year old girls are more knowledgeable about sex and what it means to consent than are some sixteen year olds; and sixteen year

---

rapists' charter. For a useful American discussion of the way the same issue has been dealt with in various American states, see Douglas N. Husak and George C. Thomas III, 'Date Rape, Social Convention, and Reasonable Mistakes', *Law and Philosophy*, Vol. 11, 1992, pp. 95-126. The discussion of unreasonable belief is on pp. 95-101.

[38] Spousal rape is now recognised in most US states and in much of Europe and the white Commonwealth. English law was relatively slow to change.

[39] Sexual Offences (Amendment) Act, 1976, Section 7(2), s. 44.

[40] For a good but somewhat dated account of consent in US rape laws, see Lucy Reed Harris, 'Towards a Consent Standard in the Law of Rape', *University of Chicago Law Review*, Vol. 43, 1976, pp. 613-45.

[41] J.C. Smith and B. Hogan, *Criminal Law*, 8th Edition, Butterworths, London, 1996, p. 469.

[42] The point that this area is closely tied to the issue of rape is strongly made by American practice. In the US sex with a minor is termed 'statutory rape'. The age of consent has historically varied from seven to twenty one, and there are currently quite a variety of approaches to the issues described above. For a good discussion, see Keith Burgess-Jackson, *Rape: A Philosophical Investigation*, Dartmouth, Brookfield, Vermont, 1996, Ch. 9.

olds are deemed to be sexually adult, although they are not adult for most other purposes. In some US states the law includes the idea that an under-age girl who has previously had sex with other men has a better idea of what is involved in consent than one who has not. Although this carries a danger of serial abuse and of the inappropriate use of sexual history evidence, the underlying notion makes some sense.[43] Whilst not all of the offences described here are legally defined as rape, there seems to be a reasonably commonsense idea that the ability to consent to sex develops as girls pass through their teens, and that sex without consent is a serious offence which, if not rape, is equivalent. I have no proposals for changing the law in this area, but *any* law will inevitably suffer boundary problems, and the distinction between rape and non-rape is consequently inevitably at least somewhat arbitrary. It is also illegal to have sex with a woman who is a 'defective', i.e. suffers from 'severe impairment of intelligence and social functioning'. The arguments in this paragraph about grey areas when it comes to age obviously apply with a little adaptation to the problem of impaired functioning. English law seems to deal tolerably well with the grey area of under-age sex, but when it comes to sex obtained by means which fall short of rape as defined in law but which are plainly unacceptable, it falls down in theory and is very ineffective in practice.

The concept of force appears unproblematical (but practical arguments about the degree of force are common). The concept of fear is more difficult. One problem is that a woman with a knife at her throat may consent to sex, but is obviously not consenting freely. Some judges have attempted to capture what is going on here by distinguishing between consent and submission, but although this is a sensible gesture at a problem the distinction is too vague to function as part of the legal definition of rape. A problem to which we will need to return is that it is difficult to equate different possible threats. An immediate threat of serious force against the woman herself plainly counts as force in the relevant sense. An immediate threat of serious force against someone else also appears to count. What about an immediate threat of *some* force, such as a moderate slap or push? There are obviously problems of interpretation here: are we looking at a situation where if the woman puts up with the slap that is an end to the matter? Or is the slap a form of communication, indicating that the assailant will do whatever is necessary to get his way?[44]

The Criminal Law Revision Committee[45] took the view that threats of force to be carried out sometime in the future should count as procurement[46] and carry a

---

[43] See Burgess-Jackson, *Rape,* Ch. 9.

[44] There are likely to be serious problems of interpretation here, as most graphically illustrated in the US *Rusk* case in which his 'heavy caresses' was her 'light choking'. For a full description of this see Estrich, *Real Rape*, pp. 63-6.

[45] Fifteenth Report, para. 2.29.

[46] Under the Sexual Offences Act, 1956, it is an offence to procure a woman to have sexual intercourse by threats, intimidation, false pretences or false representations. These

23

lesser penalty than rape. In Britain this view generally makes more sense than in a feudal or totalitarian country, where such threats might be virtually certain to be carried out, but even here a man known to be prone to domestic violence might be seen as having a very good chance of carrying out his threat.[47] What about a threat to dismiss someone from her job? For a woman in a serious career job with no easy alternative employment this would probably be a more serious threat than a slap; for a woman about to leave a casual job it might be less serious. These threats would lead to a charge of procurement, not of rape. The courts seem to have varied in their treatment of threats by police and others to report offences committed by the woman as a way of blackmailing her into having sex, one case having led to a conviction for rape and another not;[48] but, again, a sufficiently plausible and serious threat to cause a woman trouble with the police might be much more alarming than a slap. Emotional blackmail, such as a threat to break off an engagement, would not lead to a charge of rape, yet could be more distressing than mild physical violence. Smith and Hogan suggest that perhaps the line between prosecutable and trivial threats should be drawn in the same way as in cases of blackmail, i.e. a prosecutable threat 'must be a threat which a person of the age and with the other characteristics of the woman could not reasonably be expected, in the circumstances, to resist'.[49] Although this is a sensible approach, it still has a lot of problems: similar people's resistance varies greatly in similar circumstances, and emotional blackmail can be very powerful, but also works both ways (i.e. the victim has at least some capacity for counter-threats).

Moving on to fraud, judges have found themselves taxed with some rather bizarre distinctions which have little direct bearing on date rape, but which are worth bearing in mind when considering comparisons. There is little problem in English law that a man who induces a woman to have sex with her by impersonating her husband or boyfriend is guilty of rape.[50] Deception as to the nature of the act, for example, inducing a woman to believe that she is having a surgical operation when she is in fact having intercourse, is clearly rape. On the

---

offences carry a maximum of two years' imprisonment. The woman can be procured by the defendant for his own benefit; however, these offences are rarely made use of. (See J.C. Smith and B. Hogan, *Criminal Law*, 8th Edition, Butterworths, London ,1996, p. 473.

[47] For a further exploration of this issue, see Jill Radford and Liz Kelly, 'Self-Preservation: Feminist Activism and Feminist Jurisprudence', in Mary Maynard and June Purvis, eds, *(Hetero)sexual Politics*, Taylor and Francis, London, 1995, pp. 186-99. Radford and Kelly propose a new defence of self-preservation, which would reduce a murder charge to manslaughter. Whilst being defined in gender-neutral terms, self-preservation would be a defence largely used by women who killed their violent or sexually abusive partners because they could find no other way out. A woman who might need to use this defence would - with good reason - see future violence as inevitable.

[48] See Smith and Hogan, p. 471.

[49] Smith and Hogan, p. 475.

[50] Smith and Hogan, p. 469.

other hand, deception involving a fake wedding ceremony was not held to be rape on the grounds that bigamy is not held to be rape: yet the trauma caused by such a deception must surely be as bad or worse than that caused by the other frauds discussed in this paragraph.[51]   A rather wider range of frauds appears to be covered by the charge of procurement, although Smith and Hogan are rather vague as to how far they extend.[52]

Reverting briefly to the definitions used by Koss and Russell, we have seen that much of what they describe is illegal under English law, although not everything involved is rape. In addition, of course, acts involving oral sex would be covered by the English law on indecent assault. One area where English law is possibly wider than the American definitions is that rape occurs if the man 'declines to withdraw on consent being revoked or on realising that [the woman] does not consent'.[53] Although rarely prosecuted, one would guess that offences of this sort could figure quite substantially in surveys of date rape, although they are not covered by Koss's survey which is the basis of Warshaw's book.

Rape as a moral category

The focus of this book is on rape as a moral rather than a legal category. Rape is less problematic than other moral issues such as abortion or euthanasia, where there is substantial debate as to whether the law is seriously out of line with morality. I have not run across any philosophical claims that rape is acceptable in some circumstances. However, there are three important reasons for treating rape as a moral issue.

First, it allows us to discuss the seriousness of particular acts without trying to put matters into legal terminology, or to consider the - perhaps unintended - effects of legislative proposals. If, for example, it seems desirable on moral grounds to see rape less as an absolute 'either it is rape or it isn't' type of offence and more as a series of gradations from a very serious interference with another person through to bad manners, that could be reflected in English law either by rewriting the law on rape on the lines first carried out in Michigan, and having a graded series of sexual assaults in which the word 'rape' is never mentioned, or by tacking this idea on to the existing English law of rape together with the English law on procurement. Either of these approaches could produce much the same effects, but each would have its own legal advantages and drawbacks to do with

---

[51] For the judgement in *Papadimitropoulos*, which involved a fraudulent wedding ceremony, and discussion, see J.C. Smith and Brian Hogan, *Criminal Law: Cases and Materials,* Third Edition, Butterworths, London, 1986. This case actually happened in Australia, and some Australian states have now changed the law to make sex obtained through fraudulent wedding ceremonies rape.

[52] Smith and Hogan, *Criminal Law,* p. 470.

[53] Smith and Hogan, *Criminal Law,* pp. 468-9.

the way it fitted into the rest of English law. Alternatively, consider the view that the worst cases of rape are as bad as murder. This was evidently held in some southern states of the USA, which therefore imposed the death penalty for rape up to the 1960s. Even if the moral basis of this view is acceptable, the practical effect in court was that juries were very reluctant to convict rapists, who therefore tended to be put on probation for minor offences rather than executed, the main exception being black men accused of raping white women. There would thus be a good case for someone who held that rapists morally deserve to die actually advocating a lesser penalty in order to secure convictions.

Second, it will become apparent in Chapter 3 that many of the claims about date rape would require such a massive expansion of English prison accommodation if all rapes were successfully prosecuted that getting rid of date rape by prosecution alone is not a realistic aspiration. Thus the obvious role for legal change would be as an encouragement to moral change, and there is much scope for moral discussion and education.

Third, rape is so plainly morally abhorrent that philosophers and others have tended to use something of a scattergun approach in listing reasons why it is wrong, and a consistent and carefully thought-out account is a good basis for considering how extensive should be the range of acts covered by our abhorrence of rape.

In what follows I want to make things as simple as possible by asking what is the wrong done by a stranger-rapist.

There are two main issues which need to be considered. The first is the definition of the wrongful act, the second is the nature of the harm inflicted. On the first question I am happy to accept the arguments of J.H. Bogart, who argues that rape is non-consensual sex. He reaches this conclusion by considering defining rape as forcible, coerced, non-voluntary and non-consensual sex. He argues that only the last of these covers the five main categories which should be included in the 'core domain of rape', these being: sex obtained by force or threat of force against the victim; sex obtained by threats against a third party; sex while the victim is incapacitated; sex obtained by fraud; and sex involving a child. His basic argument is that children are incapable of consent to sex, even thought they may appear to be voluntarily participating without force or coercion. At the other end of the list, sex obtained by force is non-consensual as well as forcible, coerced and non-voluntary. Bogart seems to me to have captured the sense behind English law and the better US laws that the minimum definition of rape is that it is sex without the consent of the victim.[54]

Some feminists take the view that rape should be seen as against the victim's will rather than without her consent, because consent is a very passive concept. We should, they argue, be advocating sex where the active will of the woman involved is seen as central. I am happy to agree with this view as an account of the

---

[54] J.H. Bogart, 'On the Nature of Rape', *Public Affairs Quarterly,* Vol. 5, 2, April 1991, pp. 117-136, references to pp. 118-20.

sort of sex which should be encouraged. However, a woman who genuinely consents to entirely passive sex, if such a thing is possible, does not seem to be consenting to rape. Further, children who are able to do things voluntarily, but who are too young to fully understand the meaning of sexual consent are not clearly protected if the concept of will is made central.[55] There is also the problem of a woman who is unconscious. Unless she has previously stated that she does not want sex while unconscious, a man who has sex with her is not violating her will, which she is incapable of expressing, but he has emphatically not obtained her consent.

Moving on to the second question, what is the harm inflicted by having sex without consent? There are several possible answers here. They plainly overlap, and there is, of course, nothing to stop several answers being simultaneously right. Here are some suggestions:

Rape violates the *autonomy* of the person. The victim is denied the right to determine an important area of her life. Alternatively, she is treated as merely a means for the rapist.[56]

Rape violates a person's *sexual self-determination*. Sexuality is an important area in the formation of an individual's personality.

A person has a right to *control* his or her own *body* (or a right to bodily integrity). Rape violates that right.

Rape *alienates* an important aspect of a person, reducing her to a fragment of her being.[57]

---

[55] Cf. ibid., p. 119.

[56] This latter formulation involves an appeal to the Kantian principle that it is morally wrong to use someone as merely a means. To use someone as a means *with* their informed voluntary consent is frequent, normal and moral - it happens almost every time someone buys something from a shop, for example: the vendor is used as a means for the purchaser to get a commodity, but the vendor knows this is happening and is happy about it. This approach is taken by Thomas A. Mappes, 'Sexual Morality and the Concept of Using Another Person', in his *Social Ethics: Morality and Social Policy*, McGraw-Hill, New York, 1987, pp. 248-62. Cf. the analysis of treating women as sex objects in Linda LeMoncheck, *Dehumanizing Women*, Rowman and Allanheld, New Jersey, 1985, pp. 12-13. The Kantian basis of this approach is best explained in Onora O'Neill, 'Between Consenting Adults', *Philosophy and Public Affairs*, Vol. 14, No. 3, 1985, pp. 252-77. She emphasises that in intimate contexts we must respect other persons not just as persons in general but to some extent at least as 'the persons they are' (p.260). This might offer a way forward in the discussion of the ambiguities of the language and gesture of consent in Ch. 3 below. For a further discussion of the application of Kantian principles to sex, but less specifically to rape, see Raymond A. Belliotti, *Good Sex*, Kansas University Press, Kansas, 1993, pp. 98-108.

Rape violates an important part of a person's *domain*.[58]

Rape causes *unhappiness* to the victim and others for no justifiable reason.[59]

Before proceeding I want to consider the case of the Mineral Water Fanatic (MWF). This example appears frivolous in such a serious context, but is intended to prove a serious point. The MWF is a hypothetical figure who is convinced everyone should try still mineral water. He forces his victims to swallow a mouthful of mineral water. He has also been known to hold his victims down for brief periods and to hide behind them.[60] He thus violates their bodily integrity and autonomy, and uses another as a thing to conceal himself, alienating aspects of the person's personality. There is no doubt that the actions of the MWF are morally blameworthy, but despite the apparent verbal similarity between what he does and some of the above moral descriptions of rape, few would regard him as guilty of acts approaching murder in their seriousness. We thus seem to be pointed away from autonomy and bodily integrity as reasons for finding rape morally abhorrent, and pointed towards the denial of sexual self-determination and the causing of unhappiness.

Bearing the MWF in mind, let us review the list of reasons why rape is wrong more carefully. Starting with *autonomy*, there is no question that rape denies a person's autonomy. So, however, does forcing someone to swallow a mouthful of water, holding someone down briefly, or making them stand still so someone else can hide behind them. So also, as Bogart points out, does a labour contract: it involves someone sacrificing some of her autonomy in exchange for money.[61] There are two problems with autonomy on its own. First, some violations of a person's autonomy are justifiable. Some restrictions on libellous utterances, for example, are seen as a legitimate violation of free speech because the unwarranted harm done to the libel victim outweighs the right to autonomy enshrined in the

---

[57] For these first four reasons see ibid., pp. 121 et. seq.

[58] See Carolyn M. Shafer and Marilyn Frye, 'Rape and Respect', in Marilyn Pearsall, ed., *Women and Values: Readings in Recent Feminist Philosophy*, Wadsworth Publishing, Belmont, California, 1986, pp. 188-96, cf. Joan McGregor, 'Force, Consent and the Reasonable Woman', in Jules L. Coleman and Allen Buchanan, eds, *In Harm's Way*, Cambridge University Press, Cambridge, 1994, pp. 231-54.

[59] This reason is dismissed by Bogart, 'On the Nature of Rape', but is obviously important in a substantial literature on the effects of rape, to be discussed shortly.

[60] This character is adapted from Murphy's sushi stuffer - see Jeffrie G. Murphy, 'Some Ruminations on Women, Violence and the Criminal Law', in Coleman and Buchanan, eds, *In Harm's Way*, pp. 209-230, p. 214. I have changed sushi into mineral water on the grounds that the former is more dangerous to force into people's mouths.

[61] Bogart, 'On the Nature of Rape', p. 129.

defence of free speech. By itself this problem is not serious, because the violation of autonomy in instances of rape is grave, whilst the justification for it is slight. This leads us on to the second problem. Why is rape seen as a grave violation of autonomy? The main explanations are that sexuality is central to the personality, and that this particular violation causes great distress. Autonomy does not appear to be a good reason independently of these other two.

We shall return to *sexual self-determination*. What about the right to *control* one's own *body*? The same problems apply to this idea as to that of autonomy. I am not sure that we have an absolute right to control our own bodies. If I am holding onto a friend to stop him from falling from a great height it is debatable whether I have a right to let go of him in order to scratch my nose. Again the heart of the problem is that of the sexual parts of one's body, their central role in the claimed right of control, and of the distress caused by sexual violation.

The idea of *alienation* involves a claim that in some sense I own my person and personality, and that some state or states of this person are acceptable or natural or ideal, whilst other states are alienated. We thus add to the problems involved in the idea of autonomy the difficulty of showing that a certain state *is* ideal or natural or proper. Human beings are very heavily involved in various cultures and it is difficult to decide what is natural or proper. One possibility, of course, is to say that the individual decides what is natural or proper for her, but this then makes the idea of alienation redundant and replaces it with autonomy.

Shafer and Frye's idea that rape violates a person's *domain* involves the assertion that a domain is a person (a behaving body) and the space it occupies. The activities, tools and materials the person needs to carry out her goals are included, as are the 'resources of its work, play, recreation, exercise, solace and amusement'. Bending someone's will, dulling her intelligence or affecting her sense of identity 'comes very near the centre of her domain'. The idea of a domain is thus another way of stating that individuals have right to autonomy. As Shafer and Frye then acknowledge, people's rights to autonomy may conflict, in which case 'it seems only reasonable to concede the power of consent in a conflict over a given item to the person to whose domain it is more central - that is, to the one more profoundly affected by it'.[62] As with the claim about autonomy, this claim about persons' domains says something important about rape *if* it is accepted that sexual self-determination is very close to the centre of someone's domain.[63]

---

[62] Shafer and Frye, 'Rape and Respect', p. 191.

[63] The same idea is expressed by Carole Pateman in the context of prostitution: 'the services of the prostitute are related in a more intimate manner to her body than those of other professionals. Sexual services, that is to say, sex and sexuality, are constitutive of the body in a way in which the counselling skills of the social worker are not...Sexuality and the body are, further, integrally connected to conceptions of femininity and masculinity, and all these are constitutive of our individuality, our sense of self-identity'. Carole Pateman, 'Defending Prostitution: Charges Against Ericsson', *Ethics*, Vol. 93, April, 1983, pp. 561-5, quotation from p. 562. Rape would obviously also violate something

Perhaps one could hold that it is just obvious that this is the case, but a better move is to say that sexual self-determination is very central because violating it causes great distress, whereas the bodily violations carried out by the MWF are much less significant. Although my argument is now moving towards looking at the evil consequences of particular denials of sexual self-determination, it needs to be stressed that the denial of autonomy does remain in the background of my argument. People can decide to put themselves through dangerous and painful experiences, and our willingness to do this on occasion where necessary is part of what makes us moral agents. What follows should thus be seen as placing heavy stress on the consequences of one sort of denial of autonomy.

Our more detailed discussion of the list of evils involved in rape thus points in the same direction as our discussion of the MWF: the other evils seem to be premised on assertions about sexual self-determination backed up by the evidence about the distress caused by the violation of sexual self-determination. This latter point seems to me to be crucial: if violating sexual self-determination *never* did anyone any obvious harm, then rape would surely not be seen as any more harmful than the minor interference involved in, say, pressing a leaflet advocating a particular point of view into someone's hand, or causing someone to slow down a very little when driving. We thus have a basically rule utilitarian view of rape: it is evil because any benefit to the rapist is vastly outweighed by the typical consequences of rape.[64]

Bogart discusses and rejects the idea that an experiential element is intrinsic to the harm of rape. The experience of victims varies, he says: there is no common experience.[65] I am sure that the experience varies, but moral condemnation should be concerned with typical or frequent experiences. If some women are unaffected and others suicidal following rape, whilst substantial disturbance is typical, then rape is about as blameworthy as other acts which cause substantial disturbance on average.

A consequence of my approach here is that rape has a cultural and material element to it: it is more wrong for some women in some cultures than for others. In our culture, for example, a raped woman is not seen as inherently unmarriagable, although her sexual relationships will very likely be disrupted. To that extent, then, rape is less serious for us than for people who have that belief. Rape victims in modern western countries are typically offered abortions if

---

constitutive of our individuality and sense of self-identity. Cf. Keith Burgess-Jackson, *Rape: A Philosophical Investigation,* Dartmouth, Brookfield, Vermont, 1996, on the radical feminist theory of rape as something which essentially degrades the woman (p. 53). Estrich captures the same point by insisting that rape is not *simply* an assault but has its own 'unique indignity' - see Estrich, *Real Rape*, p. 81.

[64] For a fundamentally similar conclusion based on an analysis of rape as a form of sadism, see Russell Vannoy, *Sex Without Love: A Philosophical Exploration*, Prometheus Books, Buffalo, 1980, p. 59.

[65] Bogart, 'On the Nature of Rape', p. 122.

necessary. It is obviously traumatic to put a woman in the situation of having to make decisions about abortion, but arguably somewhat less traumatic than leaving her with no choice and an unwanted child. Going in the other direction, rape victims today have some fear of AIDS, which was absent some years ago and may perhaps become less of a fear in the future.[66]

The evil consequences of stranger rape[67] in modern western societies have been well charted by anti-rape activists and experts. Many victims suffer a version of post-traumatic stress disorder involving anger, depression, sleeplessness and flashbacks. Victims frequently break up with existing partners, leave their jobs, move house, move to another location. Their sexual functioning is often disrupted. Obviously the disruptions I have listed involve economic as well as psychological costs; for American victims the economic costs may include medical expenses. There is some uncertainty in the literature about how long the effects last, but they can clearly last a very long time, making it hard to claim that a particular woman has fully recovered or become a 'survivor' rather than a victim.[68] We are clearly dealing with a very serious violation.

The above list covers the main consequences for the individual victim, but the evils caused by stranger rape are more extensive. Rape is very widely feared by women. One survey suggests that violent stranger rape is the crime most feared by American women.[69] Women are generally more afraid of crime than men, and it seems that much of the reason for this is that they are afraid of sexual assault as an aspect of their fear of other crimes. As they are - in official statistics, at least -

---

[66] Linda LeMoncheck writes of the idea in our culture of sex as a defilement of women (the madonna/whore dichotomy). This idea could sensibly be linked to the analysis at this point - see LeMoncheck, *Dehumanizing Women*, pp. 48-9, 53. The idea of cultural relativity is pursued by Linda Grant in an article which suggests that thanks to a less inhibited approach to sex at that time, a date rape experience of the early 1970s might be less traumatic than a similar incident happening to a student today. See Linda Grant, 'Bad Sex', *Guardian Weekend*, 24 September 1994.

[67] In Ch. 3 I shall be discussing the evil consequences of acquaintance rape.

[68] There is a very substantial literature in this area. For a sample of it, which includes many references to further articles, see Julie A. Allison and Lawrence S. Wrightsman, *Rape: the Misunderstood Crime*, Sage, Newbury Park, CA., 1993, pp. 160-1, Patricia A. Resick, 'The Psychological Impact of Rape', *Journal of Interpersonal Violence*, Vol. 8, No. 2, June 1993, pp. 223-55, Ann W. Burgess and Lynda L. Holstrom, 'Rape Trauma Syndrome', *American Journal of Psychiatry*, Vol. 131, 1974, pp. 981-86, Ann W. Burgess and Lynda L. Holstrom, 'Adaptive Strategies and Recovery from Rape', *American Journal of Psychiatry*, Vol. 10, October 1979, pp. 1278-82, Martha R. Burt and Bonnie L. Katz, 'Rape, Robbery and Burglary: Responses to Actual and Feared Criminal Victimisation, with Special Focus on Women and the Elderly', *Victimology*, Vol. 10, 1985, pp. 325-58, Ruth E. Hall, *Ask Any Woman*, Falling Wall Press, Bristol, 1985, Ch. 11.

[69] Mark Warr, 'Fear of Rape among Urban Women', *Social Problems*, no. 32, 1985, pp. 238-50. Cf. British figures quoted in Sampson, *Acts of Abuse*, p. 126, f. 1, cf. *Anxieties About Crime: Findings from the 1994 British Crime Survey*, Home Office, 1994.

victims of crime less than men, this sets up a puzzle. One possible explanation, for which some support could be found in the literature to be discussed in Chapter 3, is that they are actually victims of sexual assault and domestic violence far more than is officially recorded. However, much of the fear rationally generated by unrecorded assaults would be fear of acquaintances and intimates rather than of 'crime' as usually discussed. Another possible explanation is the press coverage of rape. Violent rapes which end in murder receive much more coverage than attempted rapes, although the latter are much more common, as are rapes where the actual rape is the worst experience, rather than accompanying violence or sadism.[70] At any rate, one of the evils of rape is the generation of fear in women who are afraid they might become victims.[71]

A closely-related evil is the restrictions which fear of rape places on women's movements and activities. There are a whole series of issues to do with control of the streets after dark, public transport, the design of urban spaces, which are generated by (mainly women's) fear of crime. If this fear means that women to some extent lose work and education opportunities, leisure activities and the chance of participating in political activities, then rapists are restricting the benefits available to half the population as well as generating fear.[72]

In concluding this chapter I want to stress that I consider stranger rape in any society to be a very serious crime with a series of evil consequences as sketched previously. I see the core of the crime as being a denial of sexual self-determination, and its seriousness as being determined by the series of evil consequences. In debating whether or not particular acts should be considered as rape it is comparison with these features which should be the main focus.

---

[70] For a useful discussion, see Jalna Hanmer and Sheila Saunders, *Women, Violence and Crime Prevention: A West Yorkshire Study*, Avebury, Aldershot, 1993, esp. Ch. 3.

[71] Burgess-Jackson, *Rape: A Philosophical Investigation*, Ch. 10, makes a convincing and original argument that there is a major issue of distributive justice here which is largely overlooked by philosophers who discuss the distribution of social benefits when they should also look at the distribution of fear.

[72] There is quite a large literature in this area. For a few examples see: Hanmer and Saunders, *Women, Violence and Crime Prevention;* Hall, *Ask Any Woman;* Elizabeth Stanko, *Everyday Violence: How Men and Women Experience Sexual and Physical Danger,* Pandora Press, London, 1990. Cf. Stephanie Riger and Margaret Gordon 'The Impact of Crime on Urban Women', in A.W. Burgess, ed., *Rape and Sexual Assault,* Vol. 2, Garland, London and N.Y, 1988.

3 Date rape: the evidence

In the Introduction date rape was identified, following Mary Koss, as rape where there is some level of romantic relationship between the victim and the assailant. Romantic relationships are the dominant pattern for sex in Britain and the USA: both contain other frameworks, such as arranged marriages, prostitution and formalised sado-masochism, but these are relatively marginal. Mary Koss does not elaborate what she means by 'some level of romantic relationship', but from her writing in general and the wider discussion of date rape the obvious conclusion is that the level of romantic involvement can be pretty minimal: an agreement to meet for a date, flirtatious conduct at a party, a past relationship currently ended, all might qualify. A romantic relationship and consent to sex are likely to overlap, although, plainly, minimal romantic relationships such as those listed in the previous sentence fall very well short of consent. Hence the issue of consent and non-consent and how these are identified - by participants, by empirical investigators, and theoretically - is very important in the discussion of date rape.

As a preliminary in this chapter, however, I want to distinguish date rape from some other types of rape which are often discussed alongside it. I shall then review some of the US and British literature which argues that date rape is very widespread. In doing this I shall identify a series of problems concerning sexual consent which will be analysed more fully in the next two chapters.

Forms of rape excluded by the definition used

My focus in looking at date rape as defined by Mary Koss is on how a 'romantic relationship', even a minimal one, is identified, and on how a distinction is made (by researchers, by the woman involved herself or by the man) between the conduct which qualifies the relationship as 'romantic' and conduct which counts as consent to sex. I wish to exclude three forms of rape which, although they

33

overlap with date rape in some discussions, lack behaviour which could remotely be counted as consent by any normal criteria.

The first of these is non-romantic acquaintance rape. Date rape tends to be discussed alongside acquaintance rape. This makes good sense in that dates are obviously acquaintances, so that date rape is a form of acquaintance rape.[1] The converse, however, is obviously not true: rape by non-romantic acquaintances is not date rape. Rape carried out by neighbours, relatives, colleagues etc. where there has been no suggestion whatsoever of a romantic relationship, ranks with stranger rape as a traumatic event. The evidence is that the victim may be somewhat less terrified than when assaulted by a total stranger, but finds that her trust of other people is more severely disrupted than is usual among victims of stranger rape, and recovery appears to be slower.[2] There are a series of reasons for the under-reporting of non-romantic acquaintance rape which have something in common with date rape: the victim may not be able to face the consequences for her friends and family of reporting someone they know and love for rape, or may have a regard for the assailant which leads her to hesitate, or may fear that she will not be believed because the circumstances of the assault can be portrayed as more inviting than they were in fact. In what follows I wish to disregard rape by non-romantic acquaintances for two reasons. First, its causes, and ways of avoiding it or educating potential perpetrators not to attempt it, are obviously rather different from what would be appropriate for date rape. It is worth trying to distinguish statistically between the two sorts of event. Second, much of the evidence that date rape is deeply traumatic is actually evidence that acquaintance rape is deeply traumatic. It seems at least worth asking whether a woman who agrees to, for example, go to bed with her male friend for the night following petting[3] which gets as far as cunnilingus, but who has not actually consented to genital sex, is as traumatised as women suddenly assaulted by the next-door neighbour. My impression is that there is not much evidence in the literature on this question.[4]

---

[1] Date and acquaintance rape are commonly bracketed together throughout the literature; for example, the first book which brought the issue of date rape to public attention in the USA was Robin Warshaw, *I Never Called it Rape: The Ms report on Recognising, Fighting and Surviving Date and Acquaintance Rape,* Harper and Row, New York, 1988.

[2] B.L. Katz, 'The psychological impact of stranger versus nonstranger rape on victims' recovery', in A. Parrott and L. Bechhofer, eds, *Acquaintance Rape: The Hidden Crime,* New York, John Wiley, 1991, pp. 251-69.

[3] Petting is an American term which I shall stick with, as it is more precise and neutral but generic term than British equivalents: caressing, feeling, stroking, kissing, touching, cuddling, fondling, embracing and groping.

[4] Some claims made by Koss may be found in Mary P. Koss and Sarah L. Cook in 'Facing the Facts: Date and Acquaintance Rape are Significant Problems for Women', in Richard J. Gelles and Donileen R. Loseke, eds, *Current Controversies on Family Violence,* Sage, Newbury Park, California, 1993, pp. 104-119, pp. 108-9. The most substantial

Second, another form of rape which appears in the literature on date rape, but which does not fit my definition, is rape under the cover of a date. In this variant the victim is invited on a date, but rape rather than seduction has clearly been planned. This is particularly apparent where instead of a normal date the woman finds she is to be subjected to gang rape. A notorious version of this in the United States is what sometimes happens at college fraternity parties: a (usually) new woman student is given spiked punch which renders her incapacitated, and members of the fraternity then form a 'train' and rape her in turn.[5] There are, however, also examples of women subjected to planned rapes by individuals using a date as a cover, for instance the case of 'Jill' described by Robin Warshaw, who was driven on a first date to a remote spot for a picnic. On arrival the man produced a gun, which he said was loaded, and raped her.[6] Sue Lees's account of serial rapists discusses several men who developed techniques for isolating their victims in what were clearly planned rapes, but where the victim was, for example, invited on a date or being taken home from a party. Time and again the victims describe the assailant as moving very suddenly from normal, indeed possibly 'charming', friendly behaviour to an assault in an isolated place, in some instances involving threats with knives. Lees makes the point that the planned 'acquaintance' element in these cases frequently leads to acquittal in court, and that it is often a technique adopted by men previously convicted of stranger rape.[7] It may be difficult for courts or for other outsiders to always be clear as to what has happened in cases of rape under the cover of a date, but for these instances I would fully support the view of writers such as Lees that there is no sharp distinction to be drawn between this sort of event and stranger rape, and would also support her proposals for making the prosecution of these cases easier.

A third category of rape which I wish to exclude is end-of-acquaintance rape. This occurs at, or after, the end of a relationship. The man returns, perhaps attempts to resume the friendship and is rebuffed, perhaps simply seeks revenge, but in either case proceeds to rape his former lover, often with considerable

---

published survey, which compares 41 college women who had been date raped to 125 who had not, finding that rape victims exhibited significantly more trauma symptoms and lower sexual self-esteem, is B.L. Shapiro and J.C. Schwarz, 'Date Rape: Its Relationship to Trauma Symptoms and Sexual Self-Esteem', *Journal of Interpersonal Violence*, Vol. 12, No. 3, pp. 407-19. (There is also a reference to a poster presentation: J.M. Jones and C.L. Muehlenhard, 'The impact of verbal and physical sexual coercion on women's psychological health', 1993, Kansas Series in Clinical Psychology, Lawrence, KS.)

[5] On this see Warshaw, *I Never Called it Rape*, pp. 100 et. seq.

[6] Ibid., p. 28.

[7] Lees, *Carnal Knowledge*, pp. 159-80. Germaine Greer's description of being invited by a man she met at a party to go for a short walk so they could talk more easily and then being violently raped (*Guardian*, 20 March 1995) fits this pattern.

violence. There are some descriptions of this in the literature on date rape,[8] which are strikingly similar to many descriptions of spousal rape.[9] Cases of spousal rape which come to court tend to involve substantial violence which could be prosecuted even without the legal recognition of spousal rape, and a mere description makes it clear that we are dealing with violent and traumatic events which the victim would hardly have encouraged.[10] On the other hand, it seems highly likely that if rape with some encouragement and without much violence occurs on dates, then it also occurs within marriages. There is some evidence about this sort of spousal rape in the literature I am about to discuss, and it seems to fit my conception of date rape. The evidence seems to be that this sort of spousal rape features less in rape trials than in the breakdown of relationships. Certainly, much of my subsequent discussion is applicable to this sort of event.[11]

Two descriptions of date rape

Before looking at the surveys and statistics about date rape, let us look at two fictional descriptions presented by well-regarded authors on the subject as typical date rapes. These are rather different, but raise many of the themes which need to be analysed. The first comes from Andrea Parrott's introduction to *Acquaintance Rape: The Hidden Crime*:

> Mary and John had been dating for two weeks. Both Mary and John had slept with people in the past but they hadn't had sexual intercourse with each other. On their fourth date, after John took Mary out for a lobster dinner and then to a wild party to meet some of his friends, the couple went to John's apartment. Mary was wearing a sexy, provocative dress. She had spent a lot of time getting ready, because she wanted to look her best for a special evening. After they got to his apartment, they shared a bottle of wine, listened to music,

---

[8] In Robin Warshaw's own case by threatening her with a knife. See Warshaw, *I Never Called it Rape*, p. 5, cf. the case described in Susan Estrich, *Real Rape*, Cambridge, MA, Harvard University Press, 1987, pp. 8-9, or the case of 'Gabrielle' described by Monique El-Faizy, *Guardian*, 23 August 1994.

[9] E.g. David Finkelhor and Kersti Yllo, *License to Rape: Sexual Abuse of Wives*, New York, Holt, Rinehart and Winston, 1985, p. 25.

[10] The events surveyed by Finkelhor and Yllo, *License to Rape*, also generally fit into this pattern - see, for example, pp. 18-19.

[11] A further category of rape which will not be discussed is gay and lesbian date rape. This almost certainly exists, but is much less represented in the literature on date rape. See, for example, the comments in Julie A. Allison and Lawrence S. Wrightsman, *Rape, The Misunderstood Crime*, London, Sage, 1993, p. 49. My excuse is that it would be necessary to establish the dynamics of gay and lesbian dating and sexual aggression in order to start such a discussion, and that this would take us too far afield.

talked, laughed and kissed. Mary told John what a wonderful time she was having with him. John suggested that they move to his bedroom where they could get more comfortable. She nodded in agreement. In the bedroom, they started dancing erotically and kissing passionately. John caressed Mary's breasts, and Mary moaned. When he started to unbutton her blouse, Mary asked him to stop. He kissed her gently and continued to undress her. She begged him to stop. She told him 'No!' emphatically and said that she was not ready for sex with him. He continued anyway, telling her that he knew she wanted it. He told her to relax and that she was really going to like it. John assured Mary that he loved her and that he had been thinking about this moment ever since they first met. He pulled up her skirt and pulled down her panties. While holding both of her arms with one of his hands, he unzipped his fly, took out his erect penis, and penetrated her.

Parrott follows this description up by asserting that Mary was raped.[12] Several themes emerge from this vignette which run through the literature: Mary agrees to a series of invitations which John deems encouraging; John has spent a lot of money on the date; they are both quite drunk; John seems to be suffering from sexual frustration rather than an urge to violence, and the rape involves only enough force to overpower Mary; Mary makes it clear she does not want sex, but does not attempt the sorts of resistance which she might well have used had John been a stranger; Mary would have a very difficult time in court if she attempted to bring charges, and might, indeed, not herself describe what happened as rape.

In a longer description, Lois Pineau talks of a woman who goes out with a man hoping for 'mutual and reciprocal' interest. She comes under pressure to have sex with him, but does not want the kind of sex he wants; perhaps she wants kisses, caressing or foreplay but no more; perhaps she has 'religious reservations', 'concerns about pregnancy or disease, a disinclination to be another conquest'. She may feel that 'if he is in need, she should provide...he is suffering from sexual frustration and ...she is largely to blame'. 'He feels no dating obligation, but has a strong commitment to scoring...uses the myth of "so hard to control" ...[he] becomes overbearing'. She feels 'a bit queasy' from too many drinks:

She is having trouble disengaging his body from hers, and wishes he would just go away. She does not adopt a strident angry stance, partly because she thinks he is acting normally and does not deserve it, and partly because she feels she is partly to blame, and partly because there is always the danger that her anger will make him angry, possibly violent. It seems that the only thing to do, given his aggression and her queasy fatigue, is to go along with him and get it over with, but this decision is so entangled with the events in process it is hard to know if it is not simply a recognition of what is actually

12 Parrott and Bechhofer, *Acquaintance Rape: The Hidden Crime*, New York, John Wiley, 1991, p. 9.

happening. She finds the whole encounter a thoroughly disagreeable experience, but he does not take any notice and would not have changed course if he had. He congratulates himself on his sexual prowess and is confirmed in his opinion that aggressive tactics pay off. Later she feels that she has been raped, but, paradoxically, tells herself that she let herself be raped.[13]

Pineau's description has much in common with Parrott's, but contains some useful additional features. The relationship between date rape and a norm of aggressive male sexuality is strongly made, together with an implicit challenge to that norm; the woman's ambivalent feelings about the episode are very much what emerges elsewhere; the woman's uncertainty about whether her date would become violent if she resisted vigorously is also important.[14]

The exact scope of date rape needs to be debated through a survey of the literature, but the two above descriptions give a good idea of the sort of event we are dealing with.

Introduction to the surveys

The discussion of surveys which follows is quite lengthy. What are the main threads which emerge? To start with, all the surveys show a much higher rate of rape than that found in any variety of official data. An immediate response to this is that something must be wrong in the figures - we surely do not live in a society where rape is so common? Part of what I aim to do is to consider various reasons why the figures might be too high. Some of these are: maybe the samples are skewed; the questions used elicit positive answers from women who do not consider themselves raped, perhaps because the surveys use indirect questions; the definition of rape used may be too wide; rape may be bracketed together with less serious events as 'sexual assault'; intoxication is a particular difficulty, as it is hard to distinguish in a survey between mutually agreed drinking and deliberate use of, say, spiked punch; male and female views of the same events may be different; there may be some degree of failure of memory of assaults, or failure to match memories appropriately to survey questions; the woman may have clearly not consented, but, because she was dealing with an acquaintance, failed to resist the way she would have resisted a stranger (Pineau's 'she let herself be raped'); or 'attempted rape' may be particularly hard to clearly identify using a

---

[13] Lois Pineau, 'Date Rape: A Feminist Analysis', in Leslie Francis, ed., *Date Rape: Feminism, Philosophy and the Law*, Pennsylvania, Pennsylvania State University Press, 1996, pp. 1-26, extract on p. 7; Pineau's interesting article is also available in *Law and Philosophy*, Vol. 8, 1989, pp. 217-43.

[14] For a description of a 'date rape' which she argues is in fact not rape, see Kate Fillion, *Lip Service*, Pandora/Harper Collins, London, 1997, pp. 245-259.

questionnaire.[15] Despite all of these comments, the various surveys build up such a substantial picture of rates of rape well above those in official statistics that their basic message has, I think, to be accepted. Two rather different types of survey round out the picture: one shows that men suffer sexual assaults from women at rates quite similar to those found in the surveys; the other that women (and men) frequently say 'no' when they mean 'yes' or 'maybe', offering miscommunication as a significant explanation for some of the data.

The numerical majority of the surveys considered were carried out by US psychologists. Major surveys by Mary Koss and Diana Russell have been supplemented by numerous smaller studies. A theme in the debate about the US surveys is whether they are a form of advocacy research, i.e. the exaggeration of results in a good cause. Three Canadian surveys published in 1993 appear to be the best example of advocacy research. The British surveys described were largely conducted by activists rather than psychologists; their main problems are to do with sampling rather than the form of question used.

US surveys

The Ms report on date rape

Although some work had been done on date rape previously,[16] the topic was introduced to the American public in 1988 in Robin Warshaw's book *I Never Called it Rape: The Ms Report on Recognising, Fighting and Surviving Date and Acquaintance Rape.*[17] The book is based on statistics drawn from a survey of 6,159 students at thirty-two colleges across the USA directed by Mary Koss, a psychologist, together with vignettes of date and acquaintance rapes drawn from Warshaw's interviews with victims, practical advice on avoiding date rape, on attempting to recover from it, and on supporting victims. On the basis of her

---

[15] Most of these issues are raised, but, given the nature of the article, not discussed at any length in the very useful Charlene L. Muehlenhard et. al., 'Definitions of Rape: Scientific and Political Implications', *Journal of Social Issues,* Vol. 48, No. 1, 1992, pp. 23-44. Cf. Mary E. Craig, 'Coercive Sexuality in Dating Relationships: A situational model', *Clinical Psychology Review,* Vol. 10, No. 4, 1990, pp. 395-423.

[16] Notably by Eugene Kanin, 'Date Rape: Unofficial Criminals and Victims', *Victimology,* Vol. 9, No. 1, 1984, pp. 95-108, but also by, among others, Sheila K. Korman and Gerald R. Leslie, 'The Relationship of Feminist Ideology and Date Expense Sharing to Perceptions of Sexual Aggression in Dating', *The Journal of Sex Research,* Vol. 18, No. 2, 1982, pp. 114-29. The authors follow Kanin's language of, for example, 'coitally-directed' 'aggressive advances' rather than attempted rape.

[17] British readers will find it difficult to get hold of a copy of this book, which was not published in the UK, but descriptions of its content appear frequently in the literature on date rape, and numerous articles by Mary Koss describing her survey on which the book was based are easy to come by.

39

survey Koss estimates that 15% of the female students in her survey had been victims of rape and 12% of attempted rape - and that each victim had been assaulted an average of twice between the ages of 14 and 21. Koss also has a category of 'unwanted sexual touching', and concludes that '[o]nly 45.6% of the young women polled by the study had *never* experienced sexual victimisation'.[18] She also concludes that during a twelve month period 16.6% of all college women were victims of rape or attempted rape.[19] From about the time of Warshaw's book an extensive literature on date rape has grown up, much of it written by psychologists. Before moving on to discuss some of this literature, let us try to make sense of Koss's claims. Given the much lower rate of reporting of rape to the police, let alone convictions in court, an immediate reaction to Koss's claims is to question her methodology. The gap between Koss's claims and official statistics is illustrated by Neil Gilbert. He points out that Koss's findings would lead us to expect that of the 14,000 women students at the University of California at Berkeley in 1990 about 2,000 would have experienced some 3,000 rapes or attempted rapes. In contrast, two rapes were reported to the police, and between 40 and 80 students sought assistance from the campus rape counselling service.[20] Alternatively, as Koss herself points out, the FBI Uniform Crime Reports for 1986 show 246 rapes at 118 American universities, figures roughly in line with Gilbert's account of the reporting of rape to the police at Berkeley.[21]

An immediate point to make is the one seen previously in Chapter 2: Koss's definition of rape follows the relatively wide definition used in the Ohio Penal Code, and defines forced oral or anal sex as rape. However, in *I Never Called It Rape*, Koss and Warshaw say little about oral and anal sex, and in any case, a high rate of indecent assault and nonconsensual buggery (the UK classification of these acts at that time) is about as unacceptable as a high rate of rape.

---

[18] Warshaw, *I Never Called It Rape*, p. 48. It is important to pay careful attention to the language of survey reports. In this case very limited unwanted sexual touching is dubbed 'sexual victimisation'. A more spectacular example is Gloria J. Fischer's survey of college males' lies or false promises used to have sex, typically exaggerating their degree of commitment. This is undesirable behaviour, and more extreme cases might be deemed rape by deception (although Fischer speculates that the women concerned may have been happy to accept the lie in order to justify their own participation in casual sex), but Fischer uses the term 'verbal coercion' to describe the males' behaviour, thus assimilating it to threats of violence - see Gloria J. Fischer, 'Deceptive, Verbally Coercive College Males: Attitudinal Predictors and Lies Told', *Archives of Sexual Behavior*, Vol. 25, No. 5, 1996, pp. 527-33.

[19] Warshaw, *I Never Called It Rape*, p. 48. Note that this leaves us with a high rate of sexual assault before the women reached university; also that the dates of student women are not necessarily student men. Thus American campuses are slightly less dangerous than might be thought from a quick reading of Koss's figures.

[20] N. Gilbert, 'Realities and Mythologies of Rape', *Society*, May-June 1992, pp. 5-10.

[21] Warshaw, *I Never Called It Rape*, p. 171.

Was Koss's sample skewed compared to the population at large? It comprised roughly equal numbers of male and female students taking psychology courses, who were asked to spend one of their classes filling in a questionnaire. Koss asserts that students are a good sub-group of the general population to survey because the peak age for rape is 16-19 and the second highest rate is at age 20-24, whilst 47% of alleged arrested rapists is also under 25. Twenty-five per cent of Americans aged 18-24 are at college.[22] There is some evidence to suggest that college-educated women, particularly white women, claim to be more sexually victimised than males or less-educated women, but it is not clear whether this is because they *are* more victimised, they *remember* their victimisation better, or are more *sensitive* to particular acts.[23] There is no particular evidence about psychology students. Koss's survey did not include colleges devoted to training for the armed services, where researchers suspect higher rates of sexual aggression may well occur.[24]

Koss's claims about the rate of assault are based on the women respondents, so another issue is whether the men in the survey reported the same rate of engaging in rape as the women suffered. Not surprisingly, they did not. From the men's responses to Koss's questions she concluded that of 2971 male students surveyed, over the previous year: 187 had committed rape, and 157 attempted rape. This makes 11.6% of the males, compared to a victimisation rate amongst the women students, measured using similar questions, of 16.6%.[25] Koss says that only 27% of the women students who she classifies as victims of rape identified the incident as rape; only 1% of the males explicitly acknowledged they had committed rape.[26] Why did the men not consider the incidents to be rape? Apart from the obvious answer that people are cautious about admitting major crimes even in anonymous surveys, the general picture is that the male students saw the incidents as less serious. Only 3% hit the victim, compared to 9% of women victims who were hit; according to the men, 75% of the women had been drinking or taking drugs, in contrast to 55% of the women who acknowledged they had been drinking or taking drugs; the men used mild force whilst the women experienced moderate

---

[22] Mary P. Koss, 'Hidden Rape: Sexual Aggression and Victimisation in a National Sample of Students in Higher Education', in A.W. Burgess, ed., *Rape and Sexual Assault*, Vol. 2, Garland, London and N.Y., 1988, pp. 3-20.

[23] On this see particularly Susan B. Sorenson et. al., 'The Prevalence of Adult Sexual Assault: The Los Angeles Epidemiologic Catchment Area Project', *American Journal of Epidemiology*, Vol. 126, No. 6, 1987, pp. 1154-64. Koss accepts elsewhere that educated victims recall more crimes than other less well-educated people, particularly assaults (Mary P. Koss; W.J. Woodruff; M.S; and Paul G. Koss, M.D., 'Criminal Victimisation Among Primary Medical Care Patients: Prevalence, Incidence and Physician Usage', *Behavioral Sciences and the Law*, Vol. 9, 1991, pp. 85-96, p. 94).

[24] Warshaw, *I Never Called It Rape*, p. 193.

[25] Ibid., p. 83.

[26] Ibid., pp. 26, 85.

force; 12% of the men noticed the woman physically struggling, whilst 70% of the women struggled.[27] One explanation of the gap is that men are more accustomed to engaging in physical force than women, and therefore are likely to see their use of force as less serious.

How much difference does it make to distinguish between non-romantic acquaintance rape and date rape? According to Koss's survey, 57% of the rapes she identified happened on dates,[28] but there is no detail about what sort of relationship was involved in the other incidents. Sixteen per cent of rape victims did not know their attacker,[29] but this rate of victimisation by strangers looks very high, and one wonders how an attack following, say, drunken dancing with a student unknown to the woman in question up to the incident would be classified. Again, rape might occur with a boyfriend but not on a date, and women raped but not on dates may have engaged in various degrees of behaviour interpreted as flirtatious by male acquaintances.

So far the questions I have raised might somewhat modify Koss's picture but are not particularly damaging. The most serious issue about Koss's approach is the questions she uses. It is well known that the victims of rape find it difficult to tell of their experiences, and may well be reluctant to include them in responses to an anonymous survey or in discussion with an interviewer from, say, a government survey such as the US Census Bureau, which compiles Bureau of Justice Statistics through anonymous household surveys now called the National Crime Survey.[30] In addition at least some victims of spousal and date rape may feel that an event that was clearly rape was actually their fault because some minor action of theirs triggered off the attack, and therefore not classify the incident as rape. Further, spousal rape has tended to become legally recognised in the USA, but a researcher cannot assume one clear legal situation in compiling questions. Because of this, researchers such as Mary Koss use questions intended to replicate the legal definition of rape without actually asking directly about 'rape'.

Three of the five questions used in the *Ms* survey seem a reasonable way of soliciting evidence of date rape, such as 'Have you had sexual intercourse with a man when you didn't want to because he used some degree of force such as twisting your arm or holding you down to make you cooperate?'[31] (At this point I

---

[27] Ibid., p. 85.

[28] Ibid., p. 11.

[29] Ibid., p. 11.

[30] Koss quotes one survey of women who had reported an assault to the police in which only 54% of the victims would admit to an interviewer that they had been raped. (Mary P. Koss, 'The Underdetection of Rape: Methodological Choices'. This article and Diana E.H. Russell, 'The Prevalence and Incidence of Forcible Rape and Attempted Rape of Females', *Victimology*, Vol. 7, 1982, pp. 81-93, offer criticisms of the National Crime Surveys methods, arguing that one would expect the surveys to underdetect rape.)

[31] Koss, ibid., p. 68.

have to invite readers to peer briefly over an abyss. It would seem that quite a lot of dating relationships are mutually violent - some 28% in one survey of adolescents at middle school and high school. The use of force constitutes the clearest way to differentiate rape from consenting sex. However, what of a relationship where force is a common currency, yet both partners are reasonably happy with the situation? Is rape deemed to be frequent within it because force is used? Or do we have to turn to some higher level of violence to identify rape? The usual criteria do not, at any rate, work in a straightforward way. I certainly subscribe to the feminist view that violence should not feature in interpersonal relationships, and that whatever about its origins women tend to suffer much worse than men in the long term in violent relationships. However, before categorising the sex which occurs in mutually violent relationships as rape (or non-rape) a much more careful discussion with the participants, to see how *they* understand their actions, is needed.)[32]

Koss's other two questions relate to drink and drugs: 'Have you had a man attempt sexual intercourse (get on top of you, insert his penis) when you didn't want to by giving you alcohol or drugs, but intercourse did not occur? Have you had sexual intercourse when you didn't want to because a man gave you alcohol or drugs?' As Gilbert points out, women who gave positive responses to these questions accounted for 44% of those identified by Koss as victims of rape or attempted rape.[33] These questions correspond, Koss says, to the section of the Ohio Revised Code which defines rape as occurring when 'for the purpose of preventing resistance the offender substantially impairs the other person's

---

[32] See, for example, Heather M. Gray and Vangie Foshee, 'Adolescent Dating Violence: Differences Between One-sided and Mutually Violent Profiles', *Journal of Interpersonal Violence*, Vol. 12, No. 1, 1997, pp. 126-41. Obviously the debate as to whether in apparently mutually violent relationships female violence is really all in one form or another of self-defence is relevant here. The authors cited are sure they were being told of genuinely mutual violence. For a larger-scale survey of students which does not deny the existence of female-initiated violence but sees male violence as more serious and widespread, see James M. Makepeace, 'Gender Differences in Courtship Violence Victimisation', *Family Relations*, Vol. 35, 1986, pp. 383-8.

[33] Gilbert, 'Realities and Mythologies of Rape'. Part of Koss's response to this point is a recalculation of her figures. She says that if the item on drink is removed then the attempted rape figure falls from 12% to 8% of women since age 14 and the completed rape figure falls from 16% to 11%. There is a minor mystery here: the fall is around a third, not Gilbert's 44%, so one would expect Koss to correct Gilbert's figure, but she does not. She does go on to point out that a fifth of the college women in her survey were the victims of attempted or completed forcible rape since the age of 14, i.e. she has uncovered a very high rate of rape and attempted rape even if the more contentious cases are discounted. (See Koss and Cook, 'Facing the Facts: Date and Acquaintance Rape are Significant Problems for Women', p. 106.)

judgement by administering any drug or intoxicant to the other person'.[34] Koss's questions would get positive responses from women given spiked punch described as 'non-alcoholic' and thus rendered senseless, who definitely fit the legal definition of rape because unable to give their consent. However, women involved in social drinking who then had sex but regretted it the next day, or who, out of a sense of obligation, had sex at the end of an expensive evening out which included being bought drink would also give 'yes' answers to Koss's second question about drink. It might be better if such conduct did not occur, but it does not fit the normal definition of rape.[35] And in the case of attempted rape when the woman is drunk, how much of an attempt does there have to be to constitute rape?[36]

About a quarter of the women who Koss identified as raped said in the questionnaire that they did not feel victimised, and it may be that the women identified as raped on the basis of the drink question feature strongly in this quarter.[37] Such 'victims' would have been wrongly identified as a consequence of

---

[34] In methodological appendix to, Warshaw, *I Never Called It Rape*, p. 207. In one respect, Koss's question about drink could actually be seen as too narrow: the law in Kansas includes nonconsensual intercourse 'when the victim is incapable of giving consent...because of the effect of any alcoholic liquor, narcotic, drug or other substance, which condition was known by the offender or was reasonably apparent to the offender', i.e. Kansas law disregards the source of the intoxicant. See Charlene Muehlenhard, Susie C. Sympson, Joi L. Phelps and Barrie J. Highby, 'Are Rape Statistics Exaggerated? A Response to Criticism of Contemporary Rape Research', *The Journal of Sex Research,* Vol. 31, No. 2, 1994, pp. 144-6.

[35] For a useful discussion of the interrelation between alcohol and date rape, see Antonia Abbey, 'Acquaintance Rape and Alcohol Consumption on College Campuses: How are they Linked?', *Journal of American College Health,* Vol. 39, January 1991, pp. 165-9.

[36] Cf. Neil Gilbert, 'The Phantom Epidemic of Sexual Assault', *The Public Interest,* Vol. 103, 1991, pp. 54-65, esp. p.59. The importance of getting the relationship between alcohol and consent right is stressed by Paul A. Morgeau's finding from a small student survey that on first dates 'The strongest predictor of sexual involvement was alcohol consumption. The greater the alcohol consumed, the more intimate the reported sexual involvement', Paul A. Mongeau and Kristen L. Johnson, 'Predicting cross-sex first-date sexual expectations and involvement: Contextual and individual difference factors', *Personal Relationships,* Vol. 2, 1995, pp. 301-12.

[37] Responding to critics such as Gilbert who stress that 73% of the 'rape victims' thus classified by Koss did not themselves think they had been raped, Koss replies that one quarter thought they *had* been raped, one quarter thought it was some kind of crime but did not realise it qualified as rape, one quarter thought it was serious sexual abuse but did not realise it qualified as a crime, and the final quarter did not feel victimised. (Mary Koss, 'Defending Date Rape', *Journal of Interpersonal Violence,* Vol. 7, No. 1, pp. 122-6.) In another response to Gilbert she says that only 10% of the women did not feel victimised. (Koss and Cook, 'Date and Acquaintance Rape are Significant Problems', p. 107. I have no explanation for this discrepancy. The 25% figure seems closer to what she says in the original report of the survey.) The relation between women's conceptions of what has happened and legal definitions is a difficult one: plainly it is possible for women to have a

the questions Koss uses. I shall return to the question of drink and consent in Chapter 5. The question of women's own definitions of their experience needs to be treated with caution. Koss emphasises, rightly, that women are not necessarily aware of legal definitions of rape, so that the fact they do not identify an experience as rape does not necessarily mean it was consenting sex. Gilbert points out that Koss gives several different versions of her finding that many of the 'victims' of rape or attempted rape did not identify their experiences in the same way as she does, and that she particularly plays down the explanation of 'miscommunication' used by 49% of the 'victims' identified by her student survey. There will be further discussion of this question in Chapter 4.[38]

It is also worth speculating about attempted rape. 'Have you had a man attempt sexual intercourse (get on top of you, insert his penis) when you didn't want to...?' would certainly cover incidents where the man was fought off with vigour and threatened with the police, but might also include a man failing to take 'no' for an answer at first but desisting when the woman made it clear she was serious. One might, for example, imagine John in Parrott's vignette quoted above not proceeding to rape but kissing Mary and getting on top of her on his sofa before being convinced that she really did mean 'no' and stopping. Most people would, I think, see this, done in a gentle and friendly way, as akin to verbal persuasion rather than a rape attempt.

The formula 'when you didn't want to' is also open to criticism. It is sensible as a way of getting women to think about incidents which would include rape, but people frequently have sex when they don't want to in circumstances no-one would describe as rape. Examples would include a couple who are both tired and would normally not have sex but who know one of them is about to go away for a fortnight on business, men or women who really would prefer to be working or watching the television or reading but who also want to take the opportunity for sex when it is on offer, or want to comfort their partner, or do not want to upset their partner, or who would want sex a bit later but by that time their partner

---

legitimate view that they have been raped which does not fit the legal definition, as was the case before the law recognised spousal rape; or to know they have had an experience of abuse but not recognise that it counts as rape, as may well happen when spousal rape is newly legalised; or, presumably, to *feel* raped when their experience would *not* meet the legal definition. I shall return to this in Ch. 4. For the minute I agree with Koss that the researcher has to put some construction on women's immediate responses, but would emphasise that this needs to be done with great care.

[38] Koss makes this point in various places, notably in Koss and Cook, 'Facing the Facts: Date and Acquaintance Rape are Significant Problems', p. 107. Gilbert's critique of various statements from Koss is on pp. 123-4 of Neil Gilbert: 'Examining the Facts: Advocacy Research Overstates the Incidence of Date and Acquaintance Rape', in Richard J. Gelles and Donileen R. Loseke, eds, *Current Controversies on Family Violence*, Sage, Newbury Park, California, 1993, pp. 120-32. He follows this up still further in: Neil Gilbert, 'Miscounting Social Ills', *Society*, Vol. 31, 1994, pp. 18-26.

would have gone off it or had to go out.[39] Some of Koss's 'victims' might well have answered 'yes' because of episodes of this sort. There is certainly some evidence elsewhere in the psychological literature on date rape that where a couple have had sex with each other more than ten times on previous occasions they are both held to have some degree of obligation to meet the other's sexual needs even if they do not want to have sex at that time.[40]

It is worth noting that the questions used in Koss's survey of women in the general population uses rather different questions, involving the formula 'Has a man made you have sex by...', which is less open to the objections raised above.[41]

Two further findings in Koss's student survey give rise to questions. One is that in her survey 42% of the women she classified as raped had sex again with their assailant,[42] and 55% of the men who had raped said they had had sex again with their victim. A high proportion of relationships subsequently broke up, but I am not clear how this break-up rate compares with that for non-coercive relationships. Koss's immediate explanation is that the victim is trying rationalise her rape into an ongoing relationship and therefore make it acceptable.[43] Later she appears to drop this view and offers three possibilities: further unforced sexual contacts; additional rapes by the same man; and misguided attempts by the victim to control the rapist's behaviour better another time - which seems to be another version of her second new explanation.[44] Mills and Granoff explain a similar finding by saying that the women who were raped 'are perhaps mislabelling the experiences and normalising abusive situations or interactions', or alternatively

---

[39] I think a reasonable formula to cover the sort of situation I have in mind is that 'she wanted to have sex on one level but not on another'; this will need to be considered at some length in Chapters 4 and 5.

[40] See R. Lance Shotland and Lynne Goodstein, 'Sexual Precedence Reduces the Perceived Legitimacy of Sexual Refusal: An Examination of Attributions Concerning Date Rape and Consensual Sex', *Personality and Social Psychology Bulletin*, Vol. 18, No. 6, Dec. 1992, pp. 756-64. Men were seen as more obliged to have unwilling sex to keep their partner happy than were women. Shotland and Goodstein speculate that this concept of sexual precedence has positive effects on a relationship by making it less likely that the partners will seek gratification elsewhere.

[41] Koss et. al., 'Criminal Victimisation Among Primary Medical Care Patients', p. 89. These revised questions appear to classify penetration by fingers or objects using force or threats as rape. I am not, of course, wishing to defend such practices, but this appears to involve a further widening of the definition of rape. There might also be a problem of double counting: attempted or achieved digital penetration would surely often be perceived as a preliminary to rape in the sense of penile penetration, so women might answer 'yes' to two questions but with one single episode in mind.

[42] Cf. 39% of rape victims (not defined) who dated their attacker again afterwards in a smaller survey by Wayne Wilson and Robert Durrenberger, 'Comparison of Rape and Attempted Rape Victims', *Psychological Reports*, Vol. 50, 1982, p. 198.

[43] Koss in Warshaw, *I Never Called It Rape*, p. 63

[44] Koss, 'Defending Date Rape'.

that the women 'perceived themselves as damaged or soiled and stayed with their abusers because no one else would want them'.[45] Another explanation, however, might simply be that at least some of the time the researchers are mis-describing episodes of miscommunication rather than gross abuse, and that further sex between the couple is not surprising. If 25% of Koss's 'victims' did not feel victimised, then probably many of these had sex again with the 'rapist'; this would leave Koss with much less to explain. In Kanin's study of self-disclosed date rapists seven possible cases out of 86 were excluded because the male reported that after a forced penetration the female became 'receptive and co-operative'; the relationships continued with consensual coitus for at least four months after the rape, and the males expressed 'considerable affect for their companions at the time of the "rape"'. Cases of this sort might feature among Koss's victims who had sex again with their rapist, as well as those for whom a more sinister explanation is appropriate.[46]

The other is the question of reporting the rape and seeking counselling. Forty-two per cent of the victims in Koss's survey told no one; 5% reported the incident to the police; 5% sought help from rape crisis centres. Previous intimacy and lack of violence were strongly associated with telling no-one.[47] One cannot tell why this silence was so extensive. Koss's approach would direct us towards the failure of victims to recognise their experience as rape, which is doubtless true for some victims. However, another possibility is that, again, we are seeing the consequences of Koss's ambiguous questions.

I have been concentrating so far on Koss's survey because it was on a large scale and set up many of the issues for subsequent researchers. Let us now move on to look at other American researchers before examining Canadian and British work in this area.

Other US surveys relating to date rape

Another major survey which is frequently quoted is one organised by Diana Russell in San Francisco in 1978. This involved interviews with 930 randomly selected women residents of San Francisco over 18. Twenty-four per cent of the women reported at least one completed rape, and 31% at least one attempted rape; or, putting these figures together, 44% reported at least one completed or attempted rape. Russell classifies these attacks as follows: 14% acquaintance rape, 12% date rape, 11% stranger rape, 8% spouses or ex-spouses, 6% friends, 3% boyfriends, 2% friends of family. Only 11% of victims, or 16% of incidents were

---

[45] Crystal S. Mills and Barbara J. Granoff, 'Date and Acquaintance Rape among a Sample of College Students', *Social Work*, Vol. 37, No. 6, 1992, pp. 504-509.

[46] Kanin, 'Date Rape: Unofficial Criminals and Victims', p. 97.

[47] Koss in Warshaw, *I Never Called it Rape*, p. 50.

attributed to strangers.[48] Quite a large part of the gap between Russell's total and existing figures must be due to date rape as I have defined it. The figures include spousal rape, which was not recognised by the law in California at that time.[49] With spousal rape removed, 19% reported at least one completed rape, 31% at least one attempted rape and these combine to make 41% reporting at least one completed or attempted extramarital rape. Among the 44% of respondents who had suffered either kind of incident, many were attacked more than once; indeed 'the average number of incidents with different assailants is almost two (1.92)'.[50]

A major feature of Russell's project was to prove that official figures on sexual assault were far too low; for this reason she used one direct question about rape but 37 others designed to elicit answers which matched the definition of rape used by Russell. Examples are:

> Have you ever had any unwanted sexual experience, including kissing, petting, or intercourse with a _____* because you felt physically threatened? IF YES: Did he (any of them) either try or succeed in having any kind of sexual intercourse with you?

> Have you ever had any kind of unwanted sexual experience with a _____* because you were asleep, unconscious, drugged or in some other way helpless? IF YES: Did he (any of them) either try or succeed in having any kind of sexual intercourse with you?

> (Three possible classes of assailants were substituted for _____*; strangers, acquaintances or friends, and dates, lovers or ex-lovers.)[51]

Either of these questions certainly could elicit a positive response from a rape victim. However, both need sensitivity in interpreting responses. The first could get a positive answer from a woman who kissed a man because she felt threatened, decided she liked it and wasn't actually being threatened, and then went on to have sex with him; the second is open to the problems already mentioned in connection with Koss's questions about drink.

There are some problems about Russell's sample. The original sample was 2,000, and a completion rate of under 50% is worrying: any systematic exclusion,

---

[48] D.E.H. Russell, *Sexual Exploitation: Rape, Child Sexual Abuse and Workplace Harassment,* Sage, Beverley Hills, CA., 1984, p. 59. (The figures add up to more than 44% because of multiple victimisations.)

[49] As Allison and Wrightsman point out, spousal rape was fully recognised in only three states in 1980; by the early 1990s it was recognised in 43 states, although with restrictions in some. Allison and Wrightsman, *Rape,* p. 89.

[50] Russell, 'The Prevalence and Incidence of Forcible Rape', p. 84.

[51] Ibid., pp. 84-6.

either of raped or unraped women, would skew the survey considerably.[52] Older women tended to refuse to be interviewed, taking the sample's average age from 50 to 43, as did married women, who would have been 60% of a random sample but were only 39% of Russell's sample. Russell gave older and married women who *were* interviewed greater weight to compensate for this, leading her rates of rape and attempted rape to decline by a fairly trivial 3% or less.[53] In the opposite direction, Russell notes that tourists, women of no fixed abode and women living in institutions were excluded from her survey, and might be expected to be more abused than women at large.[54] Russell argues that as only about one in ten rape or attempted rape incidents in her survey were reported to the police, and as the police also 'unfound' (dismissed as false) perhaps 18% of reports, one could get a true figure for San Francisco by multiplying police figures for rape and attempted rape by ten. One could follow a similar procedure with National Crime Survey data (compiled by the Census Bureau from interviews), showing that NCS rape and attempted rape figures should be multiplied by about seven. It is generally accepted that the rate of rape in large US cities is much higher than in the countryside, which raises questions about what sort of extrapolation from Russell's survey would be appropriate. FBI figures for reported rapes and NCS survey figures tend to be roughly proportional in different parts of the USA, but Russell's much higher figures are heavily based on acquaintance rape, which might or might not be proportionally lower in the countryside.[55]

Russell (and, of course, others) shifted the perception of rape amongst researchers considerably, so that ten years or so after her survey was written up, Allison and Wrightsman comment: '...agreement has emerged that rape or attempted rape by strangers accounts for a minority of rapes - probably about 15%', whereas previously many commentators thought the majority of rapes were stranger rapes.[56]

Numerous researchers have carried out smaller-scale surveys which add insights to the larger surveys described above. Koss herself was involved in a further survey of university women which closely replicates the results of the *Ms* survey, but adds some insight into rape avoidance amongst hidden victims: active resistance (screaming, running away) seemed the most effective, although

---

[52] Sorenson makes the point that '...in general, the higher the completion rate, the lower the prevalence rate' - see Sorenson et. al., 'The Prevalence of Adult Sexual Assault', p. 1156.

[53] Russell, 'The Prevalence and Incidence of Forcible Rape'', p. 87.

[54] Ibid., p.88.

[55] Russell sometimes writes as though one could extrapolate directly from her survey to the USA (or women?) at large, e.g. 'According to our survey data...there is a 26 per cent probability that a woman will be the victim of a completed rape at some time in her life'. Diana E. H. Russell and Nancy Howell, 'The Prevalence of Rape in the United States Revisited', *Signs*, Vol. 8, No. 4, 1983, pp. 688-95, quote from pp. 690-1.

[56] Allison and Wrightsman, *Rape*, p. 51.

reasoning seemed to have some effect.[57] In a survey of 2,338 students which was mainly looking at physical violence, Makepeace found 24.4% of female students reported an attempt at forced sex.[58] Miller and Marshall use a rather different classification scheme from Koss, but produce generally similar results, with rather more stress on miscommunication.[59] One useful survey looks at women before they arrive at college. In Mary Koss's survey it is left unclear whether the high rates of rape and attempted rape she finds relate mainly to the college campus or whether they are actually findings about high school students, given that the questions cover what has happened from age fourteen onwards. Himelein et. al. found that using questions similar to Koss's, but restricting questions by including 'on a date', 6.4% of women *entering* college reported rape and 22% attempted rape.[60] A comparison of representative sample groups of women in the area around Duke University and the University of California at Los Angeles, using a broader definition of sexual assault than Koss's, found a lifetime prevalence of 5.9% among the Duke women in contrast to 16.7% among the UCLA area sample. The authors of the survey comment that Duke is a conservative area with low crime, drug and alcohol abuse, and 60% of the Duke sample were born-again Christians. This certainly reinforces the point that a straightforward extrapolation from Russell's figures from San Francisco would be misleading, and also perhaps suggests that people dating with clear norms are less likely to become involved in date rape.[61]

Mills and Granoff assessed the extent of rape or attempted rape and other rape-supportive behaviour amongst students at the University of Hawaii-Manoa, using questions broadly similar to Koss's. They found that 28% of the women in their survey were the victims of rape or attempted rape. They were particularly interested in Japanese students, who form the largest ethnic group on the campus. Japanese families are more male-dominated than average US families, and this showed up in written comments from many Japanese women students which suggest they have problems acknowledging their victimisation, and that Japanese male students do not recognise their own abusive behaviour. Mills and Granoff are interested in this conclusion as a guide to educational programmes on

---

[57] Joyce Levine-MacCombie and Mary P. Koss, 'Acquaintance Rape: Effective Avoidance Strategies', *Psychology of Women Quarterly,* Vol. 10, 1986, pp. 311-20.

[58] Makepeace, 'Gender Differences in Courtship Violence Victimisation', p. 385.

[59] Beverley Miller and Jon C. Marshall, 'Coercive Sex on the University Campus', *Journal of College Student Personnel,* Vol. 28, 1987, pp. 38-47.

[60] Melissa J. Himelein, Ron E. Vogel and Dale G. Wachowiak, 'Nonconsensual Sexual Experiences in Precollege Women: Prevalence and Risk Factors', *Journal of Counseling and Development,* Vol. 72, March/April 1994, pp. 411-415.

[61] Linda K. George, Idee Winfield and Dan G. Blazer, 'Sociocultural factors in sexual assault: a comparison of two representative samples of women', *Journal of Social Issues,* Vol. 48, No. 1, 1992, pp. 105-25.

acquaintance rape, but if they are right claims that the rate of rape is much lower in Japan than in the USA should be treated with caution.[62]

Working at about the same time as Koss was completing her survey, Charlene Muehlenhard and Melaney Linton sought to identify factors which made male-against-female sexual aggression more likely by asking students to compare their most recent date (treated as a norm) with their worst experience of sexual aggression. Their conclusions, which support many assertions in Warshaw's book, are that the length of time dating partners have known each other did not seem related to sexual aggression, but that sexual aggression was more likely if: the man initiated the date; paid all the expenses; drove; if there was miscommunication about sex in that the woman was felt to have dressed suggestively and led the man on; if there was heavy use of drink or drugs; if there was 'parking';[63] and if the man accepted traditional sex roles, accepted the use of interpersonal violence, had adversarial attitudes about relationships and accepted rape myths.[64] A fifth of the women students in this survey had experienced unwanted sexual intercourse, but there was no use of weapons, virtually no slapping or hitting, some use of physical coercion, e.g. holding the woman down, and a slight use of threats, but over half the episodes simply involved the man 'just doing it' even after she said no. This leads the authors to speculate that if the women students were more assertive, or had resisted physically and with vigour, they might well have induced the men to stop.[65]

A survey using similar methods to Muehlenhard and Linton offers further insights into how 'unwanted' sex is classified. Hannon et. al. asked students at a community college about sexual behaviour unwanted by the female, and found a high rate of lifetime prevalence: 63.6% as reported by the women. However, in this project several questions were asked about dates on which *wanted* sex occurred. Many features of these dates were similar to *unwanted* sex dates, notably the range of behaviour in which at least some of the women *willingly* engaged.

---

[62] Mills and Granoff, 'Date and Acquaintance Rape'.

[63] UK readers: this refers to snogging in a parked car, not attempting to find a parking space.

[64] Charlene L. Muehlenhard and Melaney A. Linton, 'Date Rape and Sexual Aggression in Dating Situations: Incidence and Risk Factors', *Journal of Counseling Psychology*, Vol. 34, No. 2, 1987, pp. 186-96, cf. Charlene L. Muehlenhard, Debra E. Friedman and Celeste M. Thomas, 'Is Date Rape Justifiable? The Effect of Dating Activity, Who Initiated, Who Paid, and Men's Attitudes Toward Women', *Psychology of Women Quarterly*, Vol. 9, No. 3, 1985, pp. 297-310; Warshaw, *I Never Called it Rape*, pp. 152-3.

[65] A survey of 169 female college students' experiences over a year produces findings similar to, but slightly higher than, Koss's: 14.2% had experienced attempted intercourse against their will, whilst 12% had experienced intercourse against their will. See Jan E. Stets and Maureen A. Pirog-Good, 'Patterns of Physical and Sexual Abuse for Men and Women in Dating Relationships: A Descriptive Analysis', *Journal of Family Violence*, Vol. 4, No. 1, 1989, pp. 63-76.

Thus on *unwanted* sex dates 62% of women *willingly* kissed with tongue contact, 23% had their breasts touched directly by the man, 10% touched the man's genitals, 5% willingly had sex (i.e. presumably they did not want to have sex a second or third time). Hannon et. al. conclude that whilst some of what they were hearing about was 'undoubtedly' coercive sex, some 'unwanted' sex was a way of indicating a preference, i.e. that not all unwanted sex was coercive. They felt supported in this conclusion by the point that most of the unwanted sex occurred in relationships which had lasted about a year. This seems in line with my speculation previously about Koss's use of questions about 'unwanted' sex. As a possible concrete example, consider a couple who have a long-term sexual relationship engaging in extensive petting in a car. They are both very excited. She wants to continue and have sex in her apartment, he wants to continue in the car. However, this is a fine balance, as the car is in an isolated spot and there is a possibility that her flatmate and some friends will make sex in the flat embarrassing. If she says 'no', meaning 'not now, in ten minutes time', and he pushes her down and carries on, there is some danger of him turning up in the questionnaire statistics as a rapist, whereas we are in fact looking at what both would describe as a brief dispute over fine tuning.[66]

A relatively small-scale student survey carried out by Sally Ward et. al. offers some insights which would be well worth following up.[67] The survey involved administering a questionnaire to 524 women and 337 men at the University of New Hampshire. It was skewed towards freshmen students and asked only about incidents occurring that academic year. Its findings that 34% of the women students had experienced 'unwanted sexual contact', 20% unwanted attempted intercourse and 10% unwanted completed intercourse, though high enough to give cause for concern, are not statistically comparable with the other surveys. The interest in this survey lies in its distinction between date rape strictly speaking, i.e. rape by a date or boyfriend, and rape or at least unwanted sex at parties, where the male was either a stranger, but a selected stranger in the sense that he had been

---

[66] Roseann Hannon et. al., 'Dating Characteristics Leading to Unwanted vs. Wanted Sexual Behaviour', *Sex Roles,* Vol. 33, Nos. 11/12, 1995, pp. 767-83. Obviously, none of the behaviours listed amount as such to consent to sex on this occasion. A rather similar picture emerges in Sarah K. Murnen, Annette Perot and Donn Byrne, 'Coping with Unwanted Sexual Activity: Normative Responses, Situational Determinants and Individual Differences', *The Journal of Sex Research,* Vol. 26, No. 1, 1989, pp. 85-106. The authors slide very readily from talking of 'unwanted sexual attempts', carried out by means as limited as 'persuasion' to 'attacks'. The women students they quote seem generally to be fairly unconcerned about such a high rate of 'attack', and fairly confident that they can handle male attempts. For a further discussion of a survey which elides widely different forms of 'forced sex', and makes comments on roughly the same lines as Hannon et. al., see Fillion, *Lip Service,* pp. 194-7. In a different context Fillion also makes some interesting comments about how subjects interpret questionnaires - see pp. 214-7.

[67] All the information on this survey is in Sally K. Ward et. al., 'Acquaintance Rape and the College Social Scene', *Family Relations,* Vol. 40, 1991, pp. 65-71.

invited to a student party, or an acquaintance, meaning a student the woman knew but with whom she had not previously had any romantic involvement. Depending on what measure is used, up to two thirds of incidents involve acquaintances or 'strangers' at parties, not boyfriends or dates. The parties seem to involve a considerable use of alcohol. This points to a distinction between the stereotypical total stranger of the public imagination, and what might be called a pre-selected stranger met at a party. And if one wanted to adopt a pedantically accurate name for what we are discussing, most of it should perhaps be called 'party rape', a point which is obviously important in designing any education programmes or other measures to reduce incidents.

The male tactics were very much those described by Muehlenhard and Linton previously: 'just doing it', particularly in cases of unwanted sexual contact, but also in 46% of cases of unwanted completed intercourse, with some recourse to verbal tactics (arguments, pressure and threats) and some to physical force, although what sort of force is not described. Ten per cent of women suffering unwanted completed intercourse also suffered physical injury, but to what degree is unclear. Only 9% of males reported having unwanted sexual contact, meaning forcing their attentions on women; 9% reported unwanted attempted intercourse; and 3% reported unwanted completed intercourse. Unless the University of New Hampshire has a very few, extremely active party rapists who missed the survey, the picture which emerges suggests a lot of miscommunication, of men seeing female protests as not intended seriously, and encountering sufficiently little resistance to leave this belief undisturbed. The fact that in 75% of incidents the males had been drinking, as had the women in over 50% of incidents, would not improve accurate communication.

The biggest question of omission with which Koss leaves us is that of women who have not been to college and women who are beyond normal college age. They tend to get married or settle into relationships, but there will be at least some coercive sex within these relationships; and, of course, relationships break down and women seek new ones, or engage in adulterous liaisons, thus becoming vulnerable to date rape again.

There have been various surveys of women in the general population. One was carried out by Koss herself using a mailed survey sent to 5,000 adult working women in Cleveland, Ohio, getting a 45% response rate. She found a prevalence rate of 14% for attempted and 13.6% for completed forced vaginal penetration since age 14, plus 10.4% for sex achieved through incapacitation by drink or drugs. The annual incidence of rape and attempted rape using the same definition as those used for the survey of students was 61.5 per thousand. Including only completed or attempted forced vaginal intercourse, the incidence of rape was 28 per thousand women over a year, with 39% of these being committed by husbands, partners or relatives. As one might expect, this is a much higher rate than the US National Crime Survey rate of 1.1 per thousand for white women or

1.5 per thousand for black women.[68] Another survey of adult women was carried out by Kilpatrick et. al. They used interviews about lifetime experience of crime and post-traumatic stress disorder (PTSD) on 399 women out of 933 who were a representative sample of female residents of Charleston County, South Carolina. Kilpatrick et. al. do not say anything about any differences between women who agreed to participate in their interviews and women who did not. Otherwise, they seem to have interviewed a fairly average group of women with a mean age just under 40. They defined completed rape as 'requiring non-consent, threat or use of force, and one or more types of completed sexual penetration' (i.e. incapacitation due to drink or drugs is not included). They found that 23.3% of their sample had been victims of completed rape and 13.1% of attempted rape. Only 7% of completed rapes were reported to the police. The mean length of time since the attempted rapes was 20.7 years, and 17 years for completed rapes, suggesting a peak of assaults in the women's late teens or early 20s. Fifty-seven per cent of completed rapes led to PTSD, compared with 15.7% of attempted rapes or 28.2% of burglaries. Broadly, then, this survey supports the picture Koss presents.[69] A survey carried out by Susan Sorenson et. al. also broadly supports Koss, but uses different categories of sexual assault, making it impossible to produce comparable figures.[70] A small survey of young men of student age but who were not students broadly replicates Koss's findings.[71] A small-scale Canadian survey of school students appears to broadly support Koss, although the numbers are too small to be very confident about reliability, and 'force' is defined to include persistence.[72]

---

[68] The report of the Cleveland survey is in Koss et. al., 'Criminal Victimization Among Primary Medical Care Patients'. This postal survey seems vulnerable to the criticism I make below of the *Ask Any Woman* survey: perhaps victims are particularly likely to return the survey. Koss was aware of this possibility and arranged for some supplementary interviews of her sample, which produced a higher rate of victimisation than that in the postal survey (ibid., p. 93). An annual incidence rate of 61 per 1,000 women per year is a much lower rate of rape than Koss's survey figure for students, which was 103 per 1,000 - see Warshaw, *I Never Called It Rape*, p. 13. For a summary of claims about the general population which broadly support Koss's general population findings, see Koss and Cook, 'Facing the facts: Date and Acquaintance Rape are Significant Problems', p. 110. For further discussion of the prevalence of rape in the general population see Mary P. Koss, 'The Underdetection of Rape: Methodological Choices Influence Incidence Estimates', *Journal of Social Issues*, Vol. 48, 1, 1992, pp. 61-75, pp. 68-9.

[69] Dean G. Kilpatrick et. al. 'Criminal Victimization: Lifetime Prevalence, Reporting to Police, and Psychological Impact', *Crime and Delinquency*, Vol. 33, 4, Oct. 1987, pp. 479-89.

[70] Sorenson et. al., 'The Prevalence of Adult Sexual Assault'.

[71] Karen S. Calhoun et. al., 'Sexual Coercion and Attraction to Sexual Aggression in a Community Sample of Young Men', *Journal of Interpersonal Violence*, Vol. 12, No. 3, 1997, pp. 392-406.

[72] Jill Rhynard, Marlene Krebs and Julie Glover, 'Sexual Assault in Dating Relationships', *Journal of School Health*, Vol. 67, No. 3, 1997, pp. 89-93. For a further

So far a number of questions have been raised about the findings of Koss and Russell and other authors using the same approach based largely on their own evidence. However, other surveys of sexual aggression in a dating context also raise issues which either undermine Koss and Russell's claims or throw light on matters from a different angle. The main issues are the extent to which men are victims of sexual assault and the question of sexual (mis)communication.

Koss argues that women cannot rape men because rape involves forced penetration; the nearest offence she can think of is a group of women holding down a man and penetrating him anally with carrots. This is not a frequent occurrence. More realistically she imagines unethical conduct in which a woman induces a man to have sex with her by threatening to spread rumours that he is impotent. This would not be rape because the man is not penetrated and is not threatened with force.[73] Given the evidence, mentioned in Chapter 2, that men are occasionally victims of violent forced sex by female strangers, and that this is about as traumatising for them as for female rape victims, a somewhat less light-hearted approach would seem appropriate.

As Cindy Struckman-Johnson points out, Koss and many other researchers find no evidence of women forcing men to have sex because they believe it does not happen, and ask no questions about it. In a survey by Cindy Struckman-Johnson some 16% of male students had experienced at least one forced heterosexual sex episode, compared to 22% of female students.[74] Struckman-Johnson classified the forceful tactics into four categories: i.) Psychological pressure without physical force, e.g. cajolery, demands, blackmail; ii.) Psychological pressure mixed with physical restraint or force - adding removing the other's clothing, stimulating or restraining the other in a forceful manner; iii.) Physical force or restraint used as the primary means; iv.) Intoxication, e.g. the person is too drunk or high to give knowledgeable consent. Fifty-two per cent of Struckman-Johnson's small sample of coerced males suffered only psychological pressure - although this included threats to give negative information to an employer or to parents - but 38% experienced some degree of physical restraint or force, and 10% were too drunk to

---

small-scale survey of school students which points in roughly the same direction but fails to define 'force', see Terry C. Davis et. al., 'Acquaintance Rape and the High School Student', *Journal of Adolescent Health*, Vol. 14, No. 3, 1993, pp. 220-4.

[73] In Warshaw, *I Never Called it Rape*, pp. 191-2. Andrea Dworkin seems to have much the same view of the impossibility of rape carried out by women - see Dworkin, *Intercourse*, Secker and Warburg, London, 1987, p. 136.

[74] Struckman-Johnson concludes that the students she surveyed had experienced forced sex if they gave an appropriate answer to: 'In the course of your life, how many times have you been forced to engage in sexual intercourse while on a date?' - Cindy Struckman-Johnson, 'Forced Sex on Dates: It Happens to Men, Too', *Journal of Sex Research*, Vol. 24, 1988, pp. 234-41, quote on p. 236.

consent. The degree of trauma and of short- or long-term impact seems to have been much lower than that experienced by women.[75] The males in this survey could not count as rape victims according to Koss because they were not penetrated; this is consistent with UK law under which only men can rape; but if we expand the definition of rape to include sex forced on men by women then 48% of the male victims would have claims to have been raped using Koss's criteria. Thus 8% of Struckman-Johnson's male respondents would appear to have been victims of rape *on a date* at least once; of the 15% of college women who Koss argues had been raped at least once, 8.5% were victimised on a date.

Struckman-Johnson's survey is backed up by a study carried out by Muehlenhard and Cook. Their survey asked men and women students aged on average 19-20 about unwanted kissing, petting and intercourse, and found that although more women (97.5%) than men (93.5%) had experienced unwanted sexual activity, more men (62.7%) than women (46.3%) had experienced unwanted intercourse. Possible reasons for unwanted intercourse included enticement (i.e. the person was led to want sex at the time but did not when all things were considered), altruism, a desire for more experience, and various forms of peer pressure, none of which amount to rape or anything approaching it. However, 6.5% of the men and 5.8% of the women had had unwanted sexual intercourse because of physical coercion - mainly actions such as holding down or threatening - 30.8% of the men and 21% of the women had had unwanted sex because of intoxication, responses which would presumably count as rape for Koss - but only for the women students. Summarising a lot of the men's responses Muehlenhard and Cook comment that: '[t]he most common reason for unwanted sex among men appears to be social pressure related to the male stereotype', i.e. the desire to appear both to the dating partner and to himself and to their friends as a real man who is willing and able to have sex at any time.[76]

These findings about sexual coercion of men by women have not been followed up to any great extent, but could be used to build up a picture of men as coerced by ideological stereotypes of maleness, backed up by aggressive females using physical and psychological coercion and taking advantage of them when drunk. I do not believe that this in fact represents a significant social problem, although it has to be said that the commonsense ideology of men being always eager for sex with any woman is singularly unprotective of males to the extent they are

[75] Ibid., p. 238.

[76] Charlene L. Muehlenhard and Stephen W. Cook, 'Men's Self-Reports of Unwanted Sexual Activity', *The Journal of Sex Research*, Vol. 24, 1988, pp. 58-72. Because their subjects were asked about types of pressure used to secure unwanted sex but not about numbers of incidents, this survey cannot be used to make exact claims about percentages of men or women suffering sexual assault. For further references and discussion see Fillion, *Lip Service*, pp. 210-11.

genuinely victims of sexual assault by females.[77] It is also worth asking whether, if this picture is deceptive, some part of the findings about the date rape of women might not also be deceptive. Muehlenhard and Cook's study raises another issue to which we shall need to return. If we assume that there is a basic dating script in which the man makes advances and the woman sets limits, then one would expect that women would experience a great deal of unwanted sexual activity short of intercourse. Unless there is full discussion of each possible stage of advancing intimacy, the man is liable to make small advances from holding hands to putting his arm round the woman's shoulders through to more intimate touching leading towards intercourse. Even if the man stops promptly when told his advances are unwelcome, the woman is bound to encounter a fair amount of unwanted low-level sexual activity, as recorded, for example, by 97.5% of Muehlenhard and Cook's female subjects.

Studies which undermine Koss and Russell: ii.) miscommunication?

Koss, Russell and others argue that women are frequently victims of sexual assault. However, there is some reason to think that a proportion of the 'assaults' are actually examples of miscommunication.

One systematic source of miscommunication, more widely recognised, I think, by women than by men is that men have a more sexualised view of the world than women, and are prone to interpret many female activities, be it how she dresses, her gestures, what she says, where she is willing to go, as indicative of more

---

[77] Two experiments back this up. In an experiment in which male and female students were asked about the acceptability of repeatedly asking for sex, sexually stimulating a reluctant partner and using mock force, the first two acts were seen as acceptable if done by a woman to a man, and the third almost acceptable. Men thought that a man doing these acts to a woman was less acceptable, and women thought that a man doing them to a woman was much less acceptable. See David and Cindy Struckman-Johnson, 'Men and Women's Acceptance of Coercive Sexual Strategies Varied by Initiator, Gender and Couple Intimacy', *Sex Roles*, Vol. 25, Nos 11/12, 1991, pp. 661-76. Smith and colleagues presented male and female college students with a vignette in which two males (or females) force sex on a stranded student motorist. Males forcing sex on females was seen as more culpable. '...[T]he male victim of a sexual assault by females was judged more likely to have encouraged or initiated the episode, to have derived pleasure from it, and to have experienced less stress. This pattern of results was particularly pronounced for male subjects'. Ronald E. Smith, Charles J. Pine and Mark E. Hawley, 'Social Cognitions About Adult Male Victims of Female Sexual Assault', *The Journal of Sex Research*, Vol. 24, 1988, pp. 101-12 - quotation, p. 110. At a much lower level of violation, similar results were found by Leslie Margolis - see 'Gender and the Stolen Kiss: The Social Support of Male and Female to Violate a Partner's Sexual Consent in a Noncoercive Situation', *Archives of Sexual Behavior*, Vol. 19, No. 3, 1990, pp. 281-91.

interest in sex than a woman seeing the same situation would think.[78] This is obviously prone to lead to some misreading of signals. To make matters worse, the popular stereotype is that men are, in any case, insensitive to signals that women make. Thus the woman may feel that she is making it perfectly clear what she would or would not wish the man to do, whilst he is taking no notice. He may, in fact, be desperately wondering what he should do. An account of this sort of problem is given by David Cohen. Cohen was married for some years to a lesbian, and coped with the situation by having a series of affairs rather than by seeking a separation. He comments that although he has been in quite a number of romantic situations where sexual advances might well be welcome, he has never been certain whether or not they would actually really be welcome, and virtually never experienced the woman making initial sexual advances when sex had not previously occurred.[79]

To make matters still worse, there is the problem of women offering token resistance to sex. A standard rape myth which feminists are concerned to debunk is that: 'When women say "no" they mean "yes"', hence the campaigning rhyme:

Whatever we wear, wherever we go

---

[78] E.g. A. Abbey, 'Sex differences in attributions for friendly behaviour: Do males misperceive females' friendliness?' *Journal of Personality and Social Psychology*, Vol. 42, 1982, pp. 830-8; A. Abbey and C. Melby, 'The Effects of Nonverbal Cues on Gender Differences in Perceptions of Sexual Intent', *Sex Roles*, Vol. 15, Nos. 5/6, 1986, pp. 283-298. Cf. Charlene L. Muehlenhard, 'Misinterpreted Dating Behaviours and the Risk of Date Rape', *Journal of Social and Clinical Psychology*, Vol. 6, No. 1, 1988, pp. 20-37; Mary E. Craig, 'The Effects of Selective Evaluation on the Perception of Female Cues in Sexually Coercive and Noncoercive Males', *Archives of Sexual Behavior*, Vol. 22, No. 5, 1993, pp. 415-33. Kowalski provides a more sophisticated version of this study, distinguishing between 'mundane dating behaviours', such as inviting him on a date or accepting his invitation, having dinner with him, maintaining eye contact, going to a movie with him; 'romantic behaviours', such as inviting him to her apartment, lying beside him on the couch, leaning her head on his shoulder, offering to rub his back, slipping into something more comfortable'; and 'sexual behaviours' such as touching his genitals, allowing him to touch her bare breasts, removing her blouse or undressing him. The major difference is that men, particularly traditional men, attribute more sexual intent to the *mundane* dating behaviours. See Robin M. Kowalski, 'Inferring Sexual Interest from Behavioural Cues: Effects of Gender and Sexually Relevant Attitudes', *Sex Roles*, Vol. 29, Nos 1/2, 1993. There appears to be a cultural element to this: Brazilian males see more sexual intent than Brazilian females, but to a lesser extent than for Americans. All Brazilians seem more similar in perceptions to American males. See E.R. DeSouza et. al. 'Perceived Sexual Intent in the US and Brazil as a Function of the Nature of Encounter, Subjects' Nationality and Gender', *The Journal of Sex Research*, Vol. 29, No. 2, 1992, pp. 251-60; cf. E.R. DeSouza and C.S. Hunt, 'Reactions to Refusals of Sexual Advances Among US and Brazilian Men and Women', *Sex Roles*, Vol. 34, Nos 7/8, 1996, pp. 549-65.

[79] David Cohen, *Being a Man*, Routledge, London, 1990, pp. 120 et. seq.

"Yes" means "Yes" and "No" means "No".

Whilst this is a valid slogan against stranger rape, it does not provide a complete guide to intimate relations. In a survey Muehlenhard showed that 39% of college women had on at least one occasion said 'no' to sex when they were in fact willing to have sex, the majority motivation being a desire not to seem forward, but with a minority of women being keen to provoke their partner. To make matters even worse, this total rises to 60.8% amongst sexually experienced women, the sub-group of respondents most likely to say no when they mean yes; amongst virgins there will obviously be a proportion of women who would intend to remain virgins until marriage and who would make this clear at the outset to any dating partner, whilst others perhaps would have plans for life which entirely excluded men. I have run out of expressions for matters getting any worse, but the responses so far were amongst women who 'had every intention to and were willing to engage in sexual intercourse'. In the total sample, 68.5% of the women had said 'no' when they meant 'maybe'.[80] This last situation must be very common: women will normally go through a stage in a relationship which develops to sexual intercourse where they are not sure whether they want to go that far or not, and 'no meaning maybe' is the obvious way to hedge one's bets.[81] In a further survey, Muehlenhard links token resistance to the sexual double standard: much of it, she argues, is the result of women not wishing to appear unduly forward. Women who thought their partners believed in the sexual double standard were particularly prone to token resistance.[82]

A version of Muehlenhard's initial survey of token resistance was repeated to make an international comparison between the USA, Russia and Japan, and to include men. Token resistance to sex was actually higher for American men than for American women (47% compared to 38%); in Russia and Japan token resistance was higher among women than men, with 70% of non-virgin Russian women and 60% of non-virgin Japanese women having engaged in token

---

[80] C.L. Muehlenhard, and L.C. Hollabaugh, 'Do women sometimes say no when they mean yes? The prevalence and correlates of women's token resistance to sex', *Journal of Personality and Social Psychology*, Vol. 54, 1988, pp. 872-9. Shotland and Hunter report very similar results to Muehlenhard - see R. Lance Shotland and Barbara A. Hunter, 'Women's "Token Resistant" and Compliant Sexual Behaviours are Related to Uncertain Sexual Intentions and Rape', *Personality and Social Psychology Bulletin*, Vol. 21, No. 3, 1995, pp. 226-36.

[81] In the course of a discussion of this with some of my students, one woman student asserted that there was a clear difference between 'No' said in two different tones, one meaning 'No way' and the other meaning 'No, persuade me'. She was assuming that the difference would be obvious to any man she was dating, but I am afraid it was not at all clear to me - maybe things would have been clearer in the context of an actual date.

[82] Charlene L. Muehlenhard and Marcia L. McCoy, 'Double Standard/Double Bind: The Sexual Double Standard and Women's Communication about Sex', *Psychology of Women Quarterly*, Vol. 15, 1991, pp. 447-61.

resistance. The authors of the survey conclude that perhaps American men think they are being offered sex when they are actually not, or perhaps they are playing hard to get now that sexual mores are more equal in the USA. They see Russia and Japan as more traditional, making token resistance by women more likely, and offering men fewer chances of token resistance.[83] Thus a degree of token resistance to sex is common to both sexes and found in three very different societies.

The scope for miscommunication would therefore appear to be quite substantial. There is also some evidence which might point to miscommunication in the literature on date rape. In Chapter 4 I shall be arguing that there are at least two ways to look at women's behaviour during a date. One, which is endorsed by authors stressing the dangers of date rape, sees only behaviour which specifically invites a particular form of intimacy as legitimating it; without such an invitation the man is committing an assault. The other thinks in terms of symbolically signalling a readiness for greater intimacy, for example by looking enthusiastic or by going along readily with a move to greater intimacy which the man makes. On this second view a woman who, for example, moans with pleasure when having her breast felt through her clothes might well also enjoy having her breast felt directly. Looking at things this way, a man who moved from a woman inviting him into her room for coffee to throwing her onto the bed and leaping on top of her would be engaged in an assault, but a man who moved from petting below the waist with both partners stark naked to intercourse would not. There are dangers to this second view, which will be explored later - perhaps the woman who had her breast felt was moaning with pain or fear - but it bears some relation to the idea of women setting limits to behaviour on dates.[84] Accepting this second view for the moment, what evidence is there in the literature about previous levels of intimacy leading up to date rape?

According to Koss the 'average' level of intimacy which preceded the rapes in her student survey was 'petting above the waist', but the victims had made it clear they did not want intercourse.[85] An 'average' level of intimacy of petting above the waist suggests that Koss is dealing with a mixture between some victims who offered very little encouragement indeed beyond accepting a lift, going on a date or inviting a man into her room for some evidently non-sexual purpose, so that

---

[83] Susan Sprecher, Elaine Hatfield, Anthony Cortese, Elena Potapove and Anna Levitskaya, 'Token Resistance to Sexual Intercourse and Consent to Unwanted Sexual Intercourse: College Students' Dating Experiences in Three Countries', *The Journal of Sex Research*, Vol. 31, No. 2, 1994, pp. 125-32. The finding that token resistance is more common in US men than women is replicated in a further survey, which presents a picture of very similar use of token resistance by both sexes - see Lucia F. O'Sullivan and Elizabeth R. Allgeier, 'Disassembling a Stereotype: Gender Differences in the Use of Token Resistance', *Journal of Applied Psychology*, Vol. 24, No. 12, 1994, pp. 1035-55.

[84] Cf. Charlene L. Muehlenhard et. al., 'Definitions of Rape', p. 31.

[85] Koss in Warshaw, *I Never Called it Rape*, p. 49.

claims about miscommunication would be very stretched, and others where intimacy had got considerably further and the man had become confused between, say, bodily encouragement and verbal refusal. Muehlenhard and Linton note that both men and women said the man had felt led on more often during dates in which sexual aggression had occurred, but do not analyse what behaviour this actually involved.[86] Kanin in his study of self-disclosed date rapists says that not one of them would say that he planned a rape: they almost all said they planned or hoped for a seduction.[87] All of them said that the rape was preceded by some consensual activity, 84% involving some sort of genital play. For 68% this was reciprocal, for the remainder where only one party was active the active party was equally likely to be the man or the woman. 'The contacts were overwhelmingly orogenital. The remaining cases involved lesser erotic intimacies beyond the level of kissing'.[88] The men said that they became very sexually aroused, that the female was very sexually aroused, and that intimacies had gone so far that they failed to take any rejections seriously. The major response when they realised that they had carried on despite rejection was anxiety and confusion.[89] If Kanin's subjects are to be believed, miscommunication played a large part in their assaults.[90] These observations are backed up by an experiment conducted by Marx and Gross in which male students who had personally experienced token resistance, or who were told that a woman on an audiotape of a date rape had previously displayed token resistance, took longer than others to decide that the man should refrain from attempting further intimacy.[91] Two further experiments suggest that the meaning of various forms of resistance is a fairly complex matter, depending on the woman's consistency of response, the orientation of the man towards feminism, and the degree of arousal of both partners, although the

---

[86] Muehlenhard and Linton, 'Date Rape and Sexual Aggression', p. 191.

[87] Kanin, 'Date Rape: Unofficial Criminals and Victims', p. 98.

[88] Ibid., p. 99.

[89] Ibid., pp. 99-100. On the other hand, in an earlier study of women who found particular levels of sexual initiation offensive, 54% of attempts at intercourse were initiated without previous sex play - see Eugene J. Kanin and Stanley R. Parcell, 'Sexual Aggression: A Second Look at the Offended Female', *Archives of Sexual Behavior*, Vol. 6, No. 1, 1977, pp. 67-76. Kanin concluded that date rape has become more common since his initial researches in the 1950s - see Edward M. Levine and Eugene J. Kanin, 'Sexual Violence Among Dates and Acquaintances: Trends and Their Implications for Marriage and Family', *Journal of Family Violence*, Vol. 2, No. 1, 1987, pp. 55-65.

[90] Readers wanting an overview of yet further US survey material could consult Linda Bourque, *Defining Rape*, Duke University Press, Durham, North Carolina, and London, 1989, Ch. 2.

[91] Brian P. Marx and Alan M. Gross, 'Date Rape: An Analysis of Two Contextual Variables', *Behavior Modification*, Vol. 19, No. 4, 1995, pp. 451-63.

literature is consistent in recommending women to set clear limits at an early stage of a relationship.[92]

Studies which undermine Koss and Russell: iii.) unreliable reporting?

Studies such as those of Koss and Russell rely on people who complete questionnaires or respond to interviewers to have reliable memories. They are also only as good as the match which can be made between the respondent and particular questions. Kathryn Scott and Carol Aneshensel report on two sets of interviews at intervals of a year with the same randomly-selected adults with an average age of 41 in an area of Los Angeles. To investigate sexual assaults, interviewees were asked: 'In your lifetime, has anyone ever tried to pressure or force you to have sexual contact? By sexual contact, I mean touching your sexual parts, your touching their sexual parts, or sexual intercourse'. At first sight the responses from women are highly consistent: in the first survey 19.2% said they had suffered sexual assault, whilst in the second 19.4% said they had been assaulted. The male responses are slightly less consistent. However, this is an aggregate within which many respondents changed their replies. In the second survey, two in five of those sexually assaulted according to the first survey now said they were not assaulted. These retractors were balanced by a lower, but still high, number of revealers. Lifetime prevalence of sexual assault could be described as either 22.2% by including both retractors and revealers, or as 7.7% by excluding both. Females, persons not married or living as married and non-Hispanic whites were more consistent over time than other people, but even these reports were 'quite inconsistent'. In their discussion Scott and Aneshensel point towards respondents problems about remembering and classifying experience, rather than, say, a belated attempt to appear socially desirable to the second interviewer.[93] Unfortunately one can only speculate as to the responses which those investigated by other surveys would have made if re-tested a year later. This study certainly points to a need to be very careful that respondents are understanding questions in the same way as those asking them.

---

[92] E. Sandra Byers, 'Effects of Sexual Arousal on Men's and Women's Behaviour in Sexual Disagreement Situations', *The Journal of Sex Research*, Vol. 25, No. 2, 1989, pp. 235-54; Robin M. Kowalski, 'Nonverbal Behaviours and Perceptions of Sexual Intentions: Effects of Sexual Connotativeness, Verbal Response, and Rape Outcome', *Basic and Applied Psychology*, Vol. 13, No. 4, 1992, pp. 427-45.

[93] Kathryn D. Scott and Carol S. Aneshensel, 'An Examination of the Reliability of Sexual Assault Reports', *Journal of Interpersonal Violence*, Vol. 12, No. 3, 1997, pp. 361-74.

Canadian Studies

Woman Abuse in Dating Relationships

Gilbert and others accuse researchers such as Mary Koss of 'advocacy research'.[94] It seems to me that it is more important to get things right than to sling mud (in either direction), so thus far I have simply recorded the debates with a view to clarifying some of the concepts involved in the next two chapters. However, in Canada things have become much more extreme: if the term 'advocacy research' is appropriate anywhere, it is in discussions of three Canadian survey reports published in 1993. One of these is a modified version of Mary Koss's survey, DeKeseredy and Kelly's 'woman abuse in Canadian university and college dating relationships' (henceforth WADR).

In subsequent discussion of criticisms made of their survey and its presentation, DeKeseredy displays a fairly nuanced view of the world: violence and psychological abuse is at least sometimes initiated by women, women are not simply victims, there is not just one phenomenon called 'patriarchy' but a more elaborate system, etc. However, the early presentation of the results of his survey include such matters only in subtle hints and implications, and the early presentation to the media attracted much criticism by aggregating widely disparate behaviours as 'woman abuse', said to be suffered by 81% of women in the survey.[95] How was this result reached?

The WADR survey was carried out by questionnaire in 95 university and college classes selected to provide a balanced sample of Canadian students. Of a total of 3,142 respondents, 1,835 (58%) were female and 1,307 (42%) were male. However the gender distribution of Canadian students is approximately equal. Rosemary Gartner suggests that the skewed gender distribution is probably a consequence of some classes of students being informed in advance that the

---

[94] For Gilbert's fullest explanation of 'advocacy research' see Gilbert, 'Miscounting Social Ills'. His warning that advocacy research often leads to two bursts of press publicity, the first accepting the research and printing shock stories, the second debunking the research, seems apposite to Canada.

[95] Information in John Fekete, *Moral Panic: Biopolitics Rising*, Robert Davies Publishing, Montreal, 1994, p. 50. My attention was drawn to this book by DeKeseredy, who stresses that Fekete is a Professor of Cultural Studies and not trained in criminology, thus implying that he is an ignorant critic. However, a reading of Fekete's book shows that the criticisms he is making of Canadian criminologists are of gross errors in (almost) anyone's view, not of statistical fine tuning. DeKeseredy's critique of Fekete's book is to be found in Walter S. DeKeseredy, 'The Canadian national survey on woman abuse in university/college dating relationships: Biofeminist panic transmission or critical inquiry?' *Canadian Journal of Criminology*, Vol. 19, 1996, pp. 81-104. Kelly clearly fell out with DeKeseredy over the issue of premature release of data, and presents an independent rather than a joint response to criticism. See Katharine D. Kelly, 'The Politics of Data', *Canadian Journal of Sociology*, Vol. 19, 1994, pp. 81-5.

questionnaire was to be administered and some students, primarily men, deciding to absent themselves. In their responses to Gartner neither DeKeseredy nor Kelly take up this point; we have no way of telling how many students absented themselves or why they did so.[96] For the purposes of the survey 'Any intentional physical, sexual or psychological assault on a female by a male dating partner was defined as woman abuse', and abuse was investigated using a modified version of the Conflict Tactics Scale (CTS) and Mary Koss's Sexual Experiences Survey (SES). In all cases 'abuse' is inferred from responses to questions about behaviour rather than from direct admissions.[97] Aspects of the survey deal with intentions, but no analysis of these is presented; the survey included questions about violence by women, but this is also not presented.

Since leaving high school 65% of the women had suffered 'insults or swearing' from dating partners; 72% had had something done or said to spite them; 57% had been accused of having affairs or flirting with other men. Overall 86.2% of women had been victims of psychological abuse, whilst 80% of the men admitted psychological abuse.[98] As the authors comment, psychological abuse can be an important part of an overall pattern of abuse; on the other hand, doubtless many couples occasionally swear at each other, do things to spite each other and accuse each other of flirting without this becoming part of a pattern of abuse. For example, one reason for accusing someone of having an affair is that she has actually had one. This is doubtless particularly likely amongst students who have not established permanent relationships. Without further analysis we are in no position to distinguish between occasional mutual insults, psychological abuse as a precursor of physical and sexual abuse and psychological abuse as a dimension of ongoing physical and sexual abuse. In their responses to their critics DeKeseredy and Kelly both promise that the issues of interpretation and of female violence will be elucidated.[99] In fact, Kelly abandoned the project following her unhappiness with the premature release of data, whilst DeKeseredy eventually produced an article on female violence which takes the line that it is a defensive response.

Kelly and DeKeseredy did use their survey to pursue some feminist hypotheses. They pursue the plausible hypotheses that familial patriarchy and male peer

---

[96] For Gartner's critique see Rosemary Gartner, 'Studying Woman Abuse: A comment on DeKeseredy and Kelly', *Canadian Journal of Sociology*, Vol. 18, 1993, pp. 313-20. The separate responses are: Walter S. DeKeseredy, 'Addressing the complexities of woman abuse in dating: A response to Gartner and Fox', *Canadian Journal of Sociology*, Vol. 19, 1994, pp. 75-80; Kelly's response, 'The politics of data' is at pp. 81-5 of the same issue.

[97] On this see Bonnie J. Fox, 'On Violent Men and Female Victims: A comment on DeKeseredy and Kelly', *The Canadian Journal of Sociology*, Vol. 18, 1993, pp. 321-324.

[98] Walter S. DeKeseredy and Katharine Kelly, 'The Incidence and Prevalence of Woman Abuse in Canadian University and College Dating Relationships', *Canadian Journal of Sociology*, Vol. 18, 2, 1993, pp. 137-59, data on p. 153.

[99] See responses cited in previous note.

support might contribute to woman abuse.[100] They also look at women's fear of crime, with the idea that experience of dating victimisation might lead to greater fearfulness. They actually found only a slight correlation between dating victimisation and fearfulness in the home.[101] One would have thought that closer scrutiny of what they are actually measuring would be more useful than this very inconclusive piece. In a response to Fekete's criticisms of his work published early in 1996, DeKeseredy offers the standard feminist response to the issue of violence perpetrated by women: it is 'primarily used in self-defence'.[102] In an article where he is also claiming that 'the misuse of our data does not invalidate our results'[103] this is worrying.

Having noted that any light shed by the WADR survey is accompanied by a considerable amount of heat, let us briefly note the survey's analysis of date rape. DeKeseredy summarises this by saying that 28% of female respondents said they had been 'sexually abused' in the past year and 45.1% since leaving high school.[104] It is not made clear what responses to his survey he is adding up here, or how he would count one incident in which several abuses occurred. Over a year 11.4% of his female respondents suffered rape, including oral and anal sex and 'having sex when you did not want to because you were drunk or high'; this would reduce to 3.8% with incapacitation excluded. Attempted rape was suffered

---

[100] Walter S. DeKeseredy and Katharine Kelly, 'Woman Abuse in University and College Dating Relationships: The Contribution of the Ideology of Familial Patriarchy', *The Journal of Human Justice*, Vol. 4, 2, Spring 1993, pp. 25-52; Walter S. DeKeseredy and Martin D. Schwartz, 'Male Peer Support and Woman Abuse: An Expansion of DeKeseredy's Model', *Sociological Spectrum*, Vol. 13, 1993, pp. 393-413. DeKeseredy had already carried out a smaller-scale survey to try to examine the role of male peer support in woman abuse (defined the same way as for the WADR survey), written up in Walter S. DeKeseredy, *Woman Abuse in Dating Relationships: The Role of Male Peer Support*, Canadian Scholars' Press Inc., Toronto, 1988. College fraternities particularly tend to feature in accounts of date rape, and women in sororities seem to be victimised more than other students, very likely because of their associations with fraternity men - see Linda Kalof, 'Rape-Supportive Attitudes and Sexual Victimisation Experiences of Sorority and Non-Sorority Women', *Sex Roles*, Vol. 29. Nos 11/12, 1993, pp. 767-80; Patricia Gwartney-Gibbs and Jean Stockard, 'Courtship Aggression and Mixed-Sex Peer Groups', in Maureen Pirog-Good and J. E. Stets, eds, *Violence in Dating Relationships: Emerging Social Issues*, Praeger, New York, 1989, pp. 185-204. Fraternities also feature in a further extension of DeKeseredy's work: Martin D. Schwartz and Walter S. DeKeseredy, *Sexual Assault on the College Campus: The Role of Male Peer Support*, Sage, London, 1997, esp. p. 126.

[101] See Katharine D. Kelly and Walter S. DeKeseredy, 'Women's Fear of Crime and Abuse in College and University Dating Relationships', *Violence and Victims*, Vol. 9, 1, 1994, pp. 17-30.

[102] DeKeseredy, 'The Canadian national survey', p. 96.

[103] Ibid., p. 89.

[104] DeKeseredy, 'The Canadian national survey', p.86.

by 10.5%, of which 6.6% was due to incapacitation, adding up to 21.9% suffering rape or attempted rape over a year, compared to Koss's 16.6%. Since leaving high school, 24.4% had suffered rape (9.8% excluding incapacitation) and 22.1% attempted rape (8.5% excluding incapacitation), adding up to 46.5% compared to Koss's 27%.[105] It is unclear why Canadian male students apparently behave so much worse than their US counterparts.[106]

The Statistics Canada Violence Against Women Survey

The Statistics Canada Violence Against Women Survey (SCVAW), published in November 1993, was the result of a national telephone survey of 12,300 women over the age of 18. It claimed that 51% of Canadian women have suffered from male violence since the age of 16, and 39% have been sexually assaulted, 5% in any one year. The alarming figure for physical violence is not our immediate concern, but would form a background of threat against which sexual negotiation would occur. However, the figure is a rolling together of being pushed or grabbed and serious actual violence, such as being shot, with no attempt at contextualisation. As there is quite a lot of evidence which suggests that women initiate about as much violence against male intimates as do men against women, though with less serious consequences,[107] the 51% figure is of little value. Similarly the sexual assault figure derives from a question which rolls together achieved rape at gunpoint and a reluctant kiss under the mistletoe. Claims derived from the survey should therefore be treated with care, in spite of its size, cost and government sponsorship.[108]

---

[105] DeKeseredy and Kelly, 'The Incidence and Prevalence of Woman Abuse', data from pp. 149-50.

[106] For broadly similar figures from a smaller survey, together with a high rate of low-level stranger aggression in public, see Walter S. DeKeseredy, Martin D. Schwartz and Karen Tait, 'Sexual Assault and Stranger Aggression on a Canadian University Campus', *Sex Roles*, Vol. 28, Nos 5/6, 1993, pp. 263-77. Of course, not all comment on the WADR survey is critical. For an admiring account, see Susan K. Hippensteele et. al. 'Some Comments on the National Survey on Woman Abuse in Canadian University and College Dating Relationships', *The Journal of Human Justice*, Vol. 4, 2, 1993, pp. 67-71.

[107] There is a large literature in this area. A good starting point might be Murray A. Straus, 'Physical Assaults by Wives: A Major Social Problem' and Demie Kurz, 'Physical Assaults by Husbands: A Major Social Problem' both in Gelles and Loseke, eds, *Current Controversies on Family Violence*, pp. 67-87 and 88-103 respectively.

[108] For an account of the Statistics Canada survey, see Fekete, *Moral Panic*, pp. 80 et. seq.

The largest Canadian initiative on violence against women was the Canadian Panel on Violence Against Women, which was set up by the Canadian Federal Government in the aftermath of the fatal shooting of 14 female students by Marc Lépine at the École Polytechnique in Montreal on December 6th 1989. Its hearings and organisation of data were funded by the government at a cost of $10 million. Additional government grants funded surveys commissioned or used by the Panel.[109] Fekete charts a whole series of outrages carried out by the Panel. One of its publications was *Collecting the Voices: A Scrapbook*, a collection of 'voices' of women who offered evidence to the hearings set up by the panel. Fekete discovered that this was very heavily edited indeed, and that some of its most distressing quotations were taken from testimony which, quoted in full, plainly came from a woman who was clinically disturbed.[110] In the Panel's final report, *Changing the Landscape, Ending Violence - Achieving Equality*[111] there are claims that 80% of Aboriginal women had experienced violence, most of those being physically injured and 57% of them also suffering sexual abuse, founded on very limited questionnaires directed at victims of violence rather than Aboriginal (i.e., crudely, Eskimo) women generally, plus other anecdotal evidence.[112] In looking at older women, a study showing that 32 elderly people in a thousand suffer violence, with men experiencing double the violence suffered by women, is transmuted in the Panel's report into one in ten elderly people experiencing abuse, two thirds of these being women.[113] A tentative Californian study of 28 women with IQs in the range 20 to 70 supports the Panel's claim that 83% of Canadian women with disabilities - of whom there are some two million, with, of course, a wide range of disabilities - will be sexually assaulted.[114]

The centrepiece of the panel's claims, however, is the Women's Safety Project. This was the basis of the panel's claim that 'When all kinds of sexual violation and intrusion are considered, 98% of women reported that they personally experienced some form of sexual violation. This finding, in particular, clearly supports our assertion that violence affects virtually all women's lives.'[115] The Women's Safety Project was carried out by two researchers, Lori Haskell and Melanie Randall, and was designed as a version of Russell's San Francisco survey. Fekete established that the original base for the survey was 1,200 women living in Toronto. Interviews were completed with 420 of them, giving a 35%

---

[109] Fekete, *Moral Panic*, p. 37.

[110] Ibid., pp. 111-15.

[111] Ministry of Supply and Services, Ottawa, 1993.

[112] See Fekete, *Moral Panic*, pp. 120 et. seq.

[113] See Fekete, ibid., p. 132 et. seq.

[114] Fekete, ibid., pp. 138-45.

[115] *Changing Lives*, p. 10, quoted in Fekete, ibid., p. 147.

response rate. These were overwhelmingly white and middle class, 46.5% of them being university graduates compared to 15.5% of Canadian women generally. These factors all point towards an expectation of finding a higher rate of abuse than in a genuinely representative sample of Canadian women. Indeed, Haskell and Randall claim 67% of all women will be sexually assaulted at some time in their lives, 56% will suffer rape or attempted rape and 40% completed rape. The 98% figure includes, in addition, unwanted hugs and kisses, unwelcome comments, and physical abuse in an intimate relationship, such as pushing, shoving and slapping.[116] Fekete argues that one would expect such alarming findings to be properly published, but a year after the final report of the Panel the Women's Safety Project report was available only in two drafts which had to be hunted down, and which had drastic divergences between them.[117]

The findings discussed in the rest of this chapter come from academic or activist feminist researchers, not from government-sponsored bodies. If they make recommendations they typically seek better education for students, changes in the law on rape, changes in college procedures, etc. The Panel, being funded by the federal government, made more than 400 recommendations covering over 100 pages of the report. These seem to have been largely ignored by the Canadian authorities and public, but the orientation of the report can be seen from its summary: 'Violence against women is a product of a sexist, racist, heterosexist and class society and is perpetuated through all social institutions and the attitudes and behaviours of members of all Canadian communities'. The general orientation of the policy recommendations is for a rigorous application of zero tolerance of abuses.[118] One obvious comment on the quotation is that it does not seem to leave room for making any distinctions between Canada and, say, Saudi Arabia, whereas many feminists would see societies such as Canada as both less oppressive and more open to change. Another obvious comment, as Fekete observes, is to question why one should expect zero tolerance policies to have any success in such a hopeless situation - would not every part of the society tend to subvert them? A further problem, to which I shall return in Chapter 4, is one which concerns Fekete in much of the rest of his book: if the behaviours and attitudes proscribed under a zero tolerance policy are so extensive and so loosely defined, there is a grave danger of individuals falling foul of them on an arbitrary basis. This is what Fekete argues has happened to quite a number of Canadian academics.

Overall, however, the effect of the three Canadian survey reports of 1993 seems to have been a brief public furore in which supporters of the surveys' dramatic conclusions did battle with more sceptical critics, followed by a general loss of interest. The main concern of this book is the concepts used by various actors

---

[116] See Fekete, ibid., pp. 148-52.

[117] Ibid., pp. 154-61.

[118] Quoted from Fekete, ibid., pp. 166-7.

rather than campaigning strategies, but the Canadian experience does suggest that an excessive use of advocacy research can be self-defeating: amid the 80% of Canadian women students presented in the WADR survey as victims of 'woman abuse' there will be some, certainly, who are victims of rape or serious physical assault. Their cause seems to have been forgotten in the claim and counter-claim based on implausible figures.

British studies

Claims that the rate of rape in the USA is much higher than that in other industrialised countries are often made, but, given the wildly varying possible rates seen above and the tendency in many countries, including Britain, for the reporting or recording rate to rise quite suddenly, these should be approached with caution.[119] It is also open to argument whether a lower rate of officially recorded stranger rape would necessarily signal a lower rate of date and acquaintance rape. British rates of date rape need to be established from British studies rather than extrapolated by applying a multiplier to British official statistics. Studies in Britain have generally been carried out by feminist activists or sociologists and criminologists (there can be much overlap between these categories); relatively little work has been done by British psychologists. The studies have generally been of some part of the female population at large - which of course includes students - rather than of students as a sample for young people in general. There has also been a strong emphasis on women's safety, so that domestic violence and sexual abuse are often considered together.

Ask Any Woman

One of the most thorough British studies was the Women's Safety Survey, carried out in the London area in 1982-83 by the activist group Women Against Rape, with some financial help from the Greater London Council (abolished shortly afterwards by Mrs Thatcher for being too left wing) and some help from London academics. Very much a collective effort, the survey was finally written up by Ruth Hall under the title *Ask Any Woman*.[120] Two thousand copies of the 76-question survey were distributed all over London at 'festivals, high streets, doctors' surgeries, ante-natal clinics, markets, hospital wards, pensioners' and housewives' groups, bingo halls and other places where women could be found...'[121] Of these 1,236 were returned either directly or by post.

---

[119] See, for example, Allison and Wrightsman, *Rape,* pp. 9-10, where a variety of sources are used to claim that the rate of rape in the USA is 13 times that of England, four times that of West Germany, five to ten times that of France and 20 times that of Japan.

[120] Ruth E. Hall, *Ask Any Woman,* Falling Wall Press, Bristol, 1985.

[121] Ibid., p. 162.

Demographically the respondents were 'fairly representative of women in London'. The survey under-represents women of African or Asian descent. The percentage of married women is considerably lower than the census figures (33% of respondents were married, compared to 48% for Inner London and 55% for Greater London in the 1981 Census); however, the survey aimed for real living situations whereas the Census may be over-dependent on formal categories, e.g. 'married' might mean 'formally married but about to be divorced', or 'cohabiting for quite a long time'. Judging from the question about access to motorised transport, the respondents may be somewhat more working class than the average; the direct comparison of occupational groupings is not possible because, very sensibly, the survey looked at the resources the women themselves could command, whereas the Census tends to classify women in terms of their husband's occupation. The other major disproportion is that the survey over-represents women in their 20s and 30s and under-represents older, and particularly elderly women.[122]

The questions were developed carefully over a long period of time. There are two sections covering rape. The first one asks about 'unwelcome sexual remarks', having been 'grabbed or touched up against your will', having been 'the victim of an attempted rape' before moving on to ask 'have you ever been raped?' and 'have you been sexually assaulted?'. The questionnaire then asks respondents who have been raped or sexually assaulted to specify who by, to categorise the sort of coercion used into 'physical force or violence', 'threats of physical force or violence', use of a 'position of power or authority', 'some other kind of pressure' and 'you were very young'. Other questions then cover location of the attack, rape or sexual assault as a child, and a series of questions about various forms of reporting or non-reporting and emotional and financial damage.[123] These questions are open to Koss's criticism that victims may be unfamiliar with legal definitions and therefore fail to recognise their experience as rape, but not to the criticisms made of Koss that she is expanding the nature of rape. 'Sexual assault' could potentially cover a very wide range of incidents, but most respondents who said they had suffered 'sexual assault' distinguished it from being 'grabbed or touched up' and were reporting serious abuses which had, in fact, been reported to the police more often than had rape.[124] The designers of the questionnaire had the problem that they accepted the idea of spousal rape at a time when English law basically did not. Their solution to this was to ask 'Have you ever been forced to give in to sex against your will in marriage or a common law marriage?', following this up with 'Do you consider this was rape?'. There then follows a series of possible reasons for giving in to sex in marriage against one's will, ranging from violence or threats of violence through to 'it was taken for granted'

---

[122] Ibid., pp. 168-77.

[123] Ibid., pp. 185-90.

[124] Ibid., p. 29, f. 10.

or 'he was a good husband in other ways'. These allow the designers to compare their own view of what exactly constitutes marital rape with those of the respondents.

In the analysis of the replies 39% of respondents said they had suffered at least one rape, attempted rape or sexual assault; it may be difficult to distinguish between attempted rape and sexual assault, but the rape and attempted rape responses add up to 37%. Seventeen per cent of respondents had suffered at least one rape. Fifteen per cent of women who had been married or lived in a common law marriage had been raped in marriage. Sixteen per cent of respondents had been raped or sexually assaulted before the age of 16.[125] Seventy-six per cent of respondents had been grabbed or touched up against their will.[126] The survey was not set up to assess date rape as defined in this book, but three out of four rapes were acquaintance rapes, and this total rises if spousal rape is added in, so it is likely that date rape as defined here would feature to a considerable extent.[127] Another important point raised by the survey is that 30% of sexual assaults were carried out at least partly through the abuse of a position of power or authority, particularly over employees and over young girls. It also inevitably features strongly in the rape or sexual assault of 20% of respondents when they were under seventeen.[128] I shall return to this point in the next two chapters. Forms of coercion beyond those usually recognised in the law also feature strongly in the responses from women who considered that they had been raped in marriage. Asked what had made them give in to sex against their will, two thirds cited violence or threatened violence, half cited financial pressure, particularly women with children and few financial resources, nearly half were afraid their husband would 'take it out on them' in other ways, a fifth worried that he would take it out on the children, at least half cited emotional pressure, feelings of guilt, 40% cited an expectation of unwanted sex. These pressures are, of course, not mutually exclusive, and it should not be assumed that the women in question were identifying emotional pressure as rape; it is more that emotional pressure was used to back up violence.[129]

A particular strength of the Women's Safety Survey is its emphasis on economic issues. As mentioned elsewhere it documents the psychological after-effects of rape, but it also covers extra costs such as those involved in additional safety precautions (self-defence classes, running a car, anti-burglary precautions, moving to a safer area, etc.) and loss of earnings or educational opportunities due to trauma or injury and illness.[130] The survey highlights assaults on public

---

[125] Ibid., pp. 32-3.

[126] Ibid., p. 39.

[127] Ibid., pp. 69-71.

[128] Ibid., pp. 75-6, 78-87.

[129] Ibid., pp. 88-96.

[130] Ibid., pp. 145-8.

transport: nearly one in five respondents had been raped or sexually assaulted while waiting for or using public transport. Over half the respondents had accepted lifts from strangers, and over half of these did so because they could not afford public transport. Women's own cars were much safer, but the obvious policy implication of the survey is the importance of improved public transport, notably more frequent services.[131] Looking at women who were raped in marriage but were unable to leave, the survey finds that 79% of them were forced to remain by material circumstances.[132] The authors of the survey advocate a change in the law to make coercing a woman into sex by 'abusing her position of economic dependence' an offence, and would obviously like this to include wives.[133]

The Women's Safety Survey analysis offers a convincing case that rape and sexual assault are much under-reported (as we saw in Chapter 2, reporting rates in England have risen since the time of the survey, but undoubtedly remain well below incidence rates). Although it does not specifically cover date rape as defined here, it offers useful insights into pressured sex as well as straightforward rape. The major problem with the survey is that of the sample. Although the team behind the survey stressed that they were interested in the experiences of *all* women, and although the sample is not too seriously demographically skewed, it seems a reasonable assumption that women who had been assaulted or who were worried about being assaulted would think it particularly important to fill in the questionnaire, whilst confident women who had never had much of a problem might not bother. In the same way a survey on cycling which asked for responses from everyone might well over-represent cyclists.

Glasgow Evening Times survey on violence against women

This survey was carried out by the Women's Support Project, a Glasgow project against violence perpetrated on women and children which developed from the Strathclyde Rape Crisis Centre with urban aid funding. The group initially wanted to replicate the London Women's Safety Survey in Glasgow. When they failed to raise the funding to do this, they settled for an offer from the Glasgow Evening Times newspaper to print a one-page questionnaire to be returned anonymously to a freepost address. The questionnaire was printed in January 1989 and came at the end of three days of pieces on women and various forms of domestic violence and sexual assault. The results which follow come from the 1,503 completed forms received. The comment in the last paragraph about the London Women's Safety survey sample obviously also applies to this survey.

The women who completed questionnaires were almost all white, and 85% of respondents were aged 18-49; just over 60% were married or cohabiting. The

---

[131] Ibid., pp. 55-8.

[132] Ibid., pp. 98-9.

[133] Ibid., p. 77, n. 4.

survey does not really offer any way to assess class in either the conventional way or in the manner attempted by the London Women's Safety Survey.[134]

The survey was not designed to look for date rape as such, and the strong stress on domestic violence in the articles which preceded it may well have discouraged younger women from completing it.[135] Nonetheless, 42% of respondents gave a positive answer to: 'As an adult have you ever been approached sexually or been involved in sexual activity you didn't like or want or which went beyond what you wanted?'. Some responses to this were triggered by attempted rape; presumably some may have been unsuccessful approaches for some sort of sexual activity. Together, husbands and boyfriends were responsible for over 48% of the sexual assaults. Fifteen per cent of respondents to the survey said they had been raped (elicited by following the previous question with: 'Did this include rape?'), and husbands and boyfriends accounted for 56% of these rapes.[136] The responses revealed a great deal of domestic violence, with 36% of the sample having been threatened with violence by boyfriends, and over half of the women in the survey having experienced domestic violence at some stage.[137] A third of the respondents had had sex for the sake of peace at home.[138] Just under 40% of the respondents to the survey overall had children living with them, but of the women who had suffered domestic violence 68.6% had children living with them at the time, again suggesting that dependent women are easier to abuse.[139] From the letters quoted there is an obvious overlap between domestic violence and spousal rape, an issue to which we shall return.[140] Twenty-one per cent of respondents suffered sexual assault as children, again raising questions about male abuse of authority.[141]

Whilst the sampling technique and some of the questions used suggest it may be exaggerating the problems of domestic and sexual abuse in Glasgow, the very high figures in the survey certainly suggest that the British Crime Survey and still more police statistics (about 240-280 complaints of rape to the police annually, 1985-88, leading to 30-47 convictions in the whole of Scotland)[142] considerably under-represent the rate of abuse. This survey was one of the considerations which

---

[134] Patricia Bell, 'Women's Support Project/Evening Times Report on Responses from 1,503 Women to the Survey on Violence Against Women', 1990, pp. 10-11, available from Women's Support Project, Newlands Centre, 871 Springfield Road, Glasgow G31 4HZ.

[135] Ibid., p. 47.

[136] Ibid., pp. 27-30.

[137] Ibid., pp. 45, 50.

[138] Ibid., p. 90.

[139] Ibid., p. 58. However, among women who engaged in sexual activity they did not like 'for peace at home', rather more were economically independent than economically dependent at the time of the survey. Various ad hoc reasons are offered for this surprising result.

[140] Ibid., pp. 63-7.

[141] Ibid., p. 36.

[142] Ibid., p. 96.

pushed Strathclyde Regional Council towards supporting the Zero Tolerance Campaign against domestic violence and sexual abuse.

The hidden figure: domestic violence in north London

This survey was carried out under the direction of Jayne Mooney, commissioned by Islington Council and funded by the Department of the Environment and Middlesex University. Half the households in a socially and ethnically mixed area of Islington were selected, using the Post Office Address File to make sure of including households not on the electoral register. Half of those targeted for interview were males over 16, the other half females over 16. Nothing is said in Mooney's account of the survey about refusals or households where no-one was in, but from the fact that the first stage, an interviewer-administered questionnaire was administered to 571 women and 429 men one can deduce that some targeted individuals were missed. The second stage involved giving self-completion questionnaires to women whose partners were out; this produced 430 questionnaires. In addition, 15 women who said they had experienced domestic violence in Stage 1 were interviewed in depth.[143] Mooney's own assessment is that this was a representative sample of British women, given that most of the population lives in urban areas and the ethnic and class mixture in her survey.[144]

An interesting feature of this survey is the section on women's own definitions of domestic violence. Apart from more obvious behaviours, 80% of those surveyed included mental cruelty and 76% included 'being made to have sex without giving consent'. Mental cruelty was defined as: 'verbal abuse (e.g. calling of names, being ridiculed especially in front of other people), being deprived of money, clothes, sleep, prevented from going out etc.'[145] This sort of behaviour is likely to feature in some of the non-violent sexual coercion discussed in the Women's Safety Survey, and was seen as worse than isolated incidents of actual bodily violence.[146] The respondents' view makes perfectly good sense: a loving and decent husband who as part of his work as a surgeon inflicted occasional injuries similar to those described in the survey on his wife as part of a carefully-explained programme of medical treatment would not cause nearly as much suffering as many of Mooney's respondents experienced. However, this sensible view makes for problems in surveys of sexual coercion. One difficulty is that a certain amount of mental cruelty as defined probably occurs occasionally in most relationships without becoming part of serious sexual coercion; survey findings about mental cruelty thus have to be treated with care. Related to this is the problem of whether,

---

[143] Jayne Mooney, *The Hidden Figure: Domestic Violence in North London*, available from Centre for Criminology, Middlesex University, 1993, pp. 3-16.

[144] Ibid., p. 66.

[145] Ibid., p. 18.

[146] Ibid., p. 23.

when, and to what extent mental cruelty should be regarded as the basis for saying that sexual coercion amounting to rape has occurred.

Turning to Mooney's specific findings on rape, 23% of her sample had suffered rape at some point in their lives, 6% over the last 12 months. Remembering that some of the sample had been raped repeatedly over the previous year, Mooney records 25.0 incidents of rape per 100 women per 12 months compared to the 0.3 in both the 1984 and 1988 British Crime Surveys.[147] Mooney also asked about date rape, defined as rape occurring on a date with men 'whom the woman had not been out with on more than five occasions', a definition rather different from that in the US literature (which does not restrict the number of dates) or given above by me. She found that 25% of women reported unwanted sexual touching on such dates, particularly first dates. Date rape was suffered by 9% of the women, 35% of these on a first date, 32% with threats of violence and 5% with actual violence. None of the incidents were reported to the police.[148]

Mooney does not provide a sample of her questionnaire, nor does she cover the issue of people who refused to cooperate with her survey, both of which points could conceivably cast doubt on her findings. Assuming neither possible criticism to be valid, her survey is the best evidence of rates of rape which are much higher than those in any official figures.

Surviving sexual violence

Liz Kelly's study is based on extensive open-ended interviews with 60 women, comprising three groups of ten women, the groups having experienced respectively incest, rape and domestic violence, and a comparison group of 30 other women.[149] It therefore does not claim to contribute to the quantitative work discussed in this chapter, other than to say that as Kelly's lengthy interviews progressed women recalled more instances of abuse which they had for one reason or another forgotten, i.e. her research would tend to support the view that women experience much more abuse than materialises in police stations, and that probably women completing a quick questionnaire would fail to recall some incidents which would count. Kelly's book is, however, important in giving a much better insight into what is involved in various forms of sexual violence, and we shall return to it in Chapter 4.

---

[147] Ibid., pp. 26, 30, 34.

[148] Ibid., p. 66.

[149] Liz Kelly, *Surviving Sexual Violence,* Polity Press, Cambridge, UK, 1988, esp. p. 10.

Date rape: the 'prison works' solution

One reading of the literature on date rape is that its authors are wanting to make sure that the law treats it seriously, ensuring that perpetrators meet with their just deserts. The literature is certainly replete with comments about the police, the judicial system and the law itself, both in Britain and in the USA, failing to prosecute date rapists, and includes various suggestions for legal reforms which would increase conviction rates. It is worth examining, therefore, the possible consequences of a really effective set of reforms. The following calculations are not statistically sound, but offer an illustration of what would happen in Britain if some estimates of the extent of date and acquaintance rape were valid here.

The assumptions are: i.) The population of England and Wales is 48 million, 24 million each of men and women. ii.) The women die on average at age 75, and cohorts of women are evenly spread. Thus there are 320,000 women at each age. iii.) If they are going to be victims of rape or attempted rape this will happen at age 20 (say). iv.) Each crime of rape or attempted rape is brought to trial and punished. Because the crimes are mainly at the less serious end of the spectrum of rape, and include attempted rape, the sentences average one year, after remission, for each event. v.) I then take the rate of lifetime victimisation claimed in each study, and see what it would do to the prison population.

Mary Koss in Warshaw, I Never Called it Rape

Twenty-seven per cent of women suffer rape or attempted rape between age 14 and 21, on average two events per woman. Thus for England and Wales 172,800 events happen to 86,400 women, punishable by 172,800 years in prison.
RISE IN ENGLAND AND WALES PRISON POPULATION: *172,800.*

Diana Russell, San Francisco survey

Forty-four per cent of the women in her survey suffered rape or attempted rape, on average nearly twice. (This includes spousal rape.) Thus for England and Wales 140,800 women suffer 270,336 events, punishable by 270,336 years in prison.
RISE IN ENGLAND AND WALES PRISON POPULATION: *270,336.*

Canadian panel on violence against women

Fifty-six per cent of women in the Women's Safety Project report which plays a central role in the Panel's report suffered rape or attempted rape. Arbitrarily limiting them to one offence each, we get 179,200 events, punishable by 179,200 years in prison.
RISE IN ENGLAND AND WALES PRISON POPULATION: *179,200.*

Thirty-six per cent of women suffered rape or attempted rape, making 115,200 assaults each year, punishable by 115,200 years in prison.
RISE IN ENGLAND AND WALES PRISON POPULATION: 115,200.

Glasgow Evening Times survey on violence against women

Of this sample, 15.4% had been raped, and 41.1% had suffered either rape and/or sexual assault; most of the sexual assault was serious and much appears to be attempted rape. So a reasonable way to count this survey would be 15.4% rape, 25.7% attempted rape. Again assuming an average sentence of one year for any assault, we get 131,520 years in prison.
RISE IN ENGLAND AND WALES PRISON POPULATION: 131,520.

Jayne Mooney: The hidden figure: domestic violence in north London

Twenty-three per cent of her sample had suffered rape (defined for survey as sex without consent because of actual or threatened violence). Mooney offers no convenient figure for attempted rape. It seems reasonable to assume an average sentence of at least 1.5 years for rape, thus: 73,600 women suffered at least one rape, punishable by 110,400 years in prison. Pretty clearly this survey would have turned up a high incidence of attempted rape, so our figure is too low.
RISE IN ENGLAND AND WALES PRISON POPULATION: 110,400.

As a comparison, in 1998 the British prison population was a little over 63,000 amid much concern about rising numbers. Changes in sentencing left over from the Conservative government which fell in 1997 were forecast to increase the prison population by some 20,000: they took the slogan 'prison works' very seriously, even if those involved in the prison service are generally sceptical.

Virtually none of the rapes and attempted rapes recorded in or projected by the surveys would have resulted in conviction, given the 1995 Home Office statistics: 425 rapists convicted out of 5,059 rapes reported to police.

The above technique for calculating a rise in numbers of men in prison following reforms which made it possible to catch and convict all rapists and attempted rapists is extremely crude, but it is clear that the basic message would be the same however the calculations were modified: to imprison rapists on the scale the surveys claim they exist would require around a tripling, if not more, of prison accommodation in Britain. Given the stress in the literature that rapists are largely ordinary men there would also be very substantial problems arising from criminalising anything up to a third of the male population. (The surveys are obviously unable to supply data which would show to what extent a limited number of date rapists victimise larger numbers of women, but we certainly are

77

dealing with large numbers. I assume above that if serial date rapists are caught their sentences are extended on a crime-by-crime basis; this assumption would break down once the perpetrators had accumulated a life sentence for a 'campaign of rape'.)

The purpose of the calculation is not to pour scorn on the surveys, nor is it to argue against legal reforms. It is also not my intention to argue that rape should not be treated seriously. However, it is obvious that any practical solution to the problem of date rape is likely to imitate the Race Relations legislation and use the law and the threat of prison mainly as an educational device rather than to imitate the law against murder, where the aspiration is (reasonably) to imprison every murderer. As part of that process the next two chapters analyse some of the problems raised by the surveys and the claims made about them. In the final section of this chapter, I summarise some of the issues which arise from the surveys.

Issues raised by the survey literature on date rape

The calculations about imprisonment in the previous section highlight one issue raised by the surveys: some commentators find the very high rates of sexual assault implausible. This has led to what might be termed the 'date rape wars' in which authors such as Neil Gilbert, Katie Roiphe and John Fekete argue that the surveys use misleading questions and/or dubious sampling techniques. I have made some detailed comments on the issues involved above, and will be discussing some of the points involved in more detail in the next two chapters. Here it seems a good idea to ask for a moment what is at stake.

An accusation made by Koss and DeKeseredy is that authors such as Gilbert are encouraging politicians to cut grants made to centres offering counselling and assistance to victims of sexual violence. This accusation is not backed up with citations, although it is possible to imply that an issue has been hyped without spelling out the policy implications. My own view is that the surveys can be taken to have shown that the rates of sexual assault in both the USA and in Britain are a lot higher than would be thought from official figures, be these complaints to the police or victimisation surveys. This is backed up by the numbers of women who approach rape crisis centres who do not report to the police. There is every reason to think, therefore, that rape crisis centres are doing a useful job, and to carry on funding them. However, the centres cannot counsel women who do not approach them, be this because they have been misclassified in a survey and need no help or because they have been victimised but are unwilling to come forward for whatever reason. Thus the criterion for funding a centre should be the actual level of demand for it, rather than a hypothetical possible level drawn from a survey. The counter-accusation made by Gilbert and Roiphe is that heterosexual dating is largely an enjoyable and safe experience for women, and that the misleading figures from the surveys worry women unnecessarily and point towards a pattern of dating more like the largely chaperoned dating found in the nineteenth century. Education about date rape, if it happened at all, would be very differently organised by Gilbert and Roiphe. Some of what is argued in the next two chapters may be helpful in clarifying the issues involved here.

An important issue for further discussion is communication. Much communication between dating couples about having sex, particularly for the first time, is probably not overt, verbal communication; it is likely to involve metaphors such as 'getting more comfortable' or 'going to bed'. Also, as we have seen, there is considerable evidence of dishonest communication. One tactic involved in attempting to prevent date rape is thus the recommendation that communication should be more direct and explicit. In the next chapter I shall explore what would be involved in this, together with some possible problems.

It is too easy, however, to assume that better communication could solve all problems. As we saw in Chapter 2, the central defining feature of rape is that it is sexual intercourse without the consent of the woman. Even if communication is clear, how do we know consent when we see it? The Glasgow and Islington surveys discussed above show very high rates of domestic violence. Put together with the Women's Safety Survey these carry a very strong implication that in a lot of marriages women have sex 'to keep the peace'. Consider for a moment a woman whose partner batters her but never threatens her with violence when suggesting sex. From what he says she is free to refuse him; her situation is no different from that of a wife who is never battered. However, unlike the wife who is never battered, the battered wife must consider whether her refusal may be contributing to a build-up of tension which will lead to her getting battered 'about' something else. She may, therefore, agree quite 'willingly' to have sex, but from an implied fear. Is this consent? Perhaps she consents, but does not consent freely. Can we spell out what is meant by free consent?

The direct coercion used by the date rapists in the American surveys is largely 'moderate' or slight; the maximum seems to be pushing, slapping or arm-twisting. It may be that these actions should be seen more as communication: 'co-operate or I could do much worse' rather than as sanctions: 'have sex with me or endure this physical violence'. However, given that the level of violence normally does not go beyond that described, let us consider it as sanctions. The actions involved are rape because the woman is coerced into sex using violent sanctions. Mary Koss describes as 'unethical conduct', but not rape, the actions of a woman who induces a man to have sex with her by threatening to spread rumours about him being impotent. What about a woman who spreads rumours which lead to a man being fired from a secure and well-paid job? Faced with a choice between suffering a modest amount of violence or being sacked, many people (and particularly men, who tend to have such jobs) would prefer the modest violence. Women, too, are obviously vulnerable to various sorts of rumours and economic sanctions. How do we rate economic sanctions as against violence as sources of sexual coercion?

What about emotional coercion? If a large part of one's life is bound up with a particular relationship, threats to end it might well also be experienced as worse than modest violence.

A further issue which needs to be tackled is: who defines rape? Some of the literature, notably the Women's Safety Survey and Liz Kelly, puts a lot of emphasis on women's own view of their experience. In contrast, Mary Koss stresses that individuals often are not aware of the legal definition of rape, and insists on fitting women's experiences into a prescribed legal framework. A definition of rape which stands any chance of becoming law or acting as a guide to ethical behaviour must also be capable of being understood by most men. Some way needs to be found through this problem.

4 Date rape and the concept of consent

In Chapter 2 I accepted the central feature of English law on rape, namely that rape is having sex without consent. In the exploration of the literature on date rape in Chapter 3, consent was frequently one of the important issues. If consent is drawn more narrowly, for example, so that 'the utmost resistance' is required (as in some of the older American state legislation) then most of the examples of date rape in Chapter 3 are defined out of existence. Conversely, if various acts such as digital penetration are assimilated to rape, and an expansive view is taken about alcohol so that sex with an inebriated woman is viewed as rape, then the scope of rape becomes much wider. Another important problem is the communication of consent or non-consent. If it is assumed that women consent to sex by, say, going voluntarily to a man's apartment as part of a date then we have a very different view of rape from one which says that any sex to which there has not been explicit verbal consent is rape. Further, there is the problem of the background situation. Consent induced by threats of violence is plainly not consent in the normal sense. Most people would regard consent induced by a threat not to smile for the next twenty minutes as genuine consent. Where between these two do the boundaries lie?

In this chapter I shall start by enquiring whether there is a general concept of consent which can be applied to sexual consent. I shall look particularly at the issue of consent in politics and medicine. I shall argue that the analysis of consent proposed in the political literature by Flathman offers a good framework for making sense of consent, and follow him in looking at: i.) knowledge of what is consented to; ii.) intending to consent; iii.) communicating one's consent; iv.) against a background of free choice. The third point is quite lengthy, as it leads on to an analysis of the view in some feminist writing and in the Antioch College student code that sexual consent must be explicit for it to be genuine. Discussion of the fourth issue, free choice, involves looking at the range of sanctions which might be used to induce someone to have sex and seeing if a boundary can be set between rape and non-rape. The general theme which will emerge is that the boundaries between rape and non-rape are very murky. This has an obvious bearing on the debates and statistical uncertainties which were examined in Chapter 3.

A general concept of consent?

I started this investigation with the idea that it might help to make sense of the concept of consent in sexual relations through an investigation of the concept of consent in other areas, notably in politics and medicine. Whilst I still think there are some useful insights to be gained by this method, my general conclusion is that there is a family relationship, in Wittgenstein's sense, between consent in various areas. What this means is that there are enough features in common between, say, political and sexual consent for the same word to be usefully used for both, but that there is no single 'essence of consent'. Rather, there is an overlapping series of meanings. In other words, ultimately we have to make sense of sexual consent in its own terms rather than those drawn from elsewhere.

Let us nevertheless consider political consent and see what insights can usefully be obtained. The concept of consent arises in political philosophy in connection with the issue of political obligation, the question of why I should obey the government of the state in which I live. Do I owe it more of an obligation of obedience than I do to another state, or to a set of ideas such as human rights or international communism?

Some authors now think that we do not have any particular obligation to the state in which we live, but I would argue that in broad and general terms the concept is meaningful. Consider, for example, the South African election of 1994, which marked the full official ending of apartheid. Before this election black people were excluded from constitutional politics in South Africa. Not having any possibility of helping to decide who was to govern them, and peaceful protests having failed, they had very good reasons for giving allegiance to the African National Congress (ANC), which aimed to overthrow the apartheid regime by armed force if necessary. Whilst there are doubtless all sorts of reasons for black South Africans having reservations about the new government, there is a very marked difference between the situation before and after the election. The government was elected in free and fair elections. The fact that it was formed by the ANC testifies to a genuine change of regime. If black people want a different government from the ANC they have the opportunity to vote for a different party in the next general election. There are, therefore, very strong reasons why black people should obey the current South African government, reasons which did not apply to the former apartheid regime. These can be summed up by saying that they consented to the current government.

That said, there are a whole series of problems about political consent which do not apply to sexual consent. Political consent is normally a collective act: people vote for a government or a constitution. It therefore generates an assortment of problems about collective consent which do not apply in any obvious way to sexual consent. For example, if I am a black South African anarchist, perhaps I voted in the 1994 election as a cynical act aimed at making propaganda rather than as a sign of my consent to the new regime. Can proponents of the current regime find appropriate philosophical arguments, for example that I had a fair chance to persuade people of my views but failed, or that I will get another chance soon, to persuade me to stick within the law? If I do not accept these arguments, is it right to coerce me into obeying the law? Again, what about people too young to vote in the 1994 election, or people visiting the country? Are such people consenting to the regime by, say, using roads it has built, or by remaining in the country, even if it is difficult to leave? Political consent operates over years rather than minutes. What sort of behaviour from the government would justify the populace, or some of it, in deciding that the democratic process of consenting to the government had broken down and that they were justified in withdrawing their consent?

Such problems, whilst very interesting and important in their own right, do not have any obvious exact sexual parallels. A possible exception might be the question of the consent of women to patriarchy. Carole Pateman argues that because courts do not rely on women's evidence in rape cases, their consent to the political system when they do anything which counts as a 'yes', i.e. their acceptance of it, must be gravely in doubt.[1] As indicated in Chapter 2, I agree with her critique of the criminal justice system's approach to rape. However, the failure of the legal system to take rape seriously does not, it seems to me, permeate the rest of society. Women vote on the same basis as men; in general in court proceedings their evidence is weighed equally with men, unlike the situation under Islamic laws; their work is covered by (admittedly imperfect) equal pay and equal opportunity legislation; divorce laws are broadly equal; domestic and sexual violence are illegal, even though the procedures for dealing with them are woefully inadequate. In other words, it is no more appropriate for Pateman to argue that the way rape is dealt with permeates the rest of society than for someone else to argue that women are fully equal because equal numbers of men and women are entering higher education. This point can be illustrated by quoting Pateman on the failure of British law to recognise rape within marriage at the time she was writing: '[d]espite the apparent importance of women's consent, it is legally and socially declared irrelevant within marriage...'[2] This view has the effect that a major revolution occurred in Britain in 1991 when the House of Lords recognised spousal rape. It is certainly right that the law *should* recognise spousal

---

[1] Carole Pateman, 'Women and Consent', in Carole Pateman, *The Disorder of Women*, Polity Press, Cambridge, 1989, pp. 71-89.

[2] Pateman, 'Women and Consent', p. 82.

rape, but to understand the operation of patriarchy in general one surely has to look at a much wider range of issues. This question will be further discussed in Chapter 5.

Another point which may at least evoke echoes for those studying sexual consent is that much of the writing on consent dates from before the time of universal franchise. The notion that because we have not consented to the current state we have a right to overthrow it at any time is obviously an alarming one: a reasonable degree of political stability offers great benefits. There is therefore, as mentioned above, a tendency in the literature on consent to find rather stretched reasons for claiming that people have tacitly consented to the current state - certainly voting in a normal election, but also using any public facilities or simply not leaving. There is some similarity here to arguments that because a woman failed to specifically protest at what seems pretty clearly to be a sexual assault, or because she failed to continue struggling throughout, or etc., she actually consented and perhaps enjoyed it. Just as a stretched political account of consent is convenient for the rulers of a state, so the stretched account of sexual consent discussed here is generally convenient for men.

Turning briefly to medical consent, there seems to be fairly general agreement that the key feature of consent for a patient who is in a condition to remove herself from a hospital is that she stays rather than that she signs a consent form. Formal consent obtained by signing a form is seen as a supplement to this, as a way of explaining medical procedures to the patient and making sure that she goes along with them. There are some obvious problems in this. There is a catch-22 problem specific to medicine: patients who disagree with the doctor are prone to be deemed incompetent to decide for themselves.[3] Medical procedures are often complex and difficult for patients to understand. Does the explanation, therefore, use a broad brush approach and leave out finer details which might possibly matter in some circumstances, opening the medical staff to the accusation that they hid things from the patient? Or should a fuller explanation be used, even if it muddles the patient and 'blinds her with science'? What if the patient is unconscious, or does not seem to be in a rational state to discuss things?[4] Usually (but not always) people have a reasonably good understanding of what a proposal to have sex involves, so the problem of complexity is less evident. The question of rationality is relevant, however, in situations where the woman involved has been drinking or using drugs. Is she still in a condition to give meaningful consent?

---

[3] See, for example, J.A. Devereux, D.P.H. Jones and D.L. Dickenson, 'Can children withhold consent to treatment?', *British Medical Journal*, Vol. 306, 29 May, 1993, pp. 1459-61.

[4] For a clear discussion of these issues, see Philip Meredith, 'Patient Participation in Decision-Making and Consent to Treatment: the Case of General Surgery', *Sociology of Health and Illness*, Vol. 15, No. 3, 1993, pp. 315-36.

Let us move on to one analysis of consent drawn from the literature on political obligation which provides a helpful framework for thinking about sexual consent. Flathman breaks down the process of consent as follows:

> Assuming the circumstances are right for the question of consent to arise, for B to consent he must: a) know what he consents to, b) intend to consent to it, c) communicate his knowledge of what he is consenting to and his intention to consent (that is, communicate his consent) to the person or persons to whom the consent is given. (The communication can be either direct or indirect.)[5]

Let us go through Flathman's account, filling in the details and attempting to apply it to consent to sex. 'Assuming the circumstances are right' is not a reference to background conditions such as whether consent is being made freely - which comes later - but to issues which do not concern us here. One of these is whether the matter in question is sufficiently serious for the question of consent to arise (thus: 'Do you mind if I brush a piece of fluff off my sleeve?' is normally so tedious a question that it is not asked, but 'Would you mind if I make love to you now?' is obviously a serious question). The other is whether some people are entitled to consent as representatives of a group, an important question in politics but not usually applicable to sex.[6]

Aspects of sexual consent i.) knowing what you consent to

The first major point is that B must know what he consents to. Flathman explains:

> It does not follow that B must know, at the time he consents and in fine detail, every action that his consent commits him to take. He could, for example, commit himself to do whatever another person (e.g. Hobbes's sovereign) tells him to do. What is essential is that his consent provide criteria by which to decide whether a particular action falls within the scope of the commitment.[7]

There are some problems which might arise here. Our B (who is female) might be so young or innocent or drunk that she is not fully aware that she is consenting to sex. What assumptions are being made about how long sex will go on? Can she decide she wants to stop before he is finished? Supposing B is offered sex which will be very pleasurable, but in fact it is not, although it otherwise meets the description of sex B was given to understand was on offer, has B consented or

---

[5] R. E. Flathman, *Political Obligation*, Croom Helm, London, 1972, p. 220.

[6] Ibid., p. 214.

[7] Ibid., p. 220, f.27.

not? What accompaniments to sex is B consenting to? In other words, it seems reasonable that having her hair stroked or being kissed could be seen as part of the deal, while anal intercourse, bondage and group sex would need further negotiation, but there might well be intermediate acts, perhaps cunnilingus or toe-sucking, which are neither plainly agreed nor plainly not. What violations here would reasonably lead to a moral claim that B has been raped?

Let us consider these problems a little further. If B is young and innocent we are looking at the issues surrounding under-age sex or statutory rape, and I have nothing to add to the discussion in Chapter 2. The question of drink is rather different. Here the assumption is that a fully sober B has a perfectly good understanding of what she would be agreeing to, but she is currently drunk. I want to consider this issue in Chapter 5. What if the sex is disappointing? Whilst I cannot imagine this ever being acceptable to courts, because it would be difficult to prove what had gone wrong and who was responsible for the problem, a woman might well feel used, cheated, if she is promised something very different from what she actually experiences, and in more extreme cases these feelings might well approach those in the more marginal cases of rape which will be discussed later. Notice that to allow such a case to be called 'rape' is also allowing a woman to decide *after* the event that it was rape. This also needs - and will get - further discussion later in this chapter.

The other issue is that of accompaniments. There is a strong cultural element to this question. Kissing and hair-stroking are normal accompaniments to sex in European and American culture, but they may not be in other places. Amir in his study of rape in Philadelphia notes forced oral sex as something which was felt by victims to be a particularly perverted and degrading accompaniment to rape. On the other hand the approach of Erica Jong[8] seems to be more that a willingness to engage in cunnilingus is a requisite of a good lover. In other words, particular acts develop a particular meaning in specific times and places.

One sensible response to these problems is that in normal sex the woman should be able to indicate what she wants as things go along. Good communication, in other words, would avoid several of the problems becoming too severe. The issue of communication will be examined shortly.

Aspects of sexual consent ii.) intending to consent

Moving on to ii.), intending to consent to sex, the problems are much worse than intent to consent politically. Typically political consent, particularly voting in a constitutional referendum, involves limited and specific 'yes' or 'no' choices which are indicated by voting. Participants know that the choice will be difficult to revoke once the die is cast - normally another constitutional referendum is

---

[8] Menachem Amir, *Patterns in Forcible Rape*, University of Chicago Press, Chicago, 1971; Erica Jong, *How to Save Your Own Life*, Granada, London, 1978, pp. 85, 87, 288.

needed, possibly a whole series of them in a federal system such as the USA. Thus voters consider the arguments, make up their minds, and soberly go and vote.

In sexual consent there are two main problems, both of which have very fraught ramifications and numerous connections with the literature on date rape. To start with, let us look at the issue of unintentional consent. Does one strictly speaking have to *intend* to consent in order to consent? Consider one of the cases of tacit communication of consent which appears in the political literature. Someone who gets into a taxi at the railway station in a town and asks to be taken to the town hall is thereby held to be consenting to pay for the journey, even though money is not discussed until arrival. If the passenger arrives and refuses to pay we would say he has committed fraud. He has used a set of conventions under which agreements are reached without intending to honour his side of the bargain. If the passenger appeared in court and explained that he was innocent because he did not intend to pay, and the taxi driver should have known that, his excuse would not be taken seriously. In other words, in some circumstances at least, consenting is a 'performative utterance', in which someone who uses a form of words also thereby performs the act of consenting. Things are less simple if the conventions are less well-established than in this case. If the passenger asks to be taken to another country by taxi, or says 'Can you please get my father to hospital, I think he is having a heart attack?', or the driver knows that the best way to get to the town hall happens to be via a fifty mile detour, the parties to the contract need to extend the initial convention.

In the case of sexual consent a woman who appears to be a normal adult and who is not being subjected to any obvious form of coercion, who goes through a series of explicit questions about consenting to sex saying 'yes' at each stage would, I think, be held by a court to have consented and be unable to use her mental state of not consenting as a reason for accusing the man in question of rape. I also think that even viewing rape as a moral question one would not hold the man in this case guilty. The woman has consented by her acts. It is distressing to think of this hypothetical woman having sex with a mental state of not consenting. She appears to need education in the normal use of English, or in the meaning of consenting. I do not think that she presents a serious problem in the real world: I am more concerned to stress that conventions about meaning have a powerful role in social life.

The further one departs from specific verbal communication, however, the more fraught and realistic the problem about consenting without meaning to becomes. What if she assumed that going to his apartment to talk meant simply that, that he suggested they should undress to become more comfortable because he knew her clothes were too tight, if she assumed that they then went to bed because she was feeling tired, etc.? Quite a lot of the cases of date rape discussed in Chapter 3 involved men assuming that women were consenting to more than the woman assumed. This problem, too, seems to point towards specific verbal communication as the way to avoid misunderstanding.

The second problem is that of reluctant consent. How do we make sense of consent where the woman does the appropriate actions to consent but has mental reservations? Let us think about a woman who gets married when very much in love. After a few months of living together and working her husband proposes to take her for a romantic weekend. Unfortunately, when the weekend comes she happens to feel a bit ill and rather distracted by problems at work. Nonetheless, she is very committed to her husband and to her marriage and has a great deal of sex over the weekend as part of cementing the relationship, without him pressuring her and perhaps without him even knowing there is a problem. During this weekend she is having sex when she does not want to (which, it will be remembered, was the beginning of some of Mary Koss's questions about rape), but no-one, her included, would say she is being raped. It is more that she, like everyone else, has conflicting wants and makes a particular choice among them. Shotland and Hunter found that 38.4% of a sample of women students had engaged in this type of behaviour, which they term 'compliant' sex. The women involved generally judged that doing so would help maintain a relationship which they valued.[9] Let us now assume that the marriage gradually deteriorates. The woman increasingly finds herself having sex when she does not want to. At first she is simply doing much the same as she was on the romantic weekend, though less willingly. Then she finds that her husband is very bad-tempered if he does not have sex, although he would not force her. Later her husband threatens that if she does not have sex he will leave, which will cause very bad economic problems for her and her children. Still later he threatens to hit her if she does not give in to sex.

Clearly by the end of this story she is being raped, i.e. forced to have sex through serious threat of violence. At the beginning she is not. Somewhere in the middle she starts being raped, but it is difficult to say when. This story is intended to encapsulate the experiences of the women interviewed by Liz Kelly who, following the distinctions drawn by her interviewees, distinguished between pressured sex, coerced sex and rape, and took the view that each shaded off into the next one.[10] Pressured sex was sex which it was possible to refuse but where the woman felt pressurised to consent, perhaps because the man had paid for a date, or because the woman was made to feel responsible for the man's unhappiness if she refused, or because the woman felt living together or being married constituted a tacit agreement that she was available for sex, or where the man would be bad-tempered if the woman refused.[11] Coerced sex involved specific pressure and often the use of threatened or actual force, together with the ignoring of women's physical or verbal resistance. The women Kelly interviewed

---

[9] R. Lance Shotland and Barbara A. Hunter, 'Women's "Token Resistant" and Compliant Sexual Behaviours are Related to Uncertain Sexual Intentions and Rape', *Personality and Social Psychology Bulletin*, Vol. 21, No. 3, 1995, pp. 226-36.

[10] Liz Kelly, *Surviving Sexual Violence*, Polity Press, Cambridge, 1988, pp. 82, 84

[11] Ibid., pp. 110-11.

were hesitant about calling these experiences rape because they knew the man well, and because they stopped resisting after a certain point: there seemed to be the possibility that if they had resisted harder they might have avoided having sex.[12] Kelly's interviewees had a mental image of rape which was closer to classic stranger rape. The assaults they called rape involved either a very sudden assault where it was not possible to resist because of surprise, or the use of weapons and physical violence.[13] A decision to call a particular episode of coerced sex 'rape' is a decision that an intimate for whom the woman has had positive feelings is a rapist, guilty of a serious crime. If you are suffering serious crimes in daily life you ought to do something about it. Thus deciding to call an episode 'rape' may also be making a decision about a whole relationship.[14] Again one can see why women's views might shift over time.

What emerges from this is that some 'consent with reservations' would not even qualify as pressurised sex, and that there is a continuum from this through to rape. There is obviously a need to avoid either a cavalier assumption that all sex which is not clearly rape is wholeheartedly consenting sex, or the converse assumption that all sex which is not wholeheartedly consenting is rape. Much of the controversy generated by Mary Koss's conclusions is surely explained by this ambiguity: whilst at the rape end of the continuum she uncovered many instances of rape which were not recorded in police statistics, she is also involved in defining instances of sex involving pressure or probably-resistible physical coercion as rape. Questions about having sex when you did not 'want' to are particularly suspect in this context. Rape is certainly having sex when you did not 'want' to, but, as I argued in Chapter 3, so are a range of situations through from not wholeheartedly wanting to, but wanting to on balance, to heavily pressurised or mildly physically-coerced sex.

The problems surrounding the genuineness of 'consent with reservations' are compounded when linked to the issue of knowing what one is consenting to. Anyone with some experience of sex is likely to be able to think of situations where they reluctantly consented against their better judgement only to have a delightful time, and of others where they wholeheartedly consented to sex which proved to be disappointing. Moreover, situations of pressured sex tend to be part of a package in which the woman's general lifestyle is involved: consent to a particular sexual act is part of a relationship, which in turn is linked to other relationships and friendships, to work, residence and so on. It is unlikely that this entire life situation will be thought through each time the woman has sex; given that situations tend to shift gradually, it is not surprising that particular episodes are re-evaluated with hindsight. A particular episode might come early in a rising

---

[12] Ibid., pp. 112-4.

[13] Ibid., pp. 114-5.

[14] Cf. ibid., pp. 148 et. seq. Liz Kelly uses the term 'continuum of sexual violence' to encapsulate, amongst other things, this continuum between consenting sex with reservations, pressurised sex, coerced sex and rape.

cycle in which the sex turns out well and the relationship generally improves or in a declining cycle where pressurised sex moves towards coerced sex; in each case subsequent events would determine how the particular episode appeared in hindsight.

There are, then, many episodes in which women are not wholeheartedly consenting where they are neither clearly *intending to consent* (as in gritting one's teeth but consenting to something disagreeable) nor clearly *intending not to consent* (as in saying 'this is rape and I'm calling the police' whilst resisting physically). It would seem more accurate to say they are ambivalent about what is happening and do not have fully clear intentions.

Aspects of sexual consent iii.) the communication of consent

Flathman's third feature of consent is the communication of consent. In politics the communication of consent is straightforward in cases where the consent itself is clear: it was evident, for example, that black South Africans knew what they were doing when they voted in 1994, and the voting process itself was easy to understand. Difficulty arises if tacit consent is assumed to arise from some quite different act such as using the roads or not leaving the country.

The communication of sexual consent is probably the most fraught of the issues considered so far. Writing of how consent is given, Flathman comments that a statement from B 'I consent to X' is adequate but unusual; more common are informal locutions such as 'OK', 'go ahead if you wish', 'It's all right with me', 'good', 'I have no objections', or a nod of the head, handshake, approving smile, or simply acting in a manner which, in the circumstances, would be taken to be evidence of consent 'by persons who understand the form of life and know the language'.[15] Two possible examples of this last way of giving consent are bidding at an auction by, say, raising one's hand and the taxi example already discussed. Both actions imply a willingness to pay an amount established by convention. Consent can also be indicated by silence, as in a meeting where the chair invites comments on the accuracy of the minutes, hears nothing, and takes this to involve consent to their accuracy.

Do we, in sexual terms, 'understand the form of life and know the language'? In one sense evidently we must, as there are millions of episodes of sex weekly in Britain of which only a small proportion are rape even on the widest of criteria from Koss or Russell. The first time two people decide to make love is also a favourite theme of film makers. One approach, therefore, is to imitate our procedure with taxis. We start off with a typical transaction in which someone gets into a taxi and states a destination, thereby also agreeing to pay the fare. Deviations from the typical taxi transaction are not necessarily theft or cheating.

---

[15] Flathman, *Political Obligation*, p. 219.

The driver and passenger might surround a standard transaction with much more elaborate courtesies than is customary: they might curtail the customary transaction because this particular passenger always wants to go to a particular destination at a particular time and is paid for by a company account, so no words are spoken or money exchanged at all; or they might develop their own terminology over time, so that they both knew what they were doing but an outsider would be surprised by the mismatch between what they said and what happened. All these deviations, however, are built around the standard transaction and can be referred back to it.

At first sight this seems like a promising approach to the identification of rape: identify the normal way or ways of agreeing to have sex, then, if these have not been followed, assume we have a prima facie case of rape, but bear in mind that those involved may have developed a non-standard way of communicating which suits them. Oddly enough, this has been very little followed up. There is, as we have seen, a great deal of literature on date rape, on what sort of couples have sex earlier in their relationship or later, on factors involved in the use of condoms, on how men and women see particular situations and possible cues differently, on how women indicate they are willing to be approached by a suitable man (approached by, not have sex with). However, there is very little literature on how women actually communicate a willingness to have sex.[16] The existing articles describe rather small-scale studies on something which may well vary from one subculture to another, so one is reluctant to put too much weight on them.

The studies suggest that typical behaviours would be non-verbal and indirect: offering the man a drink, inviting him somewhere romantic and private, inviting him to listen to music or dance, conversing with him on non-sexual topics. In the early stages of an encounter, women engage in more non-verbal flirtation than men (grooming gestures, positive facial expressions, brief and not overtly sexual touching). All of these female behaviours are, of course, ambiguous. They might

---

[16] Timothy Perper and David Weis, 'Proceptive and Rejective Strategies of US and Canadian College Women', *Journal of Sex Research*, Vol. 23, 1987, pp. 455-80; E.S. Byers and Kim Lewis, 'Dating Couples' Disagreements Over the Desired Level of Sexual Intimacy', *Journal of Sex Research*, Vol. 24, 1988, pp. 15-29, which contains a reference to a further article I have so far failed to obtain: E.S. Byers, 'Female Communication of Consent and Nonconsent to Sexual Intercourse', *Journal of the New Brunswick Psychological Association*, Vol. 5, 1980, pp. 12-18. See also Monica M. Moore and Diana L. Butler, 'Predictive Aspects of Nonverbal Courtship Behaviour in Women', *Semiotica*, Vol. 76, Nos 3/4, 1989, pp. 205-15, which deals with female non-verbal signals indicating they might like to be approached by a man - evidence in the right direction, but not remotely indicative of consent. I thus agree very strongly with Douglas N. Husak and George C. Thomas III when they say: '...too much of the literature about the nature of rape and how to avoid it neglects the related issue of how couples ever manage to engage in consensual sex' - Douglas N. Husak and George C. Thomas III, 'Date Rape, Social Convention and Reasonable Mistakes', *Law and Philosophy*, Vol. 11, 1992, pp. 95-126, p. 101.

just be part of being friendly, or of pursuing non-sexual mutual interests. It seems generally up to the man to take things further.[17] The woman then responds warmly to each stage of escalation (he puts his arm round her, she snuggles up to him, he holds her hand, she holds his willingly, etc.). If she is unwilling at this stage, suggest Perper and Weis, she may possibly engage in blunt rejection, but is more likely to engage in 'incomplete rejection', for example accepting being held but not responding really warmly. Naomi McCormick basically supports this view, with the added points that male strategies for having sex are also typically indirect, and that both sexes' strategies for avoiding sex tend to be more direct.[18] A study of Australian adolescents broadly supports this point. However, amongst the Australians, both sexes had a *similar* set of strategies for encouraging their partner to have sex (see below).[19] The discussion here obviously ties in with the discussion of miscommunication in Chapter 3: women may well think they are giving an 'incomplete rejection' response to a man who feels he is being ambiguously encouraged.

In summary, then, consenting behaviour, as it appears in the limited research available, involves issuing ambiguous invitations and responding warmly to (mainly physical) male advances. If the woman says 'no' firmly but at a late stage, and even more if she is simply silent or ambiguous at a late stage, it is easy to see how a man might feel 'led on', or feel that protests were out of line with the woman's previous behaviour and not to be taken too seriously. However, according to Byers, both attempts to initiate sex and female acceptance are typically non-verbal.[20] To the extent this is right, those who interpret communicative sexuality to mean that there must be affirmative *verbal* consent from the woman are recommending wholesale changes to sexual customs.[21]

The studies described so far assume a 'traditional' sexual script in which the man initiates and the woman acts as a gatekeeper.[22] There is some evidence, both

---

[17] See Naomi B. McCormick and Andrew J. Jones, 'Gender Differences in Nonverbal Flirtation', *Journal of Sex Education and Therapy*, Vol. 15, No. 4, 1989, pp. 271-82.

[18] Naomi B. McCormick, 'Come-ons and Put-offs: Unmarried Students' Strategies for Having and Avoiding Sexual Intercourse', *Psychology of Women Quarterly*, Vol. 4, No. 2, 1979, pp. 194-211.

[19] Doreen Rosenthal and Rachel Peart, 'The Rules of the Game: Teenagers Communicating about Sex', *Journal of Adolescence*, Vol. 19, 1996, pp. 321-32.

[20] E.S. Byers and K. Lewis, 'Dating Couples' Disagreements over the Desired Level of Sexual Intimacy', *The Journal of Sex Research*, Vol. 24, 1988, pp. 15-29, referring to the research in Byers, 'Female Communication of Consent and Nonconsent to Sexual Intercourse'.

[21] Liz Kelly is quoted as taking this line: 'I don't believe that consent can be presumed in any circumstances other than a woman saying I want to have sex with you', *Observer*, 15 June 1997.

[22] For a straightforward account of this drawn from surveys of students in the Boston area in the 1970s, see Letitia Anne Peplau, Zick Rubin and Charles T. Hill, 'Sexual

anecdotal and from psychological surveys, that this pattern of dating, although still predominant, has been supplemented by patterns where there is mutual seduction, or where the woman takes the lead much more clearly than in the above: one British journalistic comment was 'nobody knows the rules any more'.[23] Kate Fillion in *Lip Service* argues this point very strongly as part of her general thesis that women are just as aggressive as men, but have established ways of hiding it which largely act to their detriment.[24] Within established relationships both men and women on occasion try to influence their partner to more sexual activity than she or he desires, a process which appears to be seen as a normal part of a relationship, not leading to coercion or rated by either partner as unpleasant.[25] In cases of mutual seduction, where she responds to his fondling by starting to undress him, and so forth, he is surely getting implicit consent by her actions, and specific verbal discussion seems redundant. If she is clearly and consistently taking the lead there is even less need for him to establish her consent, although she may arguably need to establish his. The Australian teenagers in Rosenthal and Peart's study seem to fit this model to some extent at least. Both sexes agreed that acceptable strategies for having sex included: various forms of direct physical stimulation and responsiveness; suggesting a quiet place; producing a condom; mentioning contraception; undressing your partner. These strategies are chiefly physical rather than verbal.[26] Their strategies for avoiding sex, however were more specifically verbal, the favourite with both sexes being 'Tell clearly when gone far enough'.[27] For the rest of this chapter I have generally assumed a more traditional model because it seems more likely to feature in accusations of rape.

Early in Chapter 3, I quoted from Parrott and Bechofer's account of a hypothetical date rape in which John rapes Mary. Mary engages in the following ambiguous-but-encouraging behaviour: i.) she agrees to go on four dates with

---

Intimacy in Dating Relationships', *Journal of Social Issues*, Vol. 33, No. 2, 1977, pp. 86-109.

[23] Tessa Souter, 'Date Expectations', *Guardian*, 3 August 1995. For a more academic analysis see L. F. O'Sullivan and E. S. Byers, 'College Students' incorporation of Initiator and Restrictor Roles in Sexual Dating Interactions', *The Journal of Sex Research*, Vol. 29, No. 3, 1992, pp. 435-46. In a small survey of students, Mongeau found some 70% had been on a female-initiated first date - see P.A. Mongeau et. al., 'Who's wooing whom? An investigation of female-initiated dating', in P.J. Kalbfleisch, ed., *Interpersonal communication: Evolving interpersonal relationships*, Erlbaum, Hillsdale, N. J., 1993, pp. 51-68.

[24] Kate Fillion, *Lip Service*, Pandora/Harper Collins, London, 1997, Chs. 4,5

[25] O'Sullivan and Byers, 'Eroding Stereotypes: College Women's Attempts to Influence Reluctant Male Sexual Partners'; E.S. Byers and K. Lewis, 'Dating Couples' Disagreements over the Desired Level of Sexual Intimacy', *The Journal of Sex Research*, Vol. 24, 1988, pp. 15-29.

[26] Rosenthal and Peart, 'The Rules of the Game', p. 327.

[27] Rosenthal and Peart, 'The Rules of the Game', p. 325.

John; ii.) she wears a sexy, provocative dress; iii.) she accepts an expensive lobster dinner; iv.) she agrees to go on to a party with him; v.) she agrees to go to his apartment; vi.) she shares a bottle of wine with him; vii.) she kisses him; viii.) she tells him she is having a wonderful time; ix.) she agrees to go into his bedroom; x.) she dances erotically and kisses passionately with him; xi.) she moans when he caresses her breasts. Mary has engaged in what might be called extensive 'pre-consenting' behaviour. Nothing she does amounts to consent to sex; on the other hand, at each of the eleven points described she could easily do something else which would be a blunt rejection.

The political literature on consent is ambiguous about pre-consenting behaviour. Flathman sees pre-consenting political behaviour, for example attending meetings of a potential pressure group, or saying a certain set of arrangements would be very desirable, as *not* tacit consent. For example, someone might attend anti-pornography meetings because she is a pornographer and wants to keep an eye on a group which might restrict her freedom. Simmons, on the other hand, looking at the same sort of issues, is willing to see someone who goes along with a process of this sort as engaging in tacit consent.[28] At minimum, I think, someone who engages in extensive pre-consenting behaviour would do well to either explain as things progress that it is not what it seems ('I'm inviting you to my apartment for a discussion of Heraclitus and nothing else'), or to make herself very clear if she changes her mind after a great deal of behaviour which seems to point the other way.[29]

The concept of 'pre-consenting behaviour' is probably too wide. In the John and Mary example, Mary is certainly not indicating a willingness to have sex with John by going out with him the first time. On the other hand, behaviours ix.) to xi.) appear to be quite close to consenting. If one adds xii.) Mary helps John strip naked; xiii.) Mary strips naked; xiv.) Mary lies on John's bed; xv.) Mary inserts her diaphragm and says 'Come here', she has still not, strictly speaking, consented to sex in that she has not actually said 'Come here and make love to me', but she has got so close to that that most observers would think she has clearly consented. Of course, consenting behaviour could be matched by a set of explanations which entirely negates their apparent meaning, for example John and Mary are actually making a film, so that the next scene is in fact the producer

---

[28] Flathman, *Political Obligation*, pp. 225-7, A. John Simmons, *Moral Principles and Political Obligation*, Princeton University Press, Princeton N.J, 1979, p. 89.

[29] Paul Reynolds and Jill Radford, both of whom were kind enough to read this chapter in draft form, both pointed out that the discussion of this paragraph is over-simplified. It is quite possible to imagine circumstances where a man and a woman both intend simply to have a discussion of Heraclitus when setting off for his apartment, but then things develop differently. Or one of them might be thinking this way while the other was not. Kowalski's research, discussed above, suggests that ambivalent *possibly* pre-consenting behaviour tends to be interpreted more sexually by men than women, whereas both have the same interpretation of romantic or clearly sexual behaviour.

saying 'Cut' and the crew and cast having mugs of cocoa. The idea that acting brackets off behaviour from its apparent meaning is clearly established in our society. Other attempts to bracket off behaviour are more ambiguous. In Ol Parker's television play *In Your Dreams* on the theme of date rape, one important moment is when Claire is persuaded by Jamie to invite him up to her room for coffee. She makes it clear that it is only an invitation for coffee; partly because of her earlier behaviour he assumes it is for more. A group of students shown the play disagreed (not on male/female lines) about the extent to which 'come up for coffee' at the end of an evening is a coded invitation for sex.[30]

This last problem introduces a further complication about pre-consenting behaviour: as well as being ambiguous, some consenting words and actions are metaphorical or symbolic. Thus 'shall we go to bed?' in the right context could be deemed a sexual invitation, but it is not literally one. This seems to have been a source of problems in two recent English date rape cases. In both the woman in question invited the man to go to bed with her, apparently simply meaning to sleep, and both made accusations of rape when the man started having sex when they had actually fallen asleep. In one case the woman also showed the man her collection of sadomasochistic materials and consented to cunnilingus, both activities which might be deemed pre-consenting activities close to consent. Neither resulted in a conviction in court.[31]

In her discussion of date rape Katie Roiphe talks of the problem as partly one of 'class prejudice and race prejudice' when, say, 'the southern heiress goes out with the plumber's son from the Bronx': today's American universities, she says, contain many students who do not understand the conventions of upper class American society.[32] The problem - apart from straightforward prejudice - may be one of different metaphors and conventions about consent. It certainly makes sense that a man coming from, say, a strict Moslem background would find the standard summertime behaviour of young European women, sunbathing nude or topless by day and engaging in very clinging dancing in the evening an indication that sexual consent was but a very small step away. We do not, as I indicated, have the research available to back this up, but something similar but less dramatic might well apply between the various US subcultures.

An example of this sort appeared in the British press following an article on the late Arthur Koestler. It was argued in one letter that Koestler had a middle-European approach to women in that he engaged in vigorous physical courtship but expected to be slapped and told to stop, which he would do. If they failed to tell him to stop he might be guilty of date rape. A letter then appeared from Phyllidia Paterson, assistant professor of psychiatry, which went in part:

---

[30] The play was shown on BBC2 on 14 December 1997; for the discussion, see *The Guardian*, 11 December 1997.

[31] For a brief account and discussion, see Maureen Freely, *Guardian,* 8 December 1994.

[32] Katie Roiphe, *The Morning After*, Hamish Hamilton, London, 1993, pp. 78-9.

Mr Scammell needs to join the twentieth century. Date rape *is* rape. The fact that it is perpetrated by someone the victim trusted enough to see socially makes it an even greater betrayal, and potentially more damaging. How long will it be until we realise that when a woman says 'No' she means 'No'?[33]

Roiphe and I would argue that there is at least a possibility that Koestler accepted this point, but that he came from a culture where communication between the sexes was different from that in the Britain of his day.

Keith Burgess-Jackson stresses this diversity of conventions, and argues that because of possible misunderstandings about something so serious it is degrading to a woman to allow a man to rely on a convention in assuming her sexual consent: he should instead be required to *ask* her whether or not she consents.[34] However, Burgess-Jackson's man is still having to rely on *linguistic* conventions. Might not ambiguous language but decisive physical actions be clearer than straightforward language combined with clear bodily resistance: compare 'let's get more comfortable', whilst removing his and her clothes with 'yes, I consent to sex' whilst remaining dressed and rigid.

My final point on communication before turning to the arguments about communicative sexuality is that communication within an established relationship will be different from that between a couple making love for the first time. An article about the problems of coping with an excitable dog whilst making love contains the following account of the woman inviting sex:

> My girlfriend, wrapped in a towel, walks into the sitting room. 'I'm going to bed,' she says.
> 'What - now?'
> 'Yes.'
> 'Why?'
> 'Well...you know.'[35]

The author took a minute to realise that this was a sexual invitation. It is very context-specific. The last phrase could easily, in a different context, be a way of saying she has a migraine, or she has to get up very early and needs to sleep, or needs her rest because she is pregnant, etc. This sort of invitation based only on an oblique phrase or a look or some particular actions must be very common

---

[33] *Observer,* 23 April and 7 May 1995.

[34] Keith Burgess-Jackson, *Rape: A Philosophical Investigation,* Dartmouth, Brookfield, Vermont, 1996, p. 151-3.

[35] William Leith, 'She's panting. She's excited. But do we really need a dog in bed?', *Observer Review,* 30 March, 1997.

within an established relationship, but would be a very dubious basis for sexual advances between couples who did not have such a relationship.[36]

Communicative sexuality

A theme which is repeated several times in the above analysis of consent is that better communication would be helpful. It is plainly not a way of avoiding rape altogether. In some of the more extreme cases of rape part of the motivation for the rapist is the knowledge that the woman is not consenting. The idea that better communication, and different ways of looking at communication, would be helpful features strongly in recent feminist writing and initiatives against date rape. There are two particularly influential sources, Lois Pineau's essay: 'Date Rape: A Feminist Analysis'[37] and the Antioch College Sexual Offence Policy. To some extent, at least, this idea has been written into the law in Canada, California and the Australian state of Victoria.

Let us start with the argument of Pineau's essay. Pineau's mental image of date rape can be seen from the scenario reproduced above in Chapter 3: it is of a woman who, on a first date, goes along with the aggressive sexual advances of the man because she is drunk and because she fears she has led him on somewhat and he might get violent if she refuses, although she has no very strong evidence of this. Pineau then says it is pretty clear how a court would respond to this description, assuming the case ever reached that stage. The man's aggressive tactics are only normal seduction; and the woman's failure to resist in any forceful way shows that in the end she accepted his advances.[38] However, Pineau argues, for the woman this is a perverse way of looking at things. Her obvious motive for having uncoerced sex is sexual enjoyment, which is most obviously based on sexual attraction. '[S]ubmission to an overbearing and insensitive lout'[39] is not the obvious way to achieve sexual enjoyment: did she get some other sort of payoff, such as money or tickets for the opera? As she did not, the burden of proof shifts to the man to prove that she had good reasons for going along with his wishes.

What about the idea that she led him on to some extent? Pineau considers the idea that the woman effectively made a sexual contract at some stage. She argues

---

[36] In June M. Reinisch and Ruth Beardsley, *The Kinsey Institute New Report on Sex*, Penguin, Harmondsworth, 1991, p. 102, there is an account of a married couple who have a pair of figurines on a shelf. If either of them feel like sex they lay one of the figurines down; if the other one feels like sex, too, he or she lays the other figurine down. This is a relatively elaborate signalling system between an established couple, but would be meaningless outside such a relationship.

[37] Most conveniently available in Leslie Francis, ed., *Date Rape: Feminism, Philosophy and the Law*, Pennsylvania State University Press, Pennsylvania, 1996, pp. 1-26.

[38] Ibid., pp. 8-9.

[39] Ibid., p. 8.

that first, contracts normally take a standard form so that people know what is involved (e.g. marriage), or that they are carefully specified in writing, so this implied contract is different from all others. More important, the proper recourse when contracts are not fulfilled is to a court, which will normally provide monetary compensation to the wronged party. There is no provision in modern law for the private enforcement of contracts.[40] A more plausible approach to the question of leading on is to say that at some point the man's sexual impulses become unstoppable. Pineau agrees that this is true for a few seconds around the time of orgasm, but argues that otherwise sexual satisfaction is best achieved for both partners by comfort, communication, a lack of pressure, and caring for one's partner.[41]

Given this approach in which male sexual desire is seen as controllable, Pineau argues that where a woman complains in court that she was subjected to high-pressure seduction tactics the burden of proof should lie with the defendant to show that he persuaded the woman to have sex even though there are no 'visible reasons' why she should. Once this is accepted there is no reason why women should not be sexually provocative, since they do not 'deserve' any sex they do not want.[42] The major sexual obligation on this view becomes one of knowing what one's partner feels and wants, the practice of communicative sexuality.[43] The appropriate model for sexual relationships is the mutuality characteristic of friendship: friends doubtless do have rights and obligations against each other, but if they are worrying about these it is a sign that the friendship is breaking down.[44]

In a court, then, defendants would need to explain why they persisted in the face of voiced reluctance. Rather than questioning the rape victim about how much she resisted, the focus would be on how much the defendant had tried to communicate: did he ask her what she liked? Was contraception discussed? Did he actually ask if she wanted penetration and in what position? His failure to answer such questions satisfactorily would be part of the proof of his guilt.[45] Pineau seems to accept the idea that consent can be non-verbal, provided it is clear, and commentators on the communicative sexuality law in Victoria also judge it to allow for unequivocal non-verbal behaviour. This is very important, as I shall argue below that most sexual consent is probably non-verbal.

Although the Antioch College Sexual Offence Policy was adopted independently of Lois Pineau's essay, its underlying intentions are clearly very

---

[40] Ibid., pp. 14-15.

[41] Ibid., p. 15.

[42] Ibid., p. 17.

[43] Ibid., p. 18.

[44] Ibid., pp. 20-23.

[45] Ibid., p. 24. For broadly similar arguments to Pineau's, but without the use of the term 'communicative sexuality', see Joan McGregor, 'Force, Consent and the Reasonable Woman', in Jules L. Coleman and Allen Buchanan, eds, *In Harm's Way*, Cambridge University Press, Cambridge, 1994, pp. 231-54.

much the same. Antioch College is a very small college with a total of 300 students; the student body on campus at any one time is actually smaller, as students spend part of their time on community placements. The college has a very strong radical tradition. The Sexual Offence Policy was developed due to the dissatisfaction of some students with the way some sexual assaults were handled by the faculty. In general, Antioch probably has fewer problems with sexual assaults than most US colleges. Sexual assaults are often associated with machismo sporting teams, but Antioch College lacks a football team, and its Frisbee team does not have a bad reputation. It seems to have been more that a radically-minded student body wanted to solve a problem felt to be general amongst American students. The policy was thus student-initiated, and the role of the faculty and administration was to facilitate what the students produced by, for example, putting some of the policy into suitable legal language. The gay and lesbian groups at the college were involved in producing the policy, which is written in gender-free terms. The crucial central feature of the policy is the part on consent, which reads:

Antioch College Sexual Offence Policy (part)[46]

1. For the purposes of this policy, 'consent' shall be defined as follows: the act of willingly and verbally agreeing to engage in specific sexual contact or conduct

2. If sexual contact and/or conduct is not mutually and simultaneously initiated, then the person who initiates sexual contact/conduct is responsible for getting the verbal consent of the other individual(s) involved.

3. Obtaining consent is an ongoing process in any sexual interaction. Verbal consent should be obtained with each new level of physical and/or sexual contact/conduct in any given interaction, regardless of who initiates it. Asking 'Do you want to have sex with me?' is not enough. The request for consent must be specific to each act.

4. The person with whom sexual contact/conduct is initiated is responsible to express verbally and/or physically his/her willingness or lack of willingness when reasonably possible.

5. If someone has initially consented but then stops consenting during a sexual interaction, she/he should communicate withdrawal verbally and/or through physical resistance. The other individual(s) must stop immediately.

6. To knowingly take advantage of someone who is under the influence of alcohol, drugs and/or prescribed medication is not acceptable behaviour in the Antioch community.

---

[46] The full text of the policy and a further account of its development and context can be found in Francis, ed., *Date Rape*, pp. 135-75.

7. If someone verbally agrees to engage in specific contact or conduct, but it is not of her/his own free will due to any of the circumstances stated in a. through d. below, then the person initiating shall be considered in violation of this policy if:

    a. the person submitting is under the influence of alcohol or other substances supplied to her/him by the person initiating;

    b. the person submitting is incapacitated by alcohol, drugs and/or prescribed medication;

    c. the person submitting is asleep or unconscious;

    d. the person initiating has forced, threatened, coerced or intimidated the other individual(s) into engaging in sexual contact and/or sexual conduct.

The policy then spells out a series of offences which are implicit in the above: rape, i.e. 'Non-consensual penetration, however slight, of the vagina or anus; non-consensual fellatio or cunnilingus'; sexual assault, i.e. basically attempts at rape; and sexual imposition, i.e. non-sexual touching of 'thighs, genitals, buttocks, the pubic region, or the breast/chest area', followed by other offences less interesting from our point of view such as sexual harassment or failure to disclose HIV positive status. The rest of the policy describes how it will be enforced.

The policy seems largely to have functioned in a symbolic way, as a statement of what is expected on the Antioch campus, rather than as the basis of numerous prosecutions. The main flaw in the policy was felt by those at Antioch to be that it does not deal satisfactorily with mutual initiation. The Antioch policy generated much interest and, indeed, ridicule in the media: the public image of the college had its students setting out on dates with a pile of consent forms, a breathalyser and a lawyer, whereas the main force of the policy is simply a very strong insistence on continuing verbal consent throughout a sexual transaction.

The concept of communicative sexuality is also advanced by Beverley Balos and Mary Fellows. They argue that courts should approach sexual relations using the doctrine of 'confidential relationship'. Such relationships impose a heightened duty of care, normally over financial transactions. The man would have a duty to obtain consent through positive words or actions. This would be quite stringent, for example '[t]he defence of a reasonable, good faith belief that the words or conduct [of the woman] were overt and constituted consent would also not be available to the defendant...[he] has the obligation to listen to the victim'.[47] Where there has been a history of domestic abuse, not even positive words or conduct by the victim would count as a defence.[48] They recognise that this effectively invalidates the woman's sexual choices in favour of having sex in the relationship

---

[47] Beverley Balos and Mary L. Fellows, 'Guilty of the Crime of Trust: Non-stranger Rape', *Minnesota Law Review*, Vol. 75, 1991, pp. 599-618; quotation from pp. 607-8.

[48] Ibid., p. 609.

ever again, but regard the protection offered to battered women by their proposal as so important that it takes precedence.[49] Apart from the general discussion which follows below, their approach has some extra problems. 'Confidential relationships' are typically between powerful professionals such as lawyers and clients who might be abused, or between normal adults and people of restricted powers. There is some risk, then, of their approach defining women as inherently feeble. Further, 'positive words and conduct' always need to be interpreted: a reasonable man makes sensible inferences from the woman's conduct. It is one thing to insist that the man's belief in consent must be reasonable; but there can never, surely, be a cast-iron guarantee that one person fully understands another's words and actions. Finally, whilst I hold no brief at all for wife batterers, rendering them guilty of rape for evermore on the basis of the word of their wife - even if she consented to sex in words and actions at the time - seems an unduly drastic step. It would seem better for a court to enquire whether she had good reason to be so fearful at the time of the alleged rape that she *had* to consent in words and deeds, i.e. the quality of their relationship in the immediate run up to having sex is the main issue. Leaving aside these specific features, their approach is broadly similar to those discussed already.

Communicative sexuality criticised

There are three main philosophical lines of criticism of communicative sexuality used as a criterion of non-coercive sex. First, the question of what happens to women who are passive and romantic sexually, who like Mills and Boon (in America, Harlequin Romances) novels, who admire the scene in *Gone With the Wind* where Rhett Butler sweeps Scarlet O'Hara upstairs protesting but where she is happy the next morning. Second, and most immediately problematic, there is the issue of whether the ideal is too remote from too much of real life. Third, there is what I shall call the Dworkin/MacKinnon objection which basically assimilates consensual sex under patriarchy to rape, thus rendering communicative sexuality suspect.

The Mills and Boon objection asks whether there is anything inherently wrong with women liking passive sexuality where they are swept off their feet by a stern, handsome but basically sensitive man? The point is not that the critics particularly admire this type of approach, but they do contend that it is ironic if a 'feminist' approach to date rape actually deprives numerous women of the sort of experience they value.[50] To the extent that people have this approach to sex there will also be mistakes. In particular, a man who casts himself as the hero of one of these

---

[49] Ibid., pp. 610-11.

[50] See, for example, David M. Adams, 'Date Rape and Erotic Discourse', in Francis, ed., *Date Rape*, pp. 27-39, p.34; Catharine Pierce Wells, 'Date Rape and the Law: Another Feminist View', Francis, ed., *Date Rape*, pp. 41-50, p.45.

episodes is liable to face accusations of rape when all he was trying to do was to give his beloved an enjoyable experience.

From the standpoint of the Antioch code this criticism is dismissed out of hand. I can see no role whatsoever for romantic fantasies within it: a Rhett Butler figure who cautiously insists on a verbal confirmation that his every move is acceptable simply loses all his dashing self-assurance. The Antioch riposte to the first criticism would be that the loss to romantic souls is the gain in security of most women.

Pineau's response to this criticism is quite lengthy, but ultimately similar. To start with she questions whether romantic fantasies actually correspond to what women want: there is reason for thinking that they want to be swept off their feet only against the background of an agreement to marry, or something close to that. One can readily accept Pineau's view that people may fantasise about all sorts of things they do not want to happen. Nonetheless, and she seems to acknowledge this, the persistence and popularity of romantic fantasies would seem at least to offer some pointers to some women's sexual desires in our culture.

Even if an ideology such as that of romantic fantasy is entrenched, Pineau continues, that is not to say it is either desirable or impossible to alter in the long term. If women want this sort of non-consensual sex it might be possible to arrange for it within a contractual arrangement which permits a 'get-out', similar to the arrangements masochists make (their torturer will not stop if they scream, beg or reason, but will stop at once if they say, for example, 'green'). Pineau also finds this sort of arrangement satisfactory for women who enjoy full-blown heterosexual masochism, incidentally.[51] Short of such agreements the loss of spontaneity experienced by aspiring participants in romantic novels just has to be seen as a cost of a reform which will protect women in general from rape - it is a less serious cost than the experience of rape without legal redress which is what current legislation provides. Finally, there is nothing wrong with changing the law provided it is done in the normal way, i.e. starting with a process of public discussion, moving on to a legislative process which the public can watch and influence, and ending with officially-announced legal changes published in the media. She sees much of the objections as a charge of 'utopianism', and responds by arguing that the critics are effectively very entrenched conservatives.[52]

Women who wish to act out romantic fantasies are an acknowledged problem from Pineau's perspective, but perhaps we have to accept that their loss is other women's gain. As it is not clear how widespread is the desire to act out such fantasies we cannot be sure how serious this problem is. The idea of modelling sexual relations for women who are shy about articulating their sexual needs on sado-masochistic contracts seems unlikely to be appealing: it is surely pretty damaging to a romantic fantasy to set it down in a contract. Further, informal

---

[51] Lois Pineau, 'A Response to my Critics', in Francis, ed., *Date Rape*, pp. 63-107, pp. 78-9, 100-101.

[52] Ibid., pp. 68-84.

information from Andrea Beckmann, who studies sado-masochism, suggests that the participants are always trying to test out the limits of such contracts, and there could easily be similar problems with 'romantic contracts'.

In my view the most serious of the three criticisms of communicative sexuality as a criterion for judging whether rape has occurred is the second, the question of whether it departs too far from normal life. If this criticism is seen as ultimately rendering the ideal non-viable then the prospects for women with romantic fantasies would improve as well.

The second criticism, based on normal life, is that most consenting sexual encounters do not conform to the ideal of communicative sexuality. Pineau herself acknowledges this when she mentions that the Antioch code is not appropriate for 'professed lovers', i.e. a couple in an established relationship where nothing has happened to call the relationship into question. In these circumstances to meet and kiss immediately is natural rather than a violation of someone's right to consent.[53] As most consenting sexual encounters occur within established relationships, this means that the ideal of communicative sexuality applies to most sexual life in only an attenuated form. Pineau says that she does not think this is a problem provided that 'no' still means 'no'. However, this takes us more or less back to where we started from: strictly rape is simply sex without consent, but in an existing relationship it will be particularly necessary to manifest lack of consent. This is because of the implicit and partial continuing consent which Pineau acknowledges.

Consider again the degenerating marriage, modelled on Liz Kelly's interviews, which was sketched out above. The wife moves from consenting willingly when she does not want to, through to consenting but rather unwillingly because she knows her husband will be in a bad temper if she does not, through to consenting against a background of economic threat, through finally to consenting against a threat of violence. At least until things get to the violent stage her 'no' will be respected; perhaps her husband is also quite considerate, provided he is getting sex, about the matters Pineau says communicative lovers consider - contraception, sexual position, etc. The ideal of communicative sexuality seems to offer protection to this wife only to the extent that her husband has taken it on board as a general approach to life: to treat his wife as a friend to be considered, not simply as a means to his ends.

What about the situation Pineau mainly has in mind, couples becoming intimate for the first time? There is a research problem here, as was mentioned above: although most new couples, most of the time, appear to manage to initiate sex without any suggestion of rape, it appears that they mainly do so by some mixture of male initiative and female acceptance, often of an ambiguous sort, and the use of metaphorical language and acts. In other words, most of these apparently satisfactory sexual initiatives would fall foul of Pineau's ideal of

---

[53] Ibid., pp. 66-67.

communicative sexuality, even if they are not an acting out of romantic fantasies. In turn this raises a set of male nightmares, currently groundless but potentially serious. Supposing, the worry goes, that John from our extended John and Mary example in which Mary finally inserts her diaphragm and says 'Come here', got accused of rape. He did not get an explicit verbal consent to each stage of escalation, but on the current ambiguous and metaphorical pattern there was every indication of consent.[54] Supposing the trial was held according to the criteria of communicative sexuality. Plainly he wouldn't have a leg to stand on, yet according to most fair-minded people the encounter would be held to be consensual.

A further step in this nightmare is that the trial might become a version of a show trial, a trial where the main issue is not the guilt or innocence of the accused but the education of the public. John would be imprisoned not for any real crime he has committed but to show all men that they must follow the rules of communicative sexuality. Pineau's answer to this male nightmare is clear. The law would have been changed, and John should have taken notice of it and asked clear questions at each stage. However, there is quite a danger that a jury would not convict John - after all, he was only doing what most of them would have done, without any sense that they were doing something wrong (or having something wrong done to them). If John was convicted there might well be a sense that this is a law which has been disobeyed by most of the population, and that convictions under it were random rather than justified.[55] In other words, there is a very big stride from current practice to the use of communicative sexuality as a criterion for sexual consent. This is the line taken by some of Pineau's critics: the standard used for determining consent in courts of law should be whether a reasonable person in the defendant's position would have grounds for believing that consent had been given, and this involves paying attention to the current social customs.[56] As will be imagined, I am particularly anxious about Pineau's remarks about female provocativeness. If she simply means that women should be able to make themselves look attractive and go where they please without the accusation that they were 'asking for it', I agree with her. The argument that just

---

[54] In O'Sullivan and Byers, 'College Students' incorporation of Initiator and Restrictor Roles', of sexual activities initiated by the man, direct verbal initiation took place in a quarter of cases, physical contact, suggestive movements and ambiguous verbal cues being much more common; a broadly similar pattern applies to female initiation except that a third of the women used direct verbal initiation - see p. 441.

[55] Cf. C.L. Turk and C.L Muehlenhard, 'Force versus consent in definitions of rape', paper quoted in Charlene L. Muehlenhard et. al., 'Definitions of Rape': only 28% of a sample of college students supported a definition of rape as sex without explicit verbal consent for a student code. The percentage might have gone down if they had been asked about changes to the law. (See p. 32.)

[56] See, for example, Wells, 'Date Rape and the Law', p. 44; Husak and Thomas, 'Date Rape, Social Convention and Reasonable Mistakes'.

because a woman makes herself look sexually attractive does not mean she wants sex with any old man without more ado is a powerful one. However, as we saw in the extended story about John and Mary, specific and extended female provocativeness directed at one particular man shades off into what most people would recognise as consent to sex. As I argued above about pre-consenting behaviour, specific provocativeness varies from somewhat encouraging behaviour which is not remotely consent to sex through to an invitation to sex in all but name.

Pineau's original notion is not, I think, quite as strict and specific as the Antioch code, but it is sensible to consider what sexuality looks like if the code is implemented. Like everyone else involved, Alan Guskin, the president of Antioch College at the time the policy was developed, was surprised at the intense worldwide media interest in the policy. He puts this down partly to a public interest in sex, but more specifically to the requirement that students should talk about it.[57] Whilst I am sure he is right about these two factors, the degree of ridicule which the policy aroused leads me to think that there is a further factor: the code was widely felt to impose artificial requirements on an intimate area of life in a mechanical fashion. I think this is why, despite the fact that I defend the code as an attempt at a serious solution to a serious problem, my students always seem to laugh when I first mention the code (which they have usually at least vaguely heard of) to them. In the course of his article explaining and defending the policy Guskin quotes a letter written to *The New Yorker* in its support. The author, Julia Reidhead, describes the code as an 'erotic windfall': 'What man or woman on Antioch's campus, or elsewhere, wouldn't welcome the direct question "May I kiss the hollow of your neck?" The possibilities are wonderful...'[58]

In its way this letter sums up the general reservations about the code: it is requiring everyone to rewrite their erotic conduct, most of which seemed to be working adequately before. For this reason I am happier about the code as an ideal for a university than I am as a sole legal criterion of consenting sexuality. The worst that happens to someone who falls foul of the Antioch code is expulsion (unless, presumably, the student in question would also be liable for prosecution under the laws of the state of Ohio - this is not gone into in the Code). Even as a university code it works best as a public statement of expectations which is generally respected rather than as a basis for frequent prosecutions. Perhaps if other universities adopt versions of the Antioch code in due course they can test the general effect of the policy in stopping sexual assault and in modifying people's sexual behaviour. I also have some sympathy, as I indicated in the discussion of Sue Lees's reform proposals in Chapter 2, with the idea that prosecuting lawyers in rape trials should ask questions about the extent to which the defendant followed the principles of communicative sexuality. Her idea, I

---

[57] Alan E. Guskin, 'The Antioch Response: Sex, You Don't Just Talk About It', in Francis, ed., *Date Rape,* pp. 154-165, p. 157.

[58] Ibid., p. 158.

assume, is not that defendants are automatically guilty if they have strayed one iota from the principles of communicative sexuality, but that a total failure to consider the pleasure, safety, comfort or interests of the victim acts as a strong support of the claim that she was raped.

The third objection to the ideal of communicative sexuality is the Dworkin/MacKinnon view that heterosexual sex under patriarchy amounts to rape, so that the words spoken in the course of communicative sexuality cannot be taken seriously. I want to consider this extensively in Chapter 5. Here I want simply to mention briefly a narrower and more plausible version of this criticism, which leads on in turn to consideration of the final point about consent: it is supposed to occur against a background of freedom from coercion. The final point of the Antioch Code states that if 'someone verbally agrees to engage in specific contact or conduct, but not of her/his own free will' because the person initiating the contact has 'forced, threatened, coerced or intimidated the other individual(s) into engaging in sexual contact and/or sexual conduct', then the policy is being violated. This point is pretty unremarkable, because it coincides with standard laws on rape. Consider briefly the following.

In the course of the Russian Revolution the Bolshevik's Cheka, or secret police, became worried about the loyalty of former Tsarist officers in July 1918. It hunted down many of them and executed them without trial. By the autumn of that year they were more likely to be encouraged to join the Red Army under the supervision of political commisars. While the hunt was on, however, 'Chekists invited wives of arrested officers to join in their drinking bouts'.[59] It is not hard to imagine that the invitation to a particular wife might come from a Chekist who had had no part in arresting the husband. Perhaps to preserve a jolly atmosphere the threat hanging over the husband was never mentioned, and perhaps the sexual discussion at the party fully conformed to the canons of communicative sexuality. Despite all this there is obviously no way that sexual consent obtained in such circumstances was freely given. We are looking at a narrower and more immediately deadly version of the Dworkin/MacKinnon account of patriarchy. Sadly, of course, the above account could doubtless be replicated from the histories of many dictatorships. Thus it is certainly possible, at minimum, that collective forms of threat can have the same effect as an individual threat in securing sex without consent, whatever the words spoken.

On a more individual basis, some of the incarcerated stranger rapists interviewed by Scully seem to have had a Hobbesian theory of consent, arguing that women freely consented to do what they wanted, even though the alternative was death or serious injury. Provided the women at some stage engaged in 'consenting' behaviour they were deemed by their assailant to have 'come round' and consented after all.[60] Freedom on Hobbes's account is very narrow, involving

---

[59] Edvard Radzinsky, *Stalin,* Hodder and Stoughton, London, 1996, p. 149.

[60] See Diana Scully, *Understanding Sexual Violence,* Unwin Hyman, Boston, 1990, p. 97.

'freedom from chains and prison', as opposed to freedom from serious threats. It is generally held to be a clear account of freedom, but hopelessly flawed because the choice of, say, being raped or being shot, whilst more of a choice than just being held down and raped, is not an uncoerced choice on any reasonable person's criteria.[61]

To apply this narrow version of the Dworkin/MacKinnon thesis there needs to be some specified threat or threatening situation which renders any apparently consenting words or behaviour null and void. In my view the sheer existence of patriarchy is not such a situation, although there are more specific circumstances within it which nullify consent. This will be examined in Chapter 5. I now move on to consider the fourth and final criterion of consent, the background consideration that it should be freely given.

Aspects of sexual consent iv.) a background of free choice

There are several ways of depriving someone of a free choice. One way, mentioned above, is simply to physically overpower the person: in that case there is nothing to discuss, and we are plainly dealing with rape. Beyond that, categorisation gets more difficult. The (reasonable) assumption in the law is that the worst threats are physical: there is no question that a threat of death or serious injury negates free choice so seriously that, again, we are dealing with rape. What, however, about a mild physical threat, such as being slapped or pushed? The choice is now between a seriously traumatic experience and an unpleasant one - it is obviously immoral to force such a choice on someone, but a woman keen to avoid rape could simply opt to be slapped or pushed, in which case she would have suffered a relatively minor assault. This point becomes more stark if we consider the threat of 20 seconds of tickling - again, an immoral choice, but surely the physical coercion is now frivolous compared with the 'coerced' sex.

Another sort of threat mentioned previously is an economic threat. Again, the possibilities range from threatening to arrange that the woman and her family will starve to death, which seems to rank with the most serious of the physical threats, to the threat to dismiss a woman from her career job, which is certainly serious but would result in poverty rather than death, through to the threat not to repay a small sum of money, which would be immoral but would not rank with the other threats.

Finally, there are emotional threats. Threatening to end a marriage which has lasted decades, even if there were no economic consequences, is a potentially devastating threat, which could easily be seen as worse than physical violence or economic threats.[62] At the other extreme, virtually any refusal of an offer of sex is

---

[61] Thomas Hobbes, *Leviathan*, Fontana, Collins, Glasgow, 1962, Ch. 21.

[62] Onora O'Neill points out that intimate relationships provide people with insights into each others' aims in life which make coercion possible by undercutting these in a way

likely to make the person who offers it less happy, but potential slight unhappiness hardly ranks as serious coercion.[63]

---

which might not be understood by society at large: a threat to a particular relationship or career pattern or of withdrawal of affection might in a particular context be more serious than one of the more obvious threats mentioned above. See Onora O'Neill, 'Between Consenting Adults', *Philosophy and Public Affairs,* Vol. 14, No. 3, 1985, pp. 252-77; reference to p. 270.

[63] The problem of equating threats is briefly discussed by David Finkelhor and Kirsti Yllo, *License to Rape: Sexual Abuse of Wives,* Holt, Rinehart and Winston, New York, 1985, pp. 84-90. They acknowledge that their decision on a research definition is relatively arbitrary (p. 89).

5 Sex on a sloping playing field

Up to now in this book I have been avoiding discussion of the effect of patriarchy on sexual power relations or sexual negotiation. The implicit model has been one in which men and women negotiate their sexual relations as equals, on a level playing field. Obviously one or other of them may threaten violence, or use emotional blackmail, or use economic coercion, but there has been no systematic analysis of whether men are typically able to use these threats more easily and effectively than women, because of a background of social inequality.[1] The idea that sexual consent under patriarchy is suspect because of unequal power relations was mentioned by reference in the last chapter to the Dworkin/MacKinnon thesis, but not discussed. This chapter will be devoted to this issue. I shall start by briefly juxtaposing the Dworkin/MacKinnon radical feminist thesis that sexual violence and pornography are central to patriarchal power to Walby's more rounded account of patriarchy in which it is seen as a combination of male power in a number of main areas which certainly influence each other but which lack one central cause. Of course, a full discussion of theories of patriarchy requires something much more extensive than part of a chapter. My sketch should be seen more as a statement of a (hopefully defensible) position than as an attempt to persuade those who disagree with it.

What I want to consider much more carefully in the rest of the chapter is a more narrow issue: how much do various aspects of patriarchy allow men to sexually coerce women? And which of these forms of sexual coercion should be considered as rape? The point will be argued much more fully later, but as a sample of what is to follow, consider a male university lecturer who has been promoted once, and

---

[1] For a good general critique of the idea that all that is required for legitimate sexual relations is that they should be made without force, fraud or explicit duress, i.e. the bargaining power of the parties may be radically unequal or one may be particularly vulnerable, see Raymond A. Belliotti, *Good Sex*, Kansas University Press, Kansas, 1993, p. 89.

now enjoys a salary of £34,000 per annum. A female colleague who is more talented than him is, because of various reasons to do with living in a patriarchal society, on an unpromoted salary of £25,000 per annum. Both these are reasonably comfortable but not astronomical salaries by 1998 British standards. If we assume that the male lecturer is not in any way in charge of the female, the fact he lives in a patriarchy has certainly given him an advantage in the form of a higher salary. On the other hand, his higher salary on its own hardly offers the sort of economic leverage which, by itself, would coerce her into having sex with him. In other words, the fact their economic position is not reversed is unfair, and the unfairness is caused by patriarchy. But it is not unfairness which is conducive to sexual coercion. What I want to look at in the latter part of this chapter is a variety of versions of this example - not all, of course, with the same conclusion. In terms of the chapter's metaphor, the two lecturers are on a sloping playing field which disadvantages the woman. But the slope is in this case relatively gentle: given the information presented so far there is no reason to believe that if the two lecturers start a sexual relationship it is anything but a consensual one, particularly if they both state that it is. My main focus of interest is whether an adverse slope places the woman at a serious disadvantage, and more particularly whether the adverse slope is so steep as to render any apparent statements or actions consenting to sex suspect.

Sex in a patriarchal society: rival theories

The essence of the Dworkin/MacKinnon thesis is that patriarchy is founded on male sexual violence against women, including the threat of sexual violence, and that in modern societies, particularly the USA, pornography encourages and legitimates male sexual violence. Under patriarchy, normal sex cannot be distinguished from rape. As Dworkin puts it:

> The normal fuck by a normal man is taken to be an act of invasion and ownership undertaken in a mode of predation: colonializing, forceful (manly) or nearly violent; the sexual act that by its nature makes her his...men possess women when men fuck women because both experience the man being male. This is the stunning logic of male supremacy. In this view, which is the predominant one, maleness is aggressive and violent; and so fucking, in which both the man and the woman experience *maleness*, essentially demands the disappearance of the woman as an individual; thus, in being fucked, she is possessed: ceases to exist as a discrete individual: is taken over.[2]

---

[2] Andrea Dworkin, *Intercourse*, Secker and Warburg, London, 1987, pp. 63-4, cf. pp. 78-9, 122-3, 133, 171, 189. She concludes by reiterating the basic idea but speculating that incestuous paedophile rape is becoming the male ideal (p. 194).

Or MacKinnon:

> Sexuality is to feminism what work is to Marxism: that which is most one's own, yet most taken away.[3]

> Perhaps the wrong of rape has proved so difficult to define because the unquestionable starting point has been that rape is defined as distinct from intercourse, while for women it is difficult to distinguish the two under conditions of male dominance.[4]

This sexual possession of the woman tends towards her death: 'The body dies, or the lover discards the body when it is used up, throws it away, an old, useless thing, emptied, like an empty bottle. The body is used up; and the will is raped'.[5] Women are thus defined by their sexuality, a definition which is 'socially real, socially absolute, and intrinsically coercive'.[6] Dworkin does not think that genuine sexual freedom for women is possible in our society, but it would mean 'having real and absolute control in each and every act of intercourse'.[7]

The Dworkin/MacKinnon approach sees pornography as central to the assertion and maintenance of male power over women, at least in our society. As Dworkin puts it in *Pornography*, 'male power is the *raison d'être* of pornography; the degradation of the female is the means of achieving this power'. Dworkin charts seven different sorts of male power which are reinforced by pornography: the power of a metaphysical assertion of self, of physical strength, of the capacity to terrorise a whole class of persons, of naming, of owning, of money and of sex, this last being very much what she is discussing in *Intercourse*.[8] It is this perception of the central role of pornography which led Dworkin and MacKinnon to develop and promote the Minneapolis-Indianapolis Ordinances, which were directed at curtailing pornography by making it possible for a very wide group of people to sue pornographers in the civil courts. The Ordinances were declared unconstitutional by a Federal court.

---

[3] Catharine A. MacKinnon, 'Feminism, Marxism, Method and the State: An Agenda for Theory', *Signs*, Vol. 7, No. 3, 1982, pp. 515-544, quotation from p. 515. Note that sexuality is *'that which is most one's own'* - whilst no-one would want to dispute that sexuality is very important, for some women their children, or a work of art they have created, or a particular achievement in changing the law, might be seen as the most central thing they wanted to defend.

[4] Catharine A. MacKinnon, *Towards a Feminist Theory of the State*, Harvard University Press, Cambridge, MA, 1989, p. 174.

[5] Dworkin, *Intercourse*, p. 67, cf. p. 117, 129.

[6] Ibid., p. 99.

[7] Ibid., pp. 135-6.

[8] Andrea Dworkin, *Pornography: Men Possessing Women*, The Women's Press, London, 1981, pp. 25 et. seq.

The central role of sexual violence in this view of patriarchy can also be seen in Dworkin's comment on the move by some [now basically all - M.C.] US states to recognise marital rape as a crime that this fight 'goes right to the heart of women's legal status' - the issue is no less than the ending of the 'metaphysical laws of male dominance' found in Genesis.[9] From her perspective, Dworkin sees the ending of legally-permissible rape in marriage as very central to overcoming patriarchy. From the Walby perspective to be explained shortly, whilst this right is certainly very important, it should be set alongside other reforms concerning child care, opportunities at work etc., or it is liable to remain an empty letter. Dworkin does seem to recognise the importance of other issues outside sexual violence, but briefly and rarely, and with the caveat that *all* women must be *fully* equal to men for other changes to mean anything.[10] This caveat has the effect of making real changes in women's social and economic status too minor and partial to be interesting.

In summary, the Dworkin/MacKinnon view of the playing field on which sex is negotiated is that it has such a steep slope against women that *all* sexual consent must be seen as suspect. All women are in a situation akin to that of the Tsarist officers' wives discussed in the last chapter: they may go through the motions of consenting to sex, but their consent is not valid because there is such a strong background of coercion.[11]

There are, obviously, many alternatives to the Dworkin/MacKinnon view of patriarchy. The one which I broadly endorse is that best articulated by Sylvia Walby. Walby defines patriarchy as 'a system of social structures and practices in which men dominate, oppress and exploit women'. She stresses social structure to emphasise a rejection of biological determinism and of 'the notion that every individual man is in a dominant position and every woman in a subordinate one'.[12] She identifies six patriarchal social structures: the household mode of production, paid work, the state, male violence, sexuality and cultural institutions. These six structures 'have causal effects upon each other, both reinforcing and blocking, but are relatively autonomous'.[13]

This last sentence is tremendously important. If the different structures are seen as relatively autonomous, then it is possible for women to advance on one front, perhaps becoming more equal in paid work, without (for example) this

---

[9] Dworkin, *Intercourse*, p. 165.

[10] Ibid., pp. 125-6, 173. This Dworkin view has parallels with Pateman's arguments about consent, discussed previously in Ch. 3.

[11] A standard critique of this radical feminist approach is, of course, that it presents women as powerless victims. Belliotti adds a twist to this: 'if women are truly incapable of informed consent, then why should they not be subject to the same benevolent despotism afforded other groups, such as children and the mentally incompetent?', *Good Sex,* p. 164.

[12] Sylvia Walby, *Theorising Patriarchy,* Basil Blackwells, Oxford, 1990, p.20.

[13] Ibid., p. 20.

automatically making them immune from male violence.[14] The idea of blocking is also very interesting. In her *Patriarchy At Work* Walby shows that employers tend to want equal opportunities for women so as to best exploit them as workers, and to increase competition amongst employees. In contrast, certainly in the nineteenth century, husbands and trade unionists (an overlapping group) wanted to exclude women from paid work, or from the best positions. The idea that there are causal effects demands that we should analyse to what extent, for example, state activity in the UK now facilitates women's access to employment, whereas in the nineteenth century it restricted this access.[15] Walby's six structures seem to me to offer a good understanding of contemporary societies, but there is nothing to stop the list being modified in case of need: one might, for example, want to include a specific structure for the position of women in the mosque to gain an understanding of modern Iran. Broadly, for Western countries, she identifies an overall shift from private to public patriarchy, which has involved the inclusion of women in many aspects of the public sphere, but in subordinated roles.[16]

Walby thus preserves the central insight of second wave feminism, i.e. that modern western societies where women have the vote and broadly equal legal rights remain patriarchal, whilst avoiding the sweeping essentialism and apparent biological determinism of the Dworkin/MacKinnon approach. She also accepts that factors other than 'patriarchy' affect women's position. She comments, for example, that among Western nations, the wages gap between men and women 'is least in the Scandinavian countries and greatest in the USA, with the rest of Western Europe, including Britain, in between'.[17] There is not the space here to discuss Walby's more detailed analysis of the six areas - indeed, her book inevitably leaves readers with a good knowledge of any of the areas feeling that there is much more to be said. Rather, I want to use Walby's basic approach to analyse the issue of consent to sex. It is clear immediately that Walby's image of the sexual playing field is that it has an *average* anti-female slope but that this is uneven and varied, so that some women are perhaps negotiating from a stronger position than some men some of the time.

Before proceeding further, however, it will be helpful to draw on insights from studies of masculinity, notably Bob Connell's *Masculinities*.[18] Connell's view is

---

[14] Ibid., pp. 143, 149. And conversely: '...it is not appropriate to see male violence as the basis of other forms of men's control over women'; private male violence has been (rather ineffectually) delegitimated, because of state intervention. Cf. Walby, *Patriarchy at Work*, Polity Press, Cambridge, 1986, pp. 60-66.

[15] Walby, *Theorising Patriarchy*, pp. 41, 51. For Walby's much more extended analysis of this development, see her excellent *Patriarchy at Work*.

[16] Walby, *Theorising Patriarchy*, p. 179.

[17] Ibid., p. 28. Cf. her comments on the effects of different ethnic groups, p. 181, and her comment in *Patriarchy at Work*: '...patriarchy is never the only mode in a society but always exists in articulation with another, such as capitalism', (p. 50).

[18] R.W. Connell, *Masculinities*, Polity Press, Cambridge, 1995.

that biological maleness is a (somewhat) flexible given,[19] which is then mediated by class and race. But beyond this, men have a range of choices as to how they come to terms with given masculinities. There are, for instance, oppositional masculinities so that working class boys at school may grow up accepting the school's version of masculinity or opting for an alternative sub-cultural version.[20] Thus a man can decide to aim for a conventional career with a wife who brings up his children and acts as his support, or to work at low pay on environmental projects in a feminist atmosphere, or to try to join an elite army corps, or to adopt an overtly gay lifestyle. Obviously these choices are not entirely free (the conventional career man may be unemployed, the man may have no interest in being gay, the army rejects many recruits because of lack of physical fitness, etc.). They are also not immutable. Inside the conventional career man there may be a transvestite rock star just waiting to be born. However, any particular man's resources will be much affected by the choices he has made up to that point: he may be fit, poor, well-educated, have a prison record, etc. Particular societies may have a hegemonic masculinity,[21] and any particular man needs in some way to come to terms with it, but the study of masculinity makes little sense without the idea of a degree of choice.[22]

This idea has been less taken up by feminists looking at women, yet western societies do seem to exhibit a variety of femininities, and with the increasing opportunities open to women since the advent of second wave feminism, the repercussions of these have become increasingly important. There has been much debate generated amongst feminists based on the idea of diversity, i.e. that not all women are white, middle-class and heterosexual. Thus women who are working class, or belong to particular ethnic groups, or are lesbian or disabled argue that their specific oppression has been ignored by their more privileged sisters. This line of criticism has been pursued particularly forcefully by bell hooks.[23] A poignant example of this type of criticism is the black American poet Audre Lorde's open letter to Mary Daly, accusing her of assimilating the specific oppression suffered by particular groups of women to 'the oppression of women', whereas white middle-class women basically do not share these forms of oppression.[24] Mary Daly seems to have ignored this criticism.

---

[19] Ibid., pp. 51, 54, 56.

[20] Ibid. pp. 36-7.

[21] Ibid., pp. 75 et. seq. Hegemonic masculinity is *the* form of masculinity which currently legitimates patriarchy. I have some problems with this, given that I follow Walby's account in which there are several structures of patriarchy - a view which one would imagine Connell, with his stress on structured diversity, would find congenial.

[22] David Morgan's *Discovering Men*, Routledge, London, 1992, shares many of Connell's perspectives in a largely British context.

[23] hooks, bell, *Ain't I A Woman,* Pluto Press, London, 1982; hooks, bell, *Feminist Theory: From Margin to Center*, South End Press, Boston, Ma., 1984.

[24] In Audre Lorde, *Sister Outsider,* The Crossing Press, Freedom, CA, 1984.

The diversity which bell hooks and Audre Lorde stress is a *given* diversity: women cannot choose to be born black or white or American or Ethiopian. Lorde's argument is particularly powerful because of this: she is accusing Daly of misappropriating forms of oppression which have not been chosen. Apart, however, from this important given diversity, women are increasingly divided by what can be described as chosen forms of femininity. On the analogy of the discussion of masculinity, women are born biologically female but have quite a degree of choice about what form of femininity they aim to adopt. There is in advanced capitalist countries a range of choices open to girls in their teens: do they opt for increased leisure and relatively low achievement, perhaps followed by early motherhood, or do they aim to enter the race for qualifications and jobs? A further choice for young women who opt into education and competition for jobs is what to do about motherhood: do they opt out of long-term relationships with men and opt out of parenthood? or opt for planned single parenthood? or aim to be supported by a partner for some time while their children are young, followed by returning to work? or aim to carry on working except for very short breaks around the time of birth of their children? As with the male choices discussed earlier, any one of these choices may come unstuck for reasons beyond the control of the individual woman. However, many choices are successful, and the outcomes again have implications in terms of the resources a particular woman can command at any one time. These choices are much less constrained today than they were in the early 1960s.

A further range of choices is that between career paths. In modern Britain the major excluded areas for women are the Catholic priesthood and some parts of the armed forces. Outside this there is a wide range of choices, which in turn bring with them varying degrees of security, financial reward, stress, leisure, etc. They may also be seen as different ways of being feminine: being caring, reliable, presentable, organised, sisterly, maternal and so forth. For many women there are also career-related choices to be made about their sexuality: do they risk a job where sexual harassment is particularly likely? Do they aim for a career where their gender is entirely irrelevant? Do they specifically use their sexuality for career advancement or as part of the job itself?

A very impressive example of choosing between possible patterns of femininity - in this case between patterns of working motherhood - which I have witnessed over the years is the choice open to some working-class women to undergo higher education. Most of my best students over the years have been women who left school with few qualifications who return to higher education later in life. Despite having to juggle with family commitments and lack of money, many of them are the best students I have the good fortune to teach, and go on to become teachers, social workers, personnel officers, local authority officials, etc. They thus move from the insecurities and low pay of unskilled women's work to relatively stable and well-paid jobs. Obviously not all working-class women are capable of, or have access to, higher education, so we are not looking at an entirely free choice. However, the women I teach generally end up commanding much better resources in life than others who choose not to follow this path.

Thus both the literature on diversity and the extension to women of the idea of masculinities serve to remind us that women are, and are becoming, more diverse in their resources. What does this imply where sexual bargaining is concerned?

Male and female diversity and sexual bargaining

The underlying metaphor of this chapter is that of a sexual playing field. If one accepts, as I do, that advanced capitalist societies remain patriarchal despite first and second wave feminism, the sexual playing field has an *average* slope disadvantaging women. As we have already seen, however, some women have a slope in their favour some of the time, and a slight slope against women, although unfair, is insufficient to invalidate their sexual consent. A sufficiently steep slope does, however, invalidate sexual consent, and sex in these circumstances should be assumed to be rape. It should also be remembered that this playing field metaphor is a supplement to the analysis of rape based on the issue of whether the woman consents, so that a weaker, poorer, less articulate man can still rape a rich and powerful woman by, say, catching her off guard or using weapons. The point of the metaphor is to explore the extent to which coercion underlies apparently consensual sex.

It might also be objected that the concept of sexual negotiation on a playing field seems to embody the objectionable assumption that men are not interested in anything much about women except their potential as sexual partners. Obviously there are entirely non-sexual male-female relationships which don't get on to this particular playing field at all. But for those that do, isn't reducing everything to a field game demeaning? What about love? What about the point that many men have strong ethical objections to anything resembling sexual coercion or rape? I fully accept these last two points: a man in love will want to have sex with his beloved, but only with her full acceptance, and 'sexual negotiation' seems a very demeaning way of describing a beautiful and romantic experience. Similarly, many men are fully aware of the evil consequences of rape and would strongly object to involvement in any form of sexual coercion. A realisation that they are negotiating on a playing field which slopes in their favour would lead them to take extreme care that the woman in question really was consenting to sex. For the two sorts of men described, then, the playing field metaphor is inappropriate and debasing. With that comment in mind, however, I want to stick to the metaphor and translate love or ethics into an alteration of the slope: any slope against the woman will, for these categories of men, be levelled or reversed.

For any particular encounter between a man and a woman, what are the main things we need to look at in order to see what sort of a slope they are standing on?

Following roughly Walby's six structures, but with some modifications because of our particular interest, the following seem to be important: age and basic mental capacity, authority relationships, economic status, domestic status, the law and its enforcement, physical strength, cultural norms and intoxication. I shall comment briefly on each.

We have already looked at age and basic mental capacity in Chapter 2, where I endorsed the basic concept of statutory rape, i.e. that sex between an older man and a girl below a certain age should carry penalties similar to those for the rape of an adult woman, on the basis that girls below a certain age must be deemed incapable of consent. Different societies make different judgements about how this is implemented, and a sensible approach is one where girls are seen as becoming increasingly capable of informed consent to sex as they grow older; also this happens at different speeds for different girls. The basic idea behind British practice in which the offence is deemed the more serious the younger the girl and the wider the gap in age fits well with my approach, although any law in this area is bound to be disputed, and bound to fit badly with some individual cases. A similar concept makes sense for adult women of limited mental capacity, but is harder to implement: how does one identify mental capacity? How can the right of such women to be protected from sexual coercion be balanced against their having a right to a sex life? For both the concept of a slope which diminishes as the understanding of the woman grows makes sense.

As we saw in the last chapter, authority relationships of a sufficiently stark kind invalidate consent. Thus, faced with a secret policeman who can dispose of her or her relatives, a woman's sexual consent must be presumed invalid. ('Presumed' rather than just plain 'is' because one can imagine circumstances where the woman's consent was, in fact, genuine: in the case of the Tsarist officers' wives invited to parties by the Cheka, one can imagine one particular officer's wife who had freely started an affair with a man before the Revolution, only to find that he became a Chekist after it.) In more mundane liberal democratic terms, relations between women prisoners and their warders, between mental patients and their nurses,[25] between drill sergeants and women soldiers,[26] between residential social workers and young people in care, and between schoolteachers and their pupils should be seen as non-consenting, although some degree of pragmatism should be exercised to cover cases where, say, it is discovered that a mental nurse and an ex-patient who have been happily married for some years were in fact having sex before she left the mental hospital.

If the above authority relationships constitute such a severe slope that it invalidates sexual consent, what about milder authority relations such as those between university lecturers and students or employers and employees? Here the slope is gentler because the subordinate partner is assumed to have fully adult

---

[25] These relationships are illegal in the UK.

[26] As in the case of the US sergeant Delmar Simpson, accused of 51 rapes and sentenced to 25 years.

capacities, and it is possible, though difficult and disruptive, to leave a particular university or place of work. In addition, most people who work in higher education know some long-term and happy marriages which started as affairs between lecturers and students. Similarly, many happy marriages begin with affairs between people at work. Furthermore, things sometimes happen the other way round: the partner of an existing employer comes to work for him, or the wife of a lecturer enrols as a student. A further complication is that we have been assuming that the lecturer or employer is using his authority to secure sexual consent, whereas in fact the relationship might be more that the student or employee starts the liaison in order to secure better grades or promotion.

Universities have a standard minimum approach to this problem, which is to attempt to detach the sexual relationship from the student's assessment.[27] An analogous procedure makes sense for employees: decisions about promotion or dismissal should ideally be separated from the sexual relationship. Beyond this, however, it is worth considering whether having sexual relationships with students or employees should be seen as a disciplinary offence, given the undermining effect on general morale if it is thought that individuals are 'sleeping their way to the top'. It is difficult to reach categorical conclusions because cases differ considerably: the student or employee may, for example, be attached to a part of the organisation remote from the lecturer or boss. Organisations should certainly have, either as part of their own code or as part of the general law of the country, regulations covering sexual harassment which can be implemented where lecturers or bosses are overtly attempting to take advantage of their position of authority.[28] Beyond this, however, it would be excessive to categorise all relationships between lecturers and students or employers and employees as a form of rape whatever the apparent degree of consent.

The issue of economic status is important, and raises a number of interesting questions. In extreme cases economic coercion is as serious as physical coercion, and clearly invalidates sexual consent. The Chinese landlords described in William Hinton's *Fanshen* took 'the peasants' wives and daughters to their beds almost at will', because they had such extreme economic leverage on the peasants, expropriating their land through usury and watching their debtors starve during famines. The pent-up anger of the peasants led many landlords to be beaten to

---

[27] For a British discussion of some examples of staff/student liaisons and proposals on policy, see Pam Carter and Tony Jeffs, *A Very Private Affair: Sexual Exploitation in Higher Education,* Education Now Books, Ticknall, Derbyshire, 1995. It is noteworthy that the authors, whilst regarding such liaisons as undesirable for a variety of solid reasons, do not place them on the 'continuum of sexual violence' or talk in terms of rape or near-rape.

[28] As Kate Fillion reminds us, office relationships can appear as harassment from the outside but the power can sometimes lie with the 'subordinate' woman - see *Lip Service,* Pandora/Harper Collins, London, 1997, Ch. 3.

death during the revolution on the land in 1946.[29] What about economic coercion in our society?

The degree of economic leverage available in our society is much lower than that in pre-Revolutionary China: a woman being offered a tradeoff between sex and money is likely to have state income support as a minimum standard. Whilst this offers a bleak existence, it is much superior to starvation. Thus the choice she faces between getting money by agreeing to sex or not is much less coercive than in the Chinese example. Because of this, choices in our society happen more in slow motion, so to speak: a woman threatened with the sack unless she agrees to sleep with her employer can live on state benefits while she takes him to an industrial tribunal, rather than having to agree because otherwise she or her family will starve. So far, the conclusion seems to be that economic coercion is insufficiently powerful in our society to amount to rape.[30] There are, however, several qualifications which need to be made to this conclusion.

First, 'our society', meaning advanced capitalist societies, has links with much poorer societies, leading to the phenomenon of sex tourism. Even assuming that all transactions between sex tourists and third world women are consensual at the point of agreement, if the women involved come from very poor backgrounds they are making choices knowing that their alternatives are constrained: they can carry on working as sex workers or fail to sustain their family at home and face extreme poverty themselves. In this context the slope on which sex is negotiated is so extreme as to render agreements suspect.[31] Of course it is possible to find examples which would not support this conclusion: gifts made by the Western man well in excess of any agreement, or proposals of marriage knowing that the marriage will be under broadly egalitarian Western laws.[32]

Second, I have so far been implicitly following a liberal account of relations between employers and workers or between advanced and third world countries. In this it is more or less assumed that employers get to be well off through fair

---

[29] William Hinton, *Fanshen*, Penguin, Harmondsworth, 1972, pp. 149 et. seq.

[30] As is pointed out in Charlene L. Muehlenhard et. al., 'Definitions of Rape: Scientific and Political Implications', *Journal of Social Issues,* Vol. 48, No. 1, 1992, pp. 23-44, the USA has no statutory maternity leave and little affordable daycare. The best maternity leave schemes offered by US corporations seem to be about the same as the worst statutory European Union schemes, and daycare provisions in France and Sweden put Britain and the USA to shame. (On maternity leave see Sylvia Ann Hewlett, *A Lesser Life,* Sphere Books, Harmondsworth, 1988). There are thus quite large differences in this respect between advanced capitalist countries.

[31] Thomas A. Mappes, 'Sexual Morality and the Concept of Using Another Person', *Social Ethics: Morality and Social Policy,* McGraw-Hill, New York, 1987, pp. 248-62, identifies this as sexually using someone by 'taking advantage of [her] desperate situation', (pp. 261-2) but does not make the Marxist move found in my next paragraph.

[32] For a useful discussion, see Julia O'Connell Davidson, 'British Sex Tourists in Thailand', in Mary Maynard and June Purvis, eds, *(Hetero)sexual Politics*, Taylor and Francis, London, 1995, Ch. 3.

competition and good luck, that trade between countries is on an equal basis and so forth. If more of a Marxist outlook is adopted, so that work is a form of systematic exploitation of the worker's labour, and third world countries are victims of imperialism, then many of the relationships we are considering happen against the background of a system which gives employers, or people from advanced countries, an advantage *because of* their exploitation of workers or people from the third world. Where the slope on which sex is negotiated is very steep the picture which a Marxist approach paints comes much closer to rape: the man benefits from systematic exploitation of the woman, or of her community, and then uses the advantage this gives him to negotiate sex with her. In the liberal framework this sort of activity is discussed in the context of 'coercive offers',[33] where a man puts a woman deliberately in a difficult situation, perhaps by driving her to an isolated spot miles from home, and then offers to get her out of it if she will have sex with him. This tends to be seen as closer to rape than finding a woman in an isolated spot and offering to take her home if she agrees to have sex. Because of the liberal framework, the idea that the man is benefiting from a systematically exploitative set of arrangements is not discussed.[34]

Third, there is the issue of whether sex can legitimately be traded at all. A liberal approach to prostitution sees it as a transaction in which the woman sells sexual services in much the same way as she might sell other abilities she has. There is no difference in kind between prostitution and a range of legitimate working activities: actors sell their ability to project personalities, barristers sell their ability to argue, social workers sell their ability to empathise and so forth. Of course, because prostitution or activities connected with it are criminalised in many countries, prostitution (unfairly) tends to have a bad reputation, and some of the illegal activities associated with prostitution lead to women being exploited by pimps or clients or by other women, but this is not, on the liberal view, an essential part of the relationship. Some feminist writing, however, sees sex as so central to the woman's identity that a woman selling sexual services must be a victim of extreme and unacceptable exploitation which is close to rape. The Dworkin/MacKinnon approach is based on this assumption, I think. This difference between radical feminist and liberal views is reflected in women's attitudes to what counts as personally acceptable choices. Thus some women find prostitution an acceptable activity which brings good financial rewards and the satisfaction of making clients happy, whilst others would never contemplate the sort of 'million dollars for a night of sex' exchange offered in the film *Indecent*

---

[33] Burgess-Jackson's definition of a coercive offer is wider, covering offers made in a non-manipulated vulnerable situation - see *Rape: A Philosophical Investigation,* Dartmouth, Brookfield, Vermont, 1996, p. 96.

[34] See Burgess-Jackson's incisive but non-Marxist discussion of Feinberg, *Rape,* pp. 97-102. Cf. Murphy's support for Feinberg, Jeffrie G. Murphy, 'Some Ruminations on Women, Violence and the Criminal Law', in Jules L. Coleman and Allen Buchanan, eds, *In Harm's Way,* Cambridge University Press, Cambridge, 1994, pp. 209-30, p. 221.

Proposal, let alone any lesser offers. Different attitudes to this issue are not as clearly articulated as they might be, but underlie much discussion of prostitution and rape.[35]

The mention of *Indecent Proposal* leads on to the fourth and final qualification. Even if routine prostitution is seen as close to rape, what about an offer of major benefits to a woman who is not in particular need? One possible example would be where Peter and Jane are both workers in the same job at equal pay, leading very similar lifestyles. They both buy lottery tickets. Peter wins a huge sum and offers Jane a million dollars to sleep with him. They were both comfortably off to start with, and Peter's wealth is not based on exploitation. Distasteful though this transaction may be, it is hard to see it as rape. Another possibility might be that Peter uses his new wealth to make a film. Jane has always wanted to appear in a film, and he offers her a part subject to a session on his casting couch. Again, it would be hard to argue that he is exploiting Jane, although he would certainly be abusing his position if he had become a film producer by more normal means, or if Jane's obvious talent entitled her to become a star.[36]

The issue of economic status leads on naturally to that of domestic status. Surveys of domestic violence and sexual abuse suggest that it is at its peak in relationships where the woman is at home with small children. Although it is theoretically possible for a woman with no money to take her children and leave

---

[35] For an excellent discussion of these issues, which concludes that the normative issues involved in prostitution are so substantial that ultimate agreement is highly unlikely, see Alison M. Jaggar, 'Prostitution', in Alan Soble, ed., *The Philosophy of Sex*, Littlefield, Adams and Co., New Jersey, 1980, pp. 348-68. For a defence of the liberal position that an acceptable version of prostitution as a morally permissible service occupation is possible, see L.O. Ericsson, 'Charges against Prostitution: An Attempt at a Philosophical Assessment', *Ethics*, Vol. 90, No. 3, 1980, pp. 335-66. For a radical feminist critique see Carole Pateman, 'Defending Prostitution: Charges Against Ericsson', *Ethics*, Vol. 93, April, 1983, pp. 561-5. Pateman's explanation that 'men (not women) demand prostitutes' because under patriarchy prostitution is bound up with 'relations of domination and subordination' seems to need at least some modification given the subsequent growth of male prostitution catering for women. Cf. Laurie Shrage, 'Should Feminists Oppose Prostitution?', *Ethics*, Vol. 99, January 1989, pp. 347-61, and Primoratz's defence of it and critique of Pateman and Shrage: Igor Primoratz, 'What's Wrong with Prostitution?', *Philosophy*, Vol. 68, 1993, pp. 159-82. I think a Marxist view of this issue could go either way: providing intimate services could be seen as an extreme form of alienation. Alternatively, Marxism sees work as fundamental, so that sexual relations could be deemed secondary - see Belliotti, *Good Sex*, p. 124.

[36] The incident described here somewhat resembles the offer which Angelo makes to Rosalia in Belliotti's *Good Sex*, pp. 91-8. It differs from his example because I have deliberately tried to provide Peter with a 'clean path' to his advantageous position. In general in real life I agree with Belliotti that such transactions are often surrounded with suspect systematic inequalities or patterns of exploitation; also that if Jane has an overwhelming desire to become a star, perhaps the distinction between this and a basic need becomes blurred (cf. ibid., p. 192).

home for a refuge or for emergency accommodation, the process is a very fraught one: she probably needs *some* money to complete the process; the refuge may be full or non-existent; measures to protect women from abusive partners exist but are notoriously ineffective; the woman may decide to put up with abuse for the sake of the children; perhaps her partner is abusive only for some of the time, making it hard to decide whether the stresses of leaving warrant the benefits. Thus the sexual consent of a woman who has young children, does not work outside the home, and who lacks resources or qualifications which would enable her to leave, is secured on a very steep slope. The surveys also suggest that abuse is rather less common when the woman is working outside the home and the children are non-existent or older.[37] Remember that we are looking at apparent consent which is negated by the circumstances. Obviously, many women at home with young children have loving partners who do not remotely try to exploit the woman's vulnerability. My earlier point that patriarchy is being modified by women's choices is also applicable to this discussion: to some extent women can choose how much to put themselves in an economically dependent situation by making particular career choices.

Walby's next structure is the law and its enforcement. This is obviously relevant to whether consent is freely negotiated in two ways. First, there is the direct question of the law of rape and its enforcement. If spousal rape is not recognised by the law, for example, then married women lack protection from their husbands, and the knowledge that forced sex in marriage is not illegal will be a background factor when the wife is deciding whether to go along with her husband's demands. As we saw in Chapter 2, the court process (i.e. enforcement) in Britain is very unsatisfactory in many ways, and the knowledge of this has effects on the behaviour of some men, making it more predatory, and of some women, making them more compliant. Obviously the exact letter of the law is also important. The more the background factors under discussion in this chapter are taken account of in the law, the more protection it will offer women. However, there are a lot of fraught issues in this chapter's discussion. I shall make some suggestions in the concluding chapter.

The second issue raised by the law is the general effect of the law on women's position. Thus the more the law makes domestic violence risky for offenders, the stronger becomes women's position in resisting violent sexual coercion. The more the law supports women's position as workers the better their earnings and prospects and the better their economic position when it comes to sexual negotiation. Similar points could be made about women's situation as consumers, divorce laws, electoral law and so forth: the more independent women are, the more they can negotiate freely when it comes to sex.

Physical strength is obviously important as a background factor. On average men are bigger and stronger than women, and this means that women are

---

[37] See, for example, David Finkelhor and Kirsti Yllo, *License to Rape: Sexual Abuse of Wives*, Holt, Rinehart and Winston, New York, 1985, pp. 8-9, 199.

typically negotiating on an adverse slope in this area. On the other hand, this is an average, so that some women are stronger than some men.[38] Further, the better the protection offered by the laws of rape and domestic violence and their means of enforcement, the less effective is male violence. Finally, the woman may or may not be trained in assertiveness, self-defence, use of weapons, etc.

Walby's final category is the very wide one of 'cultural norms'. This plainly needs several books to itself, but some brief observations may be helpful. Our society certainly has general cultural norms to some extent. Thus, for example, it has generally tended to become more secular over the last hundred years, the news in both tabloid and broadsheet newspapers seems to be mainly describing the same world as television news programmes, second wave feminism has been successful to the extent that anti-feminist views are usually publicly expressed apologetically rather than as obvious truths. That said, people have a great deal of choice over what cultural norms they are exposed to. The range of choice in printed media and television and radio is vastly greater than it was forty years ago, so that people can choose to live in particular sub-cultures for much of the time. We thus need to look at the cultural heritage of a particular man and woman rather than making sweeping assumptions based on supposed general norms.

Nonetheless, it is worth discussing some relevant possible factors. I shall look briefly at pornography, feminism, religion, romantic love and teenage culture. Pornography is a factor which is frequently mentioned in the literature on rape:[39] radical feminists such as Dworkin and MacKinnon assert that pornography is very pervasive in American society and is an ideology which legitimates rape. This leads to a very fraught and extensive discussion about whether exposure to pornography encourages rape, and what counts as pornography for this discussion. So far this has not reached firm conclusions for the USA, let alone for the UK. To the limited extent that there is general agreement, the worst suspicions fall on material such as 'slasher' movies which depict women enjoying pain but are not necessarily particularly pornographic in the sense of displaying explicit sexual acts. In terms of particular couples, either, both or neither of them may have been exposed to anything from massive amounts through to none of any particular type of pornography, rendering the discussion even less conclusive.[40]

---

[38] The present author is somewhat disabled. Push him over gently, steal his spectacles, and walk away at a sedate pace and he will give you no further trouble for a long time.

[39] Including by Schwartz and DeKeseredy, who argue that pornography is linked to male peer support for rape on college campuses - see Martin D. Schwartz and Walter S. DeKeseredy, *Sexual Assault on the College Campus: The Role of Male Peer Support*, Sage, London, 1997, pp. 47, 88.

[40] This issue has attracted a vast literature. For a useful introduction to it, see: G. Hawkins and F.E. Zimring, *Pornography in a Free Society*, Cambridge University Press, Cambridge, 1988; Daniel Linz, Barbara J. Wilson and Edward Donnerstein, 'Sexual Violence in the Mass Media', *Journal of Social Issues*, Vol. 48, No. 1, 1992, pp. 145-171; Feminists Against Censorship, (eds), *Pornography and Feminism: The Case Against*

Second wave feminism is itself a variable cultural influence. Variants of it are accepted by some women and some men, against, as indicated, a general background of a greater acceptance of female equality. Women influenced by feminism are likely to be more assertive about their right to control their sexuality, and men influenced by feminism are likely to agree. In statistical terms this may in some situations lead to findings of more rape and attempted rape rather than less because feminism has sensitised women to regard particular acts as abuses. A particular variant of this on US campuses is that many of them feature programmes designed to combat date rape, leading students generally to express more disapproving attitudes to it than those they brought to college.

Religion can also affect the slope on which sex is negotiated. Muslim women in Britain tend not to have a problem with date rape because they are closely observed by their parents to preserve their virginity, and then pressured to accept arranged marriages. To describe an arranged marriage negotiated by loving parents in the 'best interests' of their daughter as leading to something akin to rape is perhaps going too far, but if the daughter has been influenced by the ideas of romantic love accepted by most of British society it must come close. Another religion which steepens the slope against women is Catholicism as practised in Republican ghettos in Northern Ireland. The Church's sexual strictures are taken much more seriously than on the mainland, so that many women have ten children and numerous miscarriages, rather than the two or three children seen as a 'normal' family in Western Europe generally. Thus these women are vulnerable to male pressure or violence for much longer than women generally. In addition, of course, abortion is not permitted by the Church and is basically illegal in Northern Ireland. Further, women complaining of their lot to the priest tend to be told that they should accept suffering as part of life, and 'new men' are very thin on the ground.[41]

Romantic love is very widely accepted in advanced capitalist societies as the proper basis of sexual relations. (This is the reason why arranged marriages seem so out of line with the host society.) Romantic love asserts that a couple are made for each other, and enjoins each partner to consider and care for the other. It thus tends to promote consenting sex. We have seen the possible downside of this in

---

Censorship, Lawrence and Wishart, London, 1991; N.M. Malamuth and E. Donnerstein, eds, *Pornography and Sexual Aggression*, Academic Press, Orlando, Florida, 1984.

A standard problem in research on the effects of pornography is the difficulty of carrying it out in a real life setting. One small survey which attempted this found that men who rented out more pornographic videos did not seem to have different attitudes towards equality for women, date rape or marital rape from men who rented fewer or none. See Kimberly A. Davies, 'Voluntary Exposure to Pornography and Men's Attitudes Toward Feminism and Rape', *The Journal of Sex Research*, Vol. 34, No. 2, 1997, pp. 131-7.

[41] For a graphic and interesting account see Eileen Fairweather, Roisin McDonough and Melanie McFadyean, *Only the Rivers Run Free: Northern Ireland, The Women's War*, Pluto Press, London, 1984, esp. Ch. 3.

which the woman expects to be swept off her feet by a powerful but ultimately considerate man, which can lead to abuse, but it generally militates against pressurising a woman into sex without strong emotional attachment.

Under the heading of 'teenage culture' I want basically to discuss some studies carried out in the 1980s by Sue Lees.[42] These work on a picture of teenage life where girls are heavily constrained by the fear of being called a 'slag', i.e. a derogative term for a girl who sleeps around. Girls who suffer this abuse seem best able to resist it by acquiring a steady boyfriend. To the extent that this picture is accurate it gives boys considerable advantages, in that they control girls' reputations and are able to pressure them towards sex with a steady boyfriend to escape being called a 'slag'. Boys appear not to suffer these constraints, which are, of course, a version of the sexual double standard. A similar, but less elaborated, picture is painted by the authors of the WRAP project.[43] That said, my impression is that this double standard is declining in Britain. Teenage magazines for girls frequently discuss the possibilities of uncommitted sex. Boys shown Lees's arguments[44] reacted in the same way as my teenage children and students with whom I have discussed this issue, by saying that 'slag' has degenerated into a term of common abuse and is now used for members of both sexes. Perhaps these changes are linked to the erosion of male careers and boys' school performance relative to girls.

Walby's list naturally does not include drink as a major structure of our society, but it needs to be included in an assessment of the sexual playing field. The idea that having sex with a woman who is unconscious as a consequence of drinking is rape is widely accepted.[45] The problem is that the effects of drink vary between different people and in different quantities. The same points apply, but generally even less predictably, to a variety of drugs. With both drink and drugs we may be

---

[42] Sue Lees, *Losing Out: Sexuality and Adolescent Girls,* Hutchinson, London, 1986, and *Sugar and Spice: Sexuality and Adolescent Girls,* Penguin, Harmondsworth, 1993.

[43] Women Risk Aids Project - See, for example, Janet Holland et. al., *Pressure, Resistance, Empowerment: Young Women and The Negotiation of Safer Sex,* Tufnell Press, London, 1991; Janet Holland et. al., *Wimp or Gladiator: Contradictions in Acquiring Masculine Sexuality,* Tufnell Press, London, 1993.

[44] See Lees, *Losing Out,* pp. 112, cf. girls who thought the double standard was eroding, p. 142. For an American survey which also suggests an erosion of the double standard and support for fewer, committed relationships for both males and females, see Lucia F. O'Sullivan, 'Less is More: The Effects of Sexual Experience on Men's and Women's Personality Characteristics and Relationship Desirability', *Sex Roles,* Vol. 33, Nos. 3/4, 1995, pp. 159-81.

[45] The basic idea is very extensively known: in the tenth-century Arabian Nights stories a piece of banj renders virgin queen Ibrîzah unconscious while King Umar al-Numân rapes her. He subsequently endures an unpleasant but well-deserved death at the hands of a Christian woman - see *The Book of the Thousand Nights and One Night,* trans. J.C. Mardrus and P. Mathers, Routledge, London, 1986, Vol. 1, pp. 374-5. The modern versions are drugs such as Rohypnol (e.g. *News of the World,* 16 November 1997).

looking to some extent at cultural expectations of what they do rather than strictly physiological effects, but for the purposes of the analysis here it is the way in which the overall experience of drink and drugs - including cultural elements - influences people having sex which matters. As we saw in Chapter 3, drink features extensively in date rape surveys. However, at the other extreme from unconsciousness, it seems quite wrong to say that because a man gives a sober woman a small glass of low-alcohol wine her sexual consent is thereby rendered suspect. How far can we get beyond saying that incapacitation through drink is one factor which may affect the slope of the sexual playing field? A very useful suggestion is made by Karen Kramer. She bases her suggestions on the model of communicative sexuality which has been written into Canadian law, but her formula could, I think, be incorporated into current British law without much difficulty. She proposes (crucial clauses only quoted):

> Presumptively, no consent is obtained where:
> b. the complainant is wholly or intermittently unconscious during the sexual activity;
> d. the complainant's ability to affirmatively communicate willingness or unwillingness to engage in the act is hindered by reason of intoxication with alcohol or other substances substantially enough to cause observable physical weakening or impaired verbal ability.[46]

She also includes a clause to indicate that it does not matter if the complainant got herself drunk. Although this formula would still have grey areas, it makes sense that women need protection when intoxicated but still conscious, and it also makes sense that women are capable of rationally consenting to sex when considerably more drunk than the legal maximum for driving.

The argument of this chapter is thus that to say our society is patriarchal and has an average slope against women is not very helpful in deciding whether apparent sexual consent is actually false. It is necessary instead to look at a series of areas and see where the man and woman in question stand in relation to each of them. My view is that of the areas looked at, age, mental capacity, authority relationships, physical strength and intoxication, can each independently be the basis of a valid claim that a woman's consent was not freely given and that she is a victim of rape. The other areas, economic status, domestic status, the law and cultural norms can all significantly affect the tilt of the particular part of the playing field on which the woman is standing, but are not (apart, of course from the law of rape itself) likely to be dramatic enough on their own to support a claim of rape. Plainly a particular sexual incident will occur against a background of all

---

[46] Karen M. Kramer, 'Rule by Myth: The Social and Legal Dynamics Governing Alcohol-Related Acquaintance Rapes', *Stanford Law Review*, Vol. 47, 1994, pp. 115-60; quotation from this very informative article is from p. 152.

of these factors at once, and in a real situation it will be necessary to see whether the various factors reinforce or undermine each other.

Leaving aside the specific question of whether the slope in any particular case is sufficiently steep to invalidate the woman's consent, it is still reasonable to argue that in general women in our society negotiate on a somewhat adverse slope in each of the areas. Most of the areas discussed have been the focus of feminist demands and reforms, and fairness clearly demands support for measures which will level the playing field.[47]

A less important but interesting issue is the extent to which men may find themselves victims of an adverse slope. This seems possible in particular cases in each of the areas discussed. Age and mental capacity can obviously apply both ways round, but older women having sex with under-age boys seem to attract less opprobrium than men who have sex with under-age girls. Women are increasingly getting into positions of authority, and will doubtless on occasion abuse them by having sex with their charges. Turning to economic and domestic status, in one in five British male-female households the woman is now the higher earner, including, famously, that of the current prime minister. This trend towards at least some women being higher earners than their partners seems set to continue, given that girls are outperforming boys at school examinations, are securing university places, including those leading to law, medicine and accountancy, in roughly equal numbers, and gaining more of the new professional jobs which come available than men.[48] Nor are women immune from the temptations of heterosexual male prostitution in Britain and international sex tourism in Kenya, the Gambia, the Caribbean and Bali. For British men the concept of a lifelong secure career has been eroded, so that some women can be expected to be simply luckier than some men. On the other hand, the primary responsibility for making decisions about child care seems to have remained with the mother, who could normally expect to retain custody in the event of the partnership breaking down, so that the image of men putting up with sexual abuse from their partners because they are unable to leave and take the children with them seems generally implausible. Some women are thus negotiating from a much stronger position

---

[47] For a good account of some current issues and attempts to bring about change see: J. Lovenduski and V. Randall, *Feminist Politics Today*, Oxford University Press, Oxford, 1993. Obviously this does not take into account the opportunities offered by a more sympathetic government since 1 May 1997.

[48] See, for example Helen Wilkinson, 'Cracks in the Glass Ceiling', *Observer*, 14 June 1996. Wilkinson also celebrates the large numbers of women in various countries setting up their own businesses, although she is less specific about the average size of these. Across Europe (i.e. the EU, the EFTA countries and Central and Eastern Europe) there are 103 women for every 100 men in higher education; 110 women hold higher diplomas compared to 100 men. However, qualified women are slightly more prone to be unemployed and top jobs are still male dominated (see *Key Data on Education in the European Union*, quoted in *EC News* No. 8, 27 February 1998).

than their mothers would typically have enjoyed, and are that much less likely to face sexual abuse from their partners.

The law in Britain defines vaginal or anal sex without consent as rape, and so defends men and women against men, but offers men no protection against sexual assault by women. In addition, whilst most people recognise that rape is a serious crime (even though many people believe at least some of the myths of rape), even authors as eminent as Mary Koss discount the possibility of female-on-male rape.[49] Cultural norms do not protect men from women. Men are generally held to be always wanting sex with any willing woman; men sexually assaulted by women tend to be seen as lucky rather than victims. The law and popular culture fail, as we have seen, to defend women properly from rape, but do not even make the attempt where female-on-male sexual assault is concerned. Finally, physical strength and intoxication generally work against women, but some women are stronger than some men, and intoxication certainly features among the reasons that males surveyed have unwilling sex with females.

The analysis of the last two paragraphs does not point to a serious and widespread social problem, but there is enough scope for, and evidence of, female-on-male sexual abuse to suggest that the question should not be dismissed out of hand.

---

[49] See the discussion above in Ch. 2.

6 Conclusion

This book started by asking what could be learned in Britain from the extensive US literature on date rape, and in particular what conclusions we should draw about the dividing line between rape and consenting sex. There are three interlocking areas which require comment: philosophical issues, the law and future research.

Philosophical issues

One major philosophical question investigated was the wrongness of rape. I argued that rape is specifically a violation of sexual self-determination, and that the seriousness of the act should be measured in terms of the degree of trauma caused to the victim. This involves, particularly, *not* simply treating rape as another physical assault. In terms of the discussion in the rest of the book, this conclusion points towards more investigation of the degree of trauma inflicted on the 'hidden' victims, that is, those women seen as rape victims by investigators on the basis of their questionnaire responses but who do not report the event to the police or a counselling service. This research could also be extended to victims of 'hidden' attempted rape, pressurised sex, unwilling lesser contacts, etc., and also to male 'victims' of similar acts. Once this is carried out we will have a clearer picture of whether the researchers discussed in Chapter 3 are discovering a concealed well of misery or inferring assaults from ambiguous answers or something in between. This should also inform legislation on sexual assault: the more an act is usually traumatic the more the law should try to protect people from it.

A second philosophical issue is the clarity of the distinction between rape and non-rape. The argument of this book has very much pointed towards a continuum between pressurised sex, coerced sex and rape, both because the dividing line between legitimate pressure and illegitimate coercion is unclear, and because the

129

degree of coercion implied by the background situation varies by a long series of small degrees. An analogy could be drawn with baldness: it is perfectly clear if a person is bald as a coot or has a full head of hair, but between these extremes it is something of an arbitrary matter at what point thinning hair gives way to baldness. This clearly has an impact on how the surveys of date rape are interpreted: the more behaviour is defined as rape, the more rape the surveys may be expected to discover. The limiting case here would be a survey conducted using the theories of Dworkin and MacKinnon, which would presumably find 100% rates of rape amongst women who had had sex with men. This problem of a continuum again points to more research as to how traumatic are particular degrees of coercion to undertake particular acts. It also suggests that there should be a degree of tolerance between figures such as Koss and Gilbert or DeKeseredy and Fekete: some of their disagreement stems not from dishonesty, ignorance or poor research but from the inherent ambiguity of the subject.[1]

The third major philosophical issue is that of the communication of consent. As we saw in Chapter 4, one of the objectives of feminist anti-rape campaigners is a change in the law's approach to consent from the current British approach in which the rape victim has to prove she has not consented to one where the man has to show he has followed the guidelines of communicative sexuality, or, alternatively, but ultimately pointing in much the same direction, the man has to prove that the woman consented. Although everything else advocated by campaigners such as the Campaign to End Rape deserves unreserved support, this particular area needs more careful analysis. To start with, we seem to be moving from a traditional approach to dating in which the man takes the initiative and the woman is a gatekeeper to a more mixed situation in which the traditional approach predominates but mutual seduction or woman-led seduction is quite common. If a woman is busy removing a man's clothing it is perhaps beside the point for him to ask if she is willing to be kissed. Within the 'woman as gatekeeper' approach it seems that much of what consenting women actually do is to accept male advances. Sufficient acceptance of enough male advances amounts eventually to consent to sex. Verbal negotiation about consent is often symbolic or metaphorical as in 'Shall we get more comfortable?' or 'Shall we continue this in bed?' This appears to work most of the time for most sexual encounters, and it would be better for the law to recognise how real relationships work than to legislate that people should fit an artificial set of criteria. Related to this is a point about research: there is very little research about how consenting sex is actually negotiated: my claims in the last few sentences may be wrong, but I do not think researchers are currently in a position to confirm or deny them. A particularly serious point concerns existing relationships: feminist campaigners are quite right to insist that rape occurs within established relationships, but the communication

---

[1] For a useful list of hypothetical examples which demonstrates this continuum between two clear end points very well, see Keith Burgess-Jackson, *Rape: A Philosophical Investigation*, Dartmouth, Brookfield, Vermont, 1996, pp. 29-30.

of consent within them is likely to be much more truncated, gestural and symbolic than that found in new relationships. Thus rather different criteria governing consent and non-consent would seem to be appropriate in existing relationships where there has been no indication of a breakdown. Finally, of course, communicative sexuality does not guarantee consent if carried out against a sufficient background of threat. For the while, therefore, I would support the basic contention that prosecuting counsel should ask careful and searching questions about consent, and not readily accept that women consented in improbable circumstances, but have reservations about writing communicative sexuality into the law of rape.

The fourth and final philosophical issue is that of whether the sheer existence of a patriarchal society negates women's consent to sex. I argued that it does not, but that women are often negotiating sexual encounters on an adverse slope. Some of these adverse slopes are definitely sufficient to render apparent consent suspect, and to point to the conclusion that an encounter is rape unless special considerations show it is not. Moreover, adverse slopes which do not on their own lead to this conclusion may be cumulative, e.g. a woman may be simultaneously dealing with a much bigger stronger man, her religious upbringing which teaches her submissiveness, a degree of economic threat and the fact that she is rather drunk. I do not think that it is possible to legislate specifically and in detail for circumstances of this sort, but it is important for these factors to be put together with questions about how consent was negotiated: the man needs to be much more careful in these circumstances than, say, if they were all reversed and in the woman's favour.

Legal issues

What of legal issues? As I indicated in Chapter 2, my basic approach in this book has been to treat rape as a moral rather than a legal category, and it would be wrong to make proposals to reform the law on the basis of such a discussion. On the other hand, it seems appropriate to indicate some legal questions raised by my arguments.

The first point, which needs to be made very strongly, is that this book concerns issues which are one stage on from the immediate legal issues surrounding rape in Britain. The abuses perpetrated on rape victims by our legal system, as charted by Sue Lees or the Campaign to End Rape, are shocking. The immediate legal changes needed are those required to reduce the rate of attrition in rape cases from the current 90% level. It also needs to be understood that behind the 5,000 or so British women who complain of rape each year to the police stand a large number who are currently deterred by police and legal procedures and choose to suffer in silence rather than suffer in court. My concerns become important once these immediate abuses have been dealt with. They concern *how* many more women are raped than those in police statistics. Related to this, how can a borderline between rape and non-rape be established? These are important issues, because there is a danger of sweeping claims such as those made by Dworkin and MacKinnon discrediting an important and legitimate issue.

The second legal point is whether there should be a graduated rape (or sexual assault) law. At the moment in Britain it seems that rapists are either prosecuted under the law of rape, providing for a maximum life sentence, or not prosecuted, or prosecuted on lesser and non-sexual assault charges. The logic of both the discussion of threats which might invalidate consent in Chapter 4 and of the sloping playing field in Chapter 5 very much points to a continuum between rape and consenting sex. This in turn suggests it would be appropriate to have some kind of lesser offence than rape, with a smaller maximum sentence, to cover more marginal cases. There is both a moral and a practical issue here. Consider two students. They spend a romantic evening together. They get quite drunk. She shows him her collection of sado-masochistic pornography. They engage in petting which includes oral-genital contact, but she says she does not want to have sex. She then invites him to spend the night in her bed and wakes up to find him having sex with her. This is undoubtedly rape, as she was asleep, she had not consented, and she said she did not consent. On the other hand, prosecuting him for the same offence as a violent stranger rapist seems morally inappropriate: he has committed his crime on the basis of behaviour which most people would regard as being very close to sexual consent. The practical issue relates to this: a jury, realising that they would be convicting him of a serious offence which carries a maximum of a life sentence and normally results in imprisonment, is very likely to acquit him, even though they recognise he is 'technically' a rapist. In other words, under current laws it is likely that the current situation, in which about the only man to have been convicted in Britain of attempted or actual date rape is Angus Diggle, will remain. Distasteful as it may be for people who insist that 'rape is rape'[2] to see our student getting off with 'having his wrist slapped', it would surely be better for him to do community service and attend an educational course on rape than to get off Scot free.[3]

A graduated sexual assault law could also follow up two other aspects of the philosophical discussion. The lesser offence could be used in situations where consent was doubtful but the cumulative slope against the woman was very steep, but not steep enough to fall under laws about under age sex or abuse of authority. It could also, if written in a gender-free manner, deal with the more serious

---

[2] E.g. the letter quoted in Ch. 3 above (Phyllidia Paterson, *Observer*, 7 May 1995), Sharon Carr-Brown, letter, *Guardian*, 19 June 1997.

[3] Certainly Keith Burgess-Jackson identifies a graduated sexual assault law as a radical feminist aim - see *Rape*, p. 56. One possible advantage of a graduated law, mentioned by Jennifer Temkin in a discussion of indecent assault, is that defendants might be willing to plead guilty to a lesser charge, thus sparing the victim a full court hearing. See Jennifer Temkin, *Rape and the Legal Process*, Sweet and Maxwell, London, 1987, p. 34.

female-on-male sexual assaults. In practice one would not expect this to be used very much, but a reminder that such assaults exist would be of some comfort to the (rare) male victims.

It should be stressed that the introduction of a graduated law in Britain should wait upon the reforms advocated by Lees and the Campaign to End Rape. In the current situation there is a great danger that the effect of a graded law would be the downgrading of the (relatively few) serious offences which *are* actually successfully prosecuted under the current laws rather than an increased rate of conviction in less serious offences. Further, consistent with the argument of this book, the less serious sexual assault offence(s) should be designated as such, not as 'date rape laws', given that some assaults which happen on dates are extremely serious: the planned rapes which I described in Chapter 3 as 'rape under the cover of a date' - but which are best considered as disguised stranger rapes - would be an example of this. As the reforms advocated by Lees have to some extent gone through fairly recently in a few jurisdictions (e.g. some Australian states) there should soon be a body of experience on which to plan.

I have already covered the third legal point in my discussion of consent and communicative sexuality: there are good reasons for being cautious about writing communicative sexuality into the law. Also on the issue of consent, however, there are good reasons for taking Karen Kramer's proposals about alcohol very seriously: certainly some kind of recognition that women become incapable of giving valid sexual consent before they actually pass out would be useful.

Issues for further research

Articles by US psychologists always end with proposals for future research, and it is fitting that a book which has spent so much time discussing them should do likewise. Two proposals have already emerged in this conclusion. One is that it would be very useful if psychologists could spend more time investigating how consenting sex is negotiated, with a view to distinguishing it from non-consenting sex. It may be quite difficult to devise appropriate questions. For example, the questions used by researchers investigating what women would do if they were interested in having sex are in the right direction, but many of the answers the women gave, such as suggesting having a drink together, fall well short of actually consenting to sex. Most men are doubtless concerned to make sure that their sexual encounters are consensual, but probably do not actually think very specifically about exactly what it was about a particular encounter that convinced them that the woman consented. Similarly, women probably think more about not having consented in episodes of forced sex more than they do about exactly how they consented in consensual episodes. Moreover, given that much consenting behaviour is probably metaphorical and symbolic, some of the metaphors and symbols may be rather local, confined to fairly small groups of people.

The second proposal was that more work should be devoted to getting to understand the 'hidden victims' found in surveys.

A third suggestion is that an American psychologist could do a very useful job by simply summarising the existing research on date rape and related topics. Frequently articles start with a rather limited literature review (understandable because there is such a large literature) and the proceed to investigate something which looks, to me at least, very similar to something already investigated by researchers unmentioned in the literature review. The useful bibliography produced by Sally Ward et. al.[4] is now rather dated. In my view it is also better for a guide to study to include controversial interventions from figures such as Gilbert and Roiphe, and to be rather more inclusive of related areas, notably work on non-coercive dates. My first two suggestions are strategic proposals about the direction of psychological research, and there may well be other such suggestions which would be worth pursuing which would emerge from a general summary.

My fourth suggestion is that American psychologists should do more comparative work between countries. Much of their work is written as if it related to human dating behaviour, when actually it relates largely to US college students. In the literature 'interstate' comparisons usually mean comparisons between US states rather than between the USA and Poland or Argentina or France.[5] As I indicate in Chapter 5, dating occurs against a social and cultural background, and the best way to understand the effects of this background is to look at places where aspects of it are absent or enhanced. They almost certainly have many useful lessons to teach people from other countries, but these need to be disentangled from peculiarly US concerns.[6]

---

[4] Sally Ward et. al., *Acquaintance and Date Rape: an Annotated Bibliography*, Greenwood Press, Conneticut, Ma., 1994.

[5] For a clear indication that human beings generally are more varied in sexual mores than are Americans, see Gwen J. Broude and Sarah J. Greene, 'Cross-cultural Codes on Twenty Sexual Attitudes and Practices', *Ethnology*, Vol. 15, 1976, pp. 409-29. The data in the article are from widely varied, and in many cases tribal, societies. There may well be rather more convergence in industrial societies where unchaperoned dating is widespread and US culture spreads easily. However, for interesting possibilities of comparison between industrialised states see E.R. DeSouza and C.S. Hunt, 'Reactions to Refusals of Sexual Advances Among US and Brazilian Men and Women', *Sex Roles*, Vol. 34, Nos 7/8, 1996, pp. 549-65. The authors conclude that one reason Brazilian students tend to think less about date rape than US students is that Brazil is a much more highly eroticized society in which dating is assumed to involve consensual sex.

[6] One interesting issue where such research might help is raised by Sarah L. Cooke, who found very low rates of acceptance of sexual coercion amongst a sample of US students, but speculates that these students have become so influenced by politically correct ideas that they give the proper responses. Less 'corrupted' samples could be found in other countries. See Sarah L. Cook, 'Acceptance and Expectation of Sexual Aggression in College Students', *Psychology of Women Quarterly*, Vol. 19, 1995, pp. 181-94.

A fifth suggestion is that a British survey on the lines of the large-scale questionnaire carried out by Mary Koss in conjunction with *Ms* magazine would be very useful in convincing educational and legal authorities that there is a significant date rape problem here. As I indicated in Chapter 3, British surveys, although interesting and suggestive, have been mainly done on a small scale or confined to samples of women who may well have had worse than average experiences of sexual violence. Obviously, in the light of my earlier discussion, I think any such survey should be preceded by very careful debate about the exact form of the questions, should include a study of how seriously apparent victims are traumatised, and should include a survey of non-consenting sexual activity where women coerce men.

A final suggestion is that more work on the lines of Liz Kelly's *Surviving Sexual Violence* would be a very useful supplement to questionnaires. Obviously her work raises more problems about the subjective interpretation of lengthy answers from a small and unrepresentative sample. However, she is surely right that what women feel about sexual assault and sexual consent is what really matters rather than legal definitions or researchers' judgements: perhaps, for example, we should be worrying more about obscene phone calls and less about some sexual misunderstandings which can be formally construed as rape.

Bibliography

Abbey, A. (1982), 'Sex differences in attributions for friendly behaviour: Do males misperceive females' friendliness?', *Journal of Personality and Social Psychology*, Vol. 42, pp. 830-8.

Abbey, A. (1991), 'Acquaintance Rape and Alcohol Consumption on College Campuses: How are they Linked?', *Journal of American College Health*, Vol. 39, January, pp. 165-9.

Abbey, A., and Melby, C. (1986), 'The Effects of Nonverbal Cues on Gender Differences in Perceptions of Sexual Intent', *Sex Roles*, Vol. 15, Nos. 5/6, pp. 283-298.

Adams, David M. (1996), 'Date Rape and Erotic Discourse', in Francis, Leslie ed., *Date Rape: Feminism, Philosophy and the Law*, Pennsylvania State University Press: Pennsylvania, pp. 27-39.

Adler, Zsuzanna (1987), *Rape on Trial*, Routledge: London.

Allison, Julie A. and Wrightsman, Lawrence S. (1993), *Rape: the Misunderstood Crime*, Sage:Newbury Park, CA.

Amir, Menachem (1971), *Patterns in Forcible Rape*, University of Chicago Press: Chicago.

Balos, Beverley, and Fellows, Mary L. (1991), 'Guilty of the Crime of Trust: Nonstranger Rape', *Minnesota Law Review*, Vol. 75, pp. 599-618.

Bell, Patricia (1990), 'Women's Support Project/Evening Times Report on Responses from 1,503 Women to the Survey on Violence Against Women', available from Women's Support Project, Newlands Centre, 871 Springfield Road, Glasgow G31 4HZ.

Belliotti, Raymond A. (1993), *Good Sex*, Kansas University Press: Kansas.

Bogart, J.H. (1991), 'On the Nature of Rape', *Public Affairs Quarterly*, Vol. 5, No. 2, pp. 117-36.

Borque, Linda B. (1989), *Defining Rape*, Duke University Press: Durham and London.

Broude, Gwen J., and Greene, Sarah J. (1976), 'Cross-Cultural Codes on Twenty Sexual Attitudes and Practices', *Ethnology,* Vol. 15, pp. 409-29.

Brown, Beverley; Burman, Michèle; and Jamieson, Lynn (1993), *Sex Crimes on Trial: The Use of Sexual Evidence in Scottish Courts,* Edinburgh University Press: Edinburgh.

Brownmiller, Susan (1976), *Against our Will: Men, Women and Rape,* Penguin: Harmondsworth.

Burgess, Ann W., and Holstrom, Lynda L. (1974), 'Rape Trauma Syndrome', *American Journal of Psychiatry,* Vol. 131, pp. 981-86.

Burgess, Ann W., and Holstrom, Lynda L. (1979), 'Adaptive Strategies and Recovery from Rape', *American Journal of Psychiatry,* Vol. 10, pp. 1278-82.

Burgess-Jackson, Keith (1996), *Rape: A Philosophical Investigation,* Dartmouth: Brookfield, Vermont.

Burt, Martha R. (1980), 'Cultural Myths and Supports for Rape', *Journal of Personality and Social Psychology,* Vol. 38, No. 2, pp. 217-30.

Burt, Martha R., and Katz, Bonnie L. (1985), 'Rape, Robbery and Burglary: Responses to Actual and Feared Criminal Victimisation, with Special Focus on Women and the Elderly', *Victimology,* Vol. 10, pp. 325-58.

Byers, E. Sandra (1980), 'Female Communication of Consent and Nonconsent to Sexual Intercourse', *Journal of the New Brunswick Psychological Association,* Vol. 5, pp. 12-18.

Byers, E. Sandra (1989), 'Effects of Sexual Arousal on Men's and Women's Behaviour in Sexual Disagreement Situations', *The Journal of Sex Research,* Vol. 25, No. 2, pp. 235-54.

Byers, E. Sandra, and Lewis, K. (1988), 'Dating Couples' Disagreements over the Desired Level of Sexual Intimacy', *The Journal of Sex Research,* Vol. 24, pp. 15-29.

Calhoun, Karen S., et. al. (1997), 'Sexual Coercion and Attraction to Sexual Aggression in a Community Sample of Young Men', *Journal of Interpersonal Violence,* Vol. 12, No. 3, 1997, pp. 392-406.

Campbell, Rebecca, and Johnson, Camille R. (1997), 'Police Officers' Perceptions of Rape: Is There Consistency Between State Law and Individual Beliefs?', *Journal of Interpersonal Violence,* Vol. 12, No. 2, pp. 255-74.

Carter, Pam, and Jeffs, Tony (1995), *A Very Private Affair: Sexual Exploitation in Higher Education,* Education Now Books: Ticknall, Derbyshire.

Cohen, David (1990), *Being a Man,* Routledge: London.

Connell, Robert W. (1995), *Masculinities,* Polity Press: Cambridge.

Cook, Sarah L. (1995), 'Acceptance and Expectation of Sexual Aggression in College Students', *Psychology of Women Quarterly,* Vol. 19, pp. 181-94.

Cowling, Mark (1995) 'Date Rape and Consent', *Contemporary Politics,* Vol. 1, No. 2, pp. 57-72.

Craig, Mary E. (1990), 'Coercive Sexuality in Dating Relationships: A Situational Model', *Clinical Psychology Review,* Vol. 10, No. 4, pp. 395-423.

Craig, Mary E. (1993), 'The Effects of Selective Evaluation on the Perception of Female Cues in Sexually Coercive and Noncoercive Males', *Archives of Sexual Behavior*, Vol. 22, No. 5, pp. 415-33.

Davidson, Julia O'Connell (1995), 'British Sex Tourists in Thailand', in Maynard, Mary and Purvis, June (eds) *(Hetero)sexual Politics*, Taylor and Francis: London, 1995, Ch. 3.

Davies, Kimberly A. (1997), 'Voluntary Exposure to Pornography and Men's Attitudes Toward Feminism and Rape', *The Journal of Sex Research*, Vol. 34, No. 2, pp. 131-7.

Davis, Terry C., et. al. (1993), 'Acquaintance Rape and the High School Student', *Journal of Adolescent Health*, Vol. 14, No. 3, pp. 220-4.

DeKeseredy, Walter S. (1988), *Woman Abuse in Dating Relationships: The Role of Male Peer Support*, Canadian Scholars' Press Inc.: Toronto.

DeKeseredy, Walter S. (1994), 'Addressing the complexities of woman abuse in dating: A response to Gartner and Fox', *Canadian Journal of Sociology*, Vol. 19, pp. 75-80.

DeKeseredy, Walter S. (1996), 'The Canadian national survey on woman abuse in university/college dating relationships: Biofeminist panic transmission or critical inquiry?', *Canadian Journal of Criminology*, Vol. 19, pp. 81-104.

DeKeseredy, Walter S., and Kelly, Katharine D. (1993), 'The Incidence and Prevalence of Woman Abuse in Canadian University and College Dating Relationships', *Canadian Journal of Sociology*, Vol. 18, 2, pp. 137-59.

DeKeseredy, Walter S., and Kelly, Katharine D. (1993), 'Woman Abuse in University and College Dating Relationships: The Contribution of the Ideology of Familial Patriarchy', *The Journal of Human Justice*, Vol. 4, 2, pp. 25-52.

DeKeseredy, Walter S., and Schwartz, Martin D. (1993), 'Male Peer Support and Woman Abuse: An Expansion of DeKeseredy's Model', *Sociological Spectrum*, Vol. 13, pp. 393-413.

DeKeseredy, Walter S., Schwartz, Martin D., and Tait, Karen (1993), 'Sexual Assault and Stranger Aggression on a Canadian University Campus', *Sex Roles*, Vol. 28, Nos 5/6, pp. 263-77.

DeSouza, E.R., et. al. (1992), 'Perceived Sexual Intent in the US and Brazil as a Function of the Nature of Encounter, Subjects' Nationality and Gender', *The Journal of Sex Research*, Vol. 29, No. 2, pp. 251-60.

DeSouza, E.R., and Hunt, C.S. (1996), 'Reactions to Refusals of Sexual Advances Among US and Brazilian Men and Women', *Sex Roles*, Vol. 34, Nos 7/8, pp. 549-65.

Devereux, J.A., Jones, D.P.H., and Dickenson, D.L. (1993), 'Can children withhold consent to treatment?', *British Medical Journal*, Vol. 306, 29 May, pp. 1459-61.

Dworkin, Andrea (1987), *Intercourse*, Secker and Warburg: London.

Dworkin, Andrea (1981) *Pornography: Men Possessing Women*, The Women's Press: London.

Ellis, Lee (1989), *Theories of Rape,* Hemisphere Publishing Corporation: N.Y.

Ericsson, L.O. (1980), 'Charges against Prostitution: An Attempt at a Philosophical Assessment', *Ethics,* Vol. 90, No. 3, pp. 335-66.

Estrich, Susan (1987), *Real Rape,* Harvard University Press: Cambridge, MA.

Fairweather, Eileen, McDonough, Roisin, and McFadyean, Melanie (1984), *Only the Rivers Run Free: Northern Ireland, The Women's War,* Pluto Press: London.

Fekete, John (1994), *Moral Panic: Biopolitics Rising,* Robert Davies Publishing: Montreal.

Feminists Against Censorship (1991) *Pornography and Feminism: The Case Against Censorship,* Lawrence and Wishart, London.

Fillion, Kate (1997), *Lip Service,* Pandora/Harper Collins: London.

Finkelhor, David, and Yllo, Kirsti (1985), *License to Rape: Sexual Abuse of Wives,* Holt, Rinehart and Winston: New York.

Fischer, Gloria J. (1996), 'Deceptive, Verbally Coercive College Males: Attitudinal Predictors and Lies Told', *Archives of Sexual Behavior,* Vol. 25, No. 5, pp. 527-33.

Flathman, R. E. (1972), *Political Obligation,* Croom Helm: London.

Fox, Bonnie J. (1993), 'On Violent Men and Female Victims: A comment on DeKeseredy and Kelly', *The Canadian Journal of Sociology,* Vol. 18, pp. 321-324.

Francis, Leslie, ed., (1996), *Date Rape: Feminism, Philosophy and the Law,* Pennsylvania State University Press: Pennsylvania.

Gartner, Rosemary (1993), 'Studying Woman Abuse: A comment on DeKeseredy and Kelly', *Canadian Journal of Sociology,* Vol. 18, pp. 313-20.

George, Linda K., Winfield, Idee, and Blazer, Dan G. (1992), 'Sociocultural factors in sexual assault: a comparison of two representative samples of women', *Journal of Social Issues,* Vol. 48, No. 1, pp. 105-25.

Gilbert, Neil (1991), 'The Phantom Epidemic of Sexual Assault', *The Public Interest,* Vol. 103, pp. 54-65.

Gilbert, Neil (1992), 'Realities and Mythologies of Rape', *Society,* May-June, pp. 5-10.

Gilbert, Neil (1993), 'Examining the Facts: Advocacy Research Overstates the Incidence of Date and Acquaintance Rape', in Gelles, Richard J. and Loseke, Donileen R. (eds), *Current Controversies on Family Violence,* Sage: Newbury Park, California, pp. 120-32.

Gilbert, Neil (1994), 'Miscounting Social Ills', *Society,* Vol. 31, pp. 18-26.

Glover, Jonathan (1977), *Causing Death and Saving Lives,* Penguin: Harmondsworth.

Gray, Heather M., and Foshee, Vangie (1997), 'Adolescent Dating Violence: Differences Between One-Sided and Mutually Violent Profiles', *Journal of Interpersonal Violence,* Vol. 12, No. 1, pp. 126-41.

Guskin, Alan E. (1996), 'The Antioch Response: Sex, You Don't Just Talk About It', in Francis, Leslie, ed., *Date Rape: Feminism, Philosophy and the Law*, Pennsylvania State University Press: Pennsylvania, pp. 154-165.

Gwartney-Gibbs, Patricia, and Stockard, Jean, 'Courtship Aggression and Mixed-Sex Peer Groups' in Pirog-Good, Maureen, and Stets, J. E., eds, (1989), *Violence in Dating Relationships: Emerging Social Issues*, Praeger: New York, pp. 185-204.

Hall, Ruth E. (1985), *Ask Any Woman*, Falling Wall Press: Bristol.

Hanmer, Jalna, and Saunders, Sheila (1993), *Women, Violence and Crime Prevention: A West Yorkshire Study*, Avebury: Aldershot.

Hannon, Roseann, et. al. (1995), 'Dating Characteristics Leading to Unwanted vs. Wanted Sexual Behaviour', *Sex Roles*, Vol. 33, Nos. 11/12, pp. 767-83.

Harris, Lucy Reed (1976), 'Towards a Consent Standard in the Law of Rape', *University of Chicago Law Review*, Vol. 43, pp. 613-45.

Hawkins, G., and Zimring, F.E. (1988), *Pornography in a Free Society*, Cambridge University Press: Cambridge.

Hewlett, Sylvia Ann (1988), *A Lesser Life*, Sphere Books: Harmondsworth.

Himelein, Melissa J., Vogel, Ron E., and Wachowiak, Dale G. (1994), 'Nonconsensual Sexual Experiences in Precollege Women: Prevalence and Risk Factors', *Journal of Counseling and Development*, Vol. 72, March/April, pp. 411-415.

Hinton, William (1972), *Fanshen*, Penguin: Harmondsworth.

Hippensteele, Susan K., et. al. (1993), 'Some Comments on the National Survey on Woman Abuse in Canadian University and College Dating Relationships', *The Journal of Human Justice*, Vol. 4, 2, pp. 67-71.

HMSO (1995), *Criminal Statistics*, Home Office: London.

HMSO (1994), *Anxieties About Crime: Findings from the 1994 British Crime Survey*, Home Office: London.

Hobbes, Thomas (1962), *Leviathan*, Fontana, Collins: Glasgow.

Holland, Janet, et. al. (1991), *Pressure, Resistance, Empowerment: Young Women and The Negotiation of Safer Sex*, Tufnell Press: London.

Holland, Janet, et. al. (1993), *Wimp or Gladiator: Contradictions in Acquiring Masculine Sexuality*, Tufnell Press: London.

hooks, bell (1982) *Ain't I A Woman*, Pluto Press: London.

hooks, bell (1984), *Feminist Theory: From Margin to Center*, South End Press: Boston, Ma.

Husak, Douglas N., and Thomas III, George C. (1992), 'Date Rape, Social Convention, and Reasonable Mistakes', *Law and Philosophy*, Vol. 11, pp. 95-126.

Jaggar, Alison M. (1980), 'Prostitution', in Soble, Alan, ed., *The Philosophy of Sex*, Littlefield, Adams and Co.: New Jersey, pp. 348-68.

Jensen, Gary F., and Karpos, Maryaltani (1993), 'Managing Rape: Exploratory Research on the Behaviour of Rape Statistics', *Criminology*, Vol. 31, No. 3, pp. 363-85.

Jones, J.M., and Muehlenhard, C.L. (1993), 'The impact of verbal and physical sexual coercion on women's psychological health', 1993 Kansas Series in Clinical Psychology: Lawrence, KS.

Jong, Erica (1978), *How to Save Your Own Life*, Granada: London.

Kalof, Linda (1993), 'Rape-Supportive Attitudes and Sexual Victimisation Experiences of Sorority and Non-Sorority Women', *Sex Roles*, Vol. 29. Nos 11/12, pp. 767-80.

Kanin, Eugene (1984), 'Date Rape: Unofficial Criminals and Victims', *Victimology*, Vol. 9, No. 1, pp. 95-108.

Kanin, Eugene J., and Parcell, Stanley R. (1977), 'Sexual Aggression: A Second Look at the Offended Female', *Archives of Sexual Behavior*, Vol. 6, No. 1, pp. 67-76.

Katz, B.L. (1991), 'The Psychological Impact of Stranger Versus Nonstranger Rape on Victims' Recovery', in Parrott, A., and Bechhofer, L. (eds), *Acquaintance Rape: The Hidden Crime*, John Wiley: New York, pp. 251-69.

Kelly, Katharine D. (1994), 'The Politics of Data', *Canadian Journal of Sociology*, Vol. 19, pp. 81-5.

Kelly, Katharine D., and DeKeseredy, Walter S. (1994), 'Women's Fear of Crime and Abuse in College and University Dating Relationships', *Violence and Victims*, Vol. 9, 1, pp. 17-30.

Kelly, Liz (1988), *Surviving Sexual Violence*, Polity Press: Cambridge.

Kilpatrick, Dean G., et. al. (1987), 'Criminal Victimisation: Lifetime Prevalence, Reporting to Police, and Psychological Impact', *Crime and Delinquency*, Vol. 33, 4, pp. 479-89.

Korman, Sheila K., and Leslie, Gerald R. (1982), 'The Relationship of Feminist Ideology and Date Expense Sharing to Perceptions of Sexual Aggression in Dating', *The Journal of Sex Research*, Vol. 18, No. 2, pp. 114-29.

Koss, Mary P., and Cook, Sarah L. (1993), 'Facing the Facts: Date and Acquaintance Rape are Significant Problems for Women', in Gelles, Richard J. and Loseke, Donileen R., eds, *Current Controversies on Family Violence*, Sage: Newbury Park, California.

Koss, Mary P. (1988), 'Hidden Rape: Sexual Aggression and Victimisation in a National Sample of Students in Higher Education', in Burgess, A.W., ed., *Rape and Sexual Assault*, *V*ol. 2, Garland: London and N.Y., pp. 3-20.

Koss, Mary P., Woodruff, W.J., and Koss, Paul G. (1991), 'Criminal Victimisation among Primary Medical Care Patients: Prevalence, Incidence and Physician Usage', *Behavioral Sciences and the Law*, Vol. 9, pp. 85-96.

Koss, Mary P. (1992), 'Defending Date Rape', *Journal of Interpersonal Violence*, Vol. 7, No. 1, pp. 122-6.

Koss, Mary P. (1992), 'The Underdetection of Rape: Methodological Choices Influence Incidence Estimates', *Journal of Social Issues*, Vol. 48, 1, pp. 61-75.

Kosson, David S., Kelly, Jennifer C., and White, Jacquelyn W. (1997), 'Psychopathy-Related Traits Predict Self-Reported Sexual Aggression Among College Men', *Journal of Interpersonal Violence*, Vol. 12, No. 2, pp. 241-54.

Kowalski, Robin M. (1992), 'Nonverbal Behaviours and Perceptions of Sexual Intentions: Effects of Sexual Connotativeness, Verbal Response, and Rape Outcome', *Basic and Applied Psychology*, Vol. 13, No. 4, pp. 427-45.

Kowalski, Robin M. (1993), 'Inferring Sexual Interest from Behavioural Cues: Effects of Gender and Sexually Relevant Attitudes', *Sex Roles*, Vol. 29, Nos 1/2.

Kramer, Karen M. (1994), 'Rule by Myth: The Social and Legal Dynamics Governing Alcohol-Related Acquaintance Rapes', *Stanford Law Review*, Vol. 47, pp. 115-60.

Kurz, Demie, (1993), 'Physical Assaults by Husbands: A Major Social Problem', in Gelles, Richard J. and Loseke, Donileen R. (eds), *Current Controversies on Family Violence*, Sage: Newbury Park, California, pp. 88-103.

Lees, Sue (1986), *Losing Out: Sexuality and Adolescent Girls*, Hutchinson: London.

Lees, Sue (1993), *Sugar and Spice: Sexuality and Adolescent Girls* Penguin: Harmondsworth.

Lees, Sue (1996), *Carnal Knowledge, Rape on Trial*, Hamish Hamilton: London.

LeMoncheck, Linda (1985), *Dehumanizing Women*, Rowman and Allanheld: New Jersey.

Levine, Edward M., and Kanin, Eugene J. (1987), 'Sexual Violence Among Dates and Acquaintances: Trends and Their Implications for Marriage and Family', *Journal of Family Violence*, Vol. 2, No. 1, pp. 55-65.

Levine-MacCombie, Joyce, and Koss, Mary P. (1986), 'Acquaintance Rape: Effective Avoidance Strategies', *Psychology of Women Quarterly*, Vol. 10, pp. 311-20.

Linz, Daniel, Wilson, Barbara J., and Donnerstein, Edward (1992), 'Sexual Violence in the Mass Media', *Journal of Social Issues*, Vol. 48, No. 1, pp. 145-171.

Lorde, Audre (1984), *Sister Outsider*, The Crossing Press, Freedom, CA.

Lovenduski, J., and Randall, V. (1993), *Feminist Politics Today*, Oxford University Press: Oxford.

MacKinnon, Catharine A. (1982), 'Feminism, Marxism, Method and the State: An Agenda for Theory', *Signs*, Vol. 7, No. 3, pp. 515-544.

MacKinnon, Catharine A. (1989), *Toward a Feminist Theory of the State*, Harvard University Press: Cambridge, MA.

McCormick, Naomi B. (1979), 'Come-ons and Put-offs: Unmarried Students' Strategies for Having and Avoiding Sexual Intercourse', *Psychology of Women Quarterly*, Vol. 4, No. 2, pp. 194-211.

McCormick, Naomi B., and Jones, Andrew J. (1989), 'Gender Differences in Nonverbal Flirtation', *Journal of Sex Education and Therapy*, Vol. 15, No. 4, pp. 271-82.

McGregor, Joan (1994), 'Force, Consent and the Reasonable Woman', in Coleman, Jules L., and Buchanan, Allen (eds), *In Harm's Way*, Cambridge University Press: Cambridge, pp. 231-54.

Makepeace, James M. (1986), 'Gender Differences in Courtship Violence Victimisation', *Family Relations*, Vol. 35, pp. 383-8.

Malamuth, N.M., and Donnerstein, E., eds, (1984) *Pornography and Sexual Aggression*, Academic Press: Orlando, Florida.

Mappes, Thomas A. (1987), 'Sexual Morality and the Concept of Using Another Person', in Mappes, Thomas A., ed., *Social Ethics: Morality and Social Policy*, McGraw-Hill: New York, pp. 248-62.

Mardrus, J.C., and Mathers, P. (trans) (1986),*The Book of the Thousand Nights and One Night*, Vol. 1, Routledge: London.

Margolis, Leslie (1990), 'Gender and the Stolen Kiss: The Social Support of Male and Female to Violate a Partner's Sexual Consent in a Noncoercive Situation', *Archives of Sexual Behavior*, Vol. 19, No. 3, pp. 281-91.

Marx, Brian P., and Gross, Alan M. (1995), 'Date Rape: An Analysis of Two Contextual Variables', *Behavior Modification*, Vol. 19, No. 4, pp. 451-63.

Meredith, Philip (1993), 'Patient Participation in Decision-Making and Consent to Treatment: the Case of General Surgery', *Sociology of Health and Illness*, Vol. 15, No. 3, pp. 315-36.

Miller, Beverley, and Marshall, Jon C. (1987), 'Coercive Sex on the University Campus', *Journal of College Student Personnel*, Vol. 28, 1987, pp. 38-47.

Mills, Crystal S., and Granoff, Barbara J. (1992), 'Date and Acquaintance Rape Among a Sample of College Students', *Social Work*, Vol. 37, No. 6, pp. 504-509.

Mongeau, Paul A., et. al., (1993), 'Who's wooing whom? An investigation of female-initiated dating', in Kalbfleisch, P.J., ed., *Interpersonal communication: Evolving interpersonal relationships*, Erlbaum: Hillsdale, N.J., pp. 51-68.

Mongeau, Paul A., and Johnson, Kristen L. (1995), 'Predicting cross-sex first-date sexual expectations and involvement: Contextual and individual difference factors', *Personal Relationships*, Vol. 2, pp. 301-12.

Mooney, Jayne (1993), *The Hidden Figure: Domestic Violence in North London*, available from Centre for Criminology, Middlesex University.

Moore, Monica M., and Butler, Diana L. (1989), 'Predictive Aspects of Nonverbal Courtship Behaviour in Women', *Semiotica*, Vol. 76, Nos 3/4, pp. 205-15.

Morgan, David (1992), *Discovering Men*, Routledge: London.

Muehlenhard, Charlene L. (1988), 'Misinterpreted Dating Behaviours and the Risk of Date Rape', *Journal of Social and Clinical Psychology*, Vol. 6, No. 1, pp. 20-37.

Muehlenhard, Charlene L., Friedman, Debra E., and Thomas, Celeste M. (1985), 'Is Date Rape Justifiable? The Effect of Dating Activity, Who Initiated, Who Paid, and Men's Attitudes toward Women', *Psychology of Women Quarterly,* Vol. 9, No. 3, pp. 297-310.

Muehlenhard, Charlene L., and Linton, Melaney A. (1987), 'Date Rape and Sexual Aggression in Dating Situations: Incidence and Risk Factors', *Journal of Counseling Psychology,* Vol. 34, No. 2, pp. 186-96.

Muehlenhard, Charlene L., and Cook, Stephen W. (1988), 'Men's Self-Reports of Unwanted Sexual Activity', *The Journal of Sex Research,* Vol. 24, pp. 58-72.

Muehlenhard, C.L., and Hollabaugh, L. C. (1988), 'Do women sometimes say no when they mean yes? The prevalence and correlates of women's token resistance to sex', *Journal of Personality and Social Psychology*, Vol. 54, pp. 872-9.

Muehlenhard, Charlene L., and McCoy, Marcia L. (1991), 'Double Standard/Double Bind: The Sexual Double Standard and Women's Communication about Sex', *Psychology of Women Quarterly,* Vol. 15, pp. 447-61.

Muehlenhard, Charlene L. et. al. (1992), 'Definitions of Rape: Scientific and Political Implications', *Journal of Social Issues,* Vol. 48, No. 1, pp. 23-44.

Muehlenhard, Charlene L., Sympson, Susie C., Phelps, Joi L. and Highby, Barrie J. (1994), 'Are Rape Statistics Exaggerated? A Response to Criticism of Contemporary Rape Research', *The Journal of Sex Research,* Vol. 31, No. 2, pp. 144-6.

Murnen, Sarah K., Perot, Annette, and Byrne, Donn (1989), 'Coping with Unwanted Sexual Activity: Normative Responses, Situational Determinants and Individual Differences', *The Journal of Sex Research,* Vol. 26, No. 1, pp. 85-106.

Murphy, Jeffrie G. (1994), 'Some Ruminations on Women, Violence and the Criminal Law', in Coleman, Jules L., and Buchanan, Allen (eds), *In Harm's Way,* Cambridge University Press: Cambridge, pp. 209-230.

Murray, L. (1982), 'When Men are Raped by Women', *Sexual Medicine Today,* Vol. 20, pp. 14-16.

Nagel, Thomas (1979), *Mortal Questions,* Cambridge University Press: Cambridge.

O'Neill, Onora (1985), 'Between Consenting Adults', *Philosophy and Public Affairs,* Vol. 14, No. 3, pp. 252-77.

O'Sullivan, Lucia F., and Allgeier, Elizabeth R. (1994), 'Disassembling a Stereotype: Gender Differences in the Use of Token Resistance', *Journal of Applied Psychology,* Vol. 24, No. 12, pp. 1035-55.

O'Sullivan, Lucia F., and Byers, E. Sandra (1992), 'College Students' Incorporation of Initiator and Restrictor Roles in Sexual Dating Interactions', *The Journal of Sex Research,* Vol. 29, No. 3, pp. 435-46.

O'Sullivan, Lucia F. (1995), 'Less is More: The Effects of Sexual Experience on Men's and Women's Personality Characteristics and Relationship Desirability', *Sex Roles,* Vol. 33, Nos. 3/4, pp. 159-81.

Palmer, Craig D. (1988), 'Twelve Reasons Why Rape is NOT Sexually Motivated: A Skeptical Examination', *The Journal of Sex Research,* Vol. 25, No. 4, pp. 512-30.

Parrott, A., and Bechhofer, L. (eds) (1991), *Acquaintance Rape: The Hidden Crime,* John Wiley: New York

Pateman, Carole (1983), 'Defending Prostitution: Charges Against Ericsson', *Ethics,* Vol. 93, April, pp. 561-5.

Pateman, Carole (1989), 'Women and Consent' in Pateman, Carole, ed., *The Disorder of Women,* Polity Press: Cambridge.

Peplau, Letitia Anne, Rubin, Zick, and Hill, Charles T. (1977), 'Sexual Intimacy in Dating Relationships', *Journal of Social Issues,* Vol. 33, No. 2, pp. 86-109.

Perper, Timothy, and Weis, David (1987), 'Proceptive and Rejective Strategies of US and Canadian College Women', *Journal of Sex Research,* Vol. 23, pp. 455-80.

Pineau, Lois (1996a), 'Date Rape: A Feminist Analysis', in Francis, Leslie, ed., *Date Rape: Feminism, Philosophy and the Law,* Pennsylvania State University Press: Pennsylvania, pp. 1-26.

Pineau, Lois (1996b), 'A Response to my Critics', in Francis, Leslie, ed., *Date Rape: Feminism, Philosophy and the Law,* Pennsylvania State University Press: Pennsylvania, pp. 63-107.

Pollard, J. (1992), 'Judgements about Victims and Attackers in Depicted Rapes: A Review', *British Journal of Social Psychology,* Vol. 31, pp. 307-26.

Primoratz, Igor (1993), 'What's Wrong with Prostitution?', *Philosophy,* Vol. 68, pp. 159-82.

Radford, Jill, and Kelly, Liz (1995), 'Self-Preservation: Feminist Activism and Feminist Jurisprudence' in Maynard, Mary, and Purvis, June, (eds), *(Hetero)sexual Politics,* Taylor and Francis: London, pp. 186-99.

Radzinsky, Edvard (1996), *Stalin,* Hodder and Stoughton: London.

Reinisch, June M. and Beardsley, Ruth (1991), *The Kinsey Institute New Report on Sex,* Penguin: Harmondsworth.

Resick, Patricia A. (1993), 'The Psychological Impact of Rape', *Journal of Interpersonal Violence,* Vol. 8, No. 2, pp. 223-55.

Rhynard, Jill, Krebs, Marlene, and Glover, Julie (1997), 'Sexual Assault in Dating Relationships', *Journal of School Health,* Vol. 67, No. 3, pp. 89-93.

Richards, Janet R. (1995), *The Sceptical Feminist,* 2nd Edition, Penguin: Harmondsworth.

Riger, Stephanie, and Gordon, Margaret (1988), 'The Impact of Crime on Urban Women' in Burgess, A.W., ed., *Rape and Sexual Assault,* Vol. 2, Garland: London and N.Y.

Roiphe, Katie (1993), *The Morning After,* Hamish Hamilton: London.

Rosenthal, Doreen, and Peart, Rachel (1996), 'The Rules of the Game: Teenagers Communicating about Sex', *Journal of Adolescence*, Vol. 19, pp. 321-32.

Russell, Diana E.H. (1982), 'The Prevalence and Incidence of Forcible Rape and Attempted Rape of Females', *Victimology*, Vol. 7, pp. 81-93.

Russell, Diana E. H. (1984), *Sexual Exploitation: Rape, Child Sexual Abuse and Workplace Harassment*, Sage: Beverley Hills, CA.

Russell, Diana E. H., and Howell, Nancy (1983), 'The Prevalence of Rape in the United States Revisited', *Signs*, Vol. 8, No. 4, pp. 688-95.

Sampson, Adam (1994), *Sex Offenders and the Criminal Justice System*, Routledge: London.

Sarrel, P.M., and Masters, W.H. (1982), 'Sexual molestation of men by women', *Archives of Sexual Behaviour*, 11, pp. 117-31.

Schwartz, Martin D., and DeKeseredy, Walter S. (1997), *Sexual Assault on the College Campus: The Role of Male Peer Support*, Sage: London.

Scott, Kathryn D., and Aneshensel, Carol S. (1997), 'An examination of the Reliability of Sexual Assault Reports', *Journal of Interpersonal Violence*, Vol. 12, No. 3, pp. 361-74.

Scully, Diana (1990), *Understanding Sexual Violence*, Unwin Hyman: Boston, MA.

Segal, Lynne (1990), *Slow Motion: Changing Masculinities, Changing Men*, Virago: London.

Shafer, Carolyn M., and Frye, Marilyn (1986), 'Rape and Respect', in Pearsall, Marilyn, ed., *Women and Values: Readings in Recent Feminist Philosophy*, Wadsworth Publishing: Belmont, California, pp. 188-96.

Shapiro, B.L., and Schwarz, J.C. (1997), 'Date Rape: Its Relationship to Trauma Symptoms and Sexual Self-Esteem', *Journal of Interpersonal Violence*, Vol. 12, No. 3, pp. 407-19.

Shotland, R. Lance, and Goodstein, Lynne (1992), 'Sexual Precedence Reduces the Perceived Legitimacy of Sexual Refusal: An Examination of Attributions Concerning Date Rape and Consensual Sex', *Personality and Social Psychology Bulletin*, Vol. 18, No. 6, Dec., pp. 756-64.

Shotland, R. Lance, and Hunter, Barbara A. (1995), 'Women's "Token Resistant" and Compliant Sexual Behaviours are Related to Uncertain Sexual Intentions and Rape', *Personality and Social Psychology Bulletin*, Vol. 21, No. 3, pp. 226-36.

Shrage, Laurie (1989), 'Should Feminists Oppose Prostitution?', *Ethics*, Vol. 99, January, pp. 347-61.

Simmons, A. John (1979), *Moral Principles and Political Obligation*, Princeton University Press: Princeton, N.J.

Singer, Peter (1979) *Practical Ethics*, Cambridge University Press: Cambridge.

Smith, Lorna (1989), *Concerns About Rape*, HMSO: London.

Smith, J.C. and Hogan, B. (1996), *Criminal Law*, 8th Edition, Butterworths: London.

Smith, J.C. and Hogan, B. (1986), *Criminal Law: Cases and Materials,* Third Edition, Butterworths: London.

Smith, Ronald E., Pine, Charles J., and Hawley, Mark E. (1988), 'Social Cognitions About Adult Male Victims of Female Sexual Assault', *The Journal of Sex Research,* Vol. 24, pp. 101-12.

Sorenson, Susan B., et. al. (1987), 'The Prevalence of Adult Sexual Assault: The Los Angeles Epidemiologic Catchment Area Project', *American Journal of Epidemiology,* Vol. 126, No. 6, pp. 1154-64.

Sprecher, Susan, et. al. (1994), 'Token Resistance to Sexual Intercourse and Consent to Unwanted Sexual Intercourse: College Students' Dating Experiences in Three Countries', *The Journal of Sex Research,* Vol. 31, No. 2, pp. 125-32.

Stanko, Elizabeth (1990), *Everyday Violence: How Men and Women Experience Sexual and Physical Danger,* Pandora Press: London.

Stets, Jan E., and Pirog-Good, Maureen A. (1989), 'Patterns of Physical and Sexual Abuse for Men and Women in Dating Relationships: A Descriptive Analysis', *Journal of Family Violence,* Vol. 4, No. 1, pp. 63-76.

Straus, Murray A. (1993), 'Physical Assaults by Wives: A Major Social Problem', in Gelles, Richard J. and Loseke, Donileen R. (eds), *Current Controversies on Family Violence,* Sage: Newbury Park, California, pp. 67-87.

Struckman-Johnson, Cindy (1988), 'Forced Sex on Dates: It Happens to Men, Too', *Journal of Sex Research,* Vol. 24, pp. 234-41.

Struckman-Johnson, David and Cindy (1991), 'Men and Women's Acceptance of Coercive Sexual Strategies Varied by Initiator Gender and Couple Intimacy', *Sex Roles,* Vol. 25, Nos 11/12, pp. 661-76.

Temkin, Jennifer (1987), *Rape and the Legal Process,* Sweet and Maxwell: London.

Vannoy, Russell (1980), *Sex Without Love: A Philosophical Exploration,* Prometheus Books: Buffalo.

Walby, Sylvia (1986), *Patriarchy at Work,* Polity Press: Cambridge.

Walby, Sylvia (1990), *Theorising Patriarchy,* Basil Blackwells: Oxford.

Ward, Sally K., et. al. (1991), 'Acquaintance Rape and the College Social Scene', *Family Relations,* Vol. 40, pp. 65-71.

Ward, Sally, et. al. (1994), *Acquaintance and Date Rape: An Annotated Bibliography,* Greenwood Press: Westport, Conn.

Warr, Mark (1985), 'Fear of Rape among Urban Women', *Social Problems,* No. 32, pp. 238-50.

Warshaw, Robin (1988), *I Never Called it Rape: The Ms report on Recognising, Fighting and Surviving Date and Acquaintance Rape,* Harper and Row: New York.

Wellings, Kaye et. al. (1994), *Sexual Behaviour in Britain: the National Survey of Attitudes and Life,* Penguin: Harmondsworth.

Wells, Catharine Pierce (1996), 'Date Rape and the Law: Another Feminist View', in Francis, Leslie, ed., *Date Rape: Feminism, Philosophy and the Law,* Pennsylvania State University Press: Pennsylvania, pp. 41-50

West, Alison (1994), 'Tougher Prosecution when the Rapist is not a Stranger: Suggested Reform to the California Penal Code', *Golden Gate University Law Review,* Vol. 24, pp. 169-88.

Wilde, Lawrence (1994), *Modern European Socialism,* Dartmouth: Aldershot.

Wilson, Wayne, and Durrenberger, Robert (1982), 'Comparison of Rape and Attempted Rape Victims', *Psychological Reports,* Vol. 50, p. 198.

Index